HAMBURGER HILL

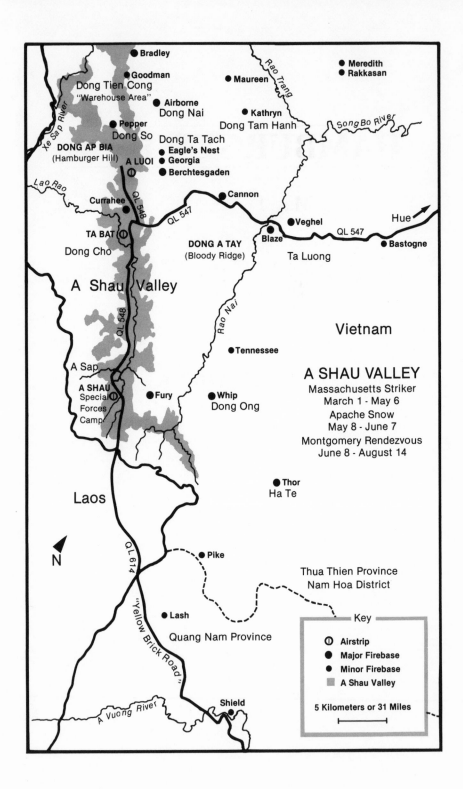

HAMBURGER HILL

May 11–20, 1969

Samuel Zaffiri

First published in Great Britain
by Arms and Armour Press, Artillery House,
Artillery Row, London SW1P 1RT

First published in the United States
by Presidio Press
31 Pamaron Way, Novato, CA 94949

Distributed in Australia by
Capricorn Link (Australia) Pty. Ltd., P.O. Box 665,
Lane Cove, New South Wales 2066, Australia

ISBN 0 85368-974 1

For Jackie

"You may not be able to read this. I am writing it in a hurry. I see death coming up the hill."

A letter home from a soldier on Hamburger Hill

"The inexorable law of combat is the disintegration and replacement of rifle companies . . ."

from *This Kind of War* by T. R. Fehrenbach

CONTENTS

ACKNOWLEDGMENTS

I especially want to thank John Comerford. Besides providing me with a lengthy account of his part in the battle with C/3/187th, his exhaustive research was invaluable in helping me pinpoint the positions and maneuvers of the different companies.

I also want to thank Dr. Richard J. Summers, the Archivist-Historian at the United States Army Military History Institute; Marian Carroll, an Associate Professor of Library Science at Illinois State University; Douglas Pike, the director of the Indochina Studies Program at the University of California, Berkeley; Frank Boccia, a former platoon leader with B/3/187th; and Ray Ytzaina, a History Instructor at St. Louis University, who is writing his doctoral dissertation on the Hamburger Hill Battle. Each provided me with documents and information crucial to the making of this book.

Finally, I would like to express my gratitude to the sixteen men who took the time to write lengthy accounts of their experiences during the battle, and to the thirty others who, though the remembering for many was a painful one, allowed me to tape their stories.

CHAPTER 1

APACHE SNOW

H-hour for Operation Apache Snow was scheduled for 0710 hours, May 10, 1969, though parts of the operation had already been in progress for fifteen days. Daily between April 25 and May 9, Air Force C130s had been "prepping" thirty possible landing zones in the A Shau Valley with daisy-cutters, giant 15,000-pound bombs designed to explode just above the ground, clearing away all trees and vegetation without cratering the LZ. To confuse the North Vietnamese as to the actual locations of the combat assault, the thirty LZs were scattered randomly across the entire length of the valley, from the southern plains around the abandoned American Special Forces camp to the far northern valley below Dong So Ridge. Of the thirty LZs, only five would actually be used this day.

0600 Hours, LZ 2, Dong Ap Bia

The Montagnard tribes in the area called it "the mountain of the crouching beast," though there is no mention in their oral traditions that explains why. On maps of Vietnam, it is labeled simply Dong Ap Bia or Ap Bia Mountain. Unlike most other mountains on the western side of the A Shau, it is not part of a larger chain, but stands alone, 970 meters above sea level at its peak, bordered on the west by the Trung Pham River and the Laotian border, on the north by Dong So Ridge, and on the south by the Rao Lao River. From this peak, like

1

the tendrils of some giant sea creature, a number of large ridges and fingers and a labyrinth of deep ravines and wide draws branch out in all directions. Two of these ridges—Hill 937 on the north and Hill 916 on the southeast—form mountains of their own, and, like all the rest of Dong Ap Bia, lie under a thick, double- and triple-canopy jungle. Under this canopy—which in places rises to heights of two hundred feet— grow layers of smaller trees, all interwoven with a tangle of vines, thick brush, and almost impenetrable stands of bamboo.

The OD green UH-ID Command and Control helicopter arrived over the mountain just after first light. Lt. Col. Weldon Honeycutt, the commander of the 3/187th, sat in the back of the ship before a bank of radios. Next to him sat his sergeant major, Bernie Meehan; and next to him, Capt. James Deleathe, the artillery liaison officer. The 3/187th was one of the five battalions that would be combat-assaulting into the northern A Shau Valley, and Honeycutt had arrived to direct the prep of its LZ before the landing.

The pilot, with his ship at one thousand feet, flew across the mountain from southeast to northeast, then back in the opposite direction. On the second pass, a heavy machine gun opened up on the ship from a position somewhere on the southwest slope of the mountain. The bullets made a thackthack sound as they passed under the ship's rotors. The door gunner on the left side of the ship tensed and brought his M60 machine gun around, looking for the telltale sign of a muzzle flash, but whoever had fired had slipped back into cover.

The pilot circled the mountain for a while and then followed a large ridge northwest for eighteen hundred meters, until he came over the small field that would be used as the LZ for Honeycutt's battalion in less than two hours. The field, covered by waist-high elephant grass and a few stunted bushes, stood in sharp contrast to the towering jungle that ringed it like the walls of a stockade. It was a deep Indochina jungle, a triple-canopy rain forest that, except for the breaks of a few narrow valleys, flowed on without interruption for miles in all directions. Most of the trees in the canopy were from 75 to 90 feet high, but in some places the scattered crowns of trees as tall as 150 feet jutted out incongruously, their brown leafless trunks in sharp contrast to the deep greens below.

As he had the mountain, the pilot circled the LZ so Honeycutt and his staff could have a closer look. The rising sun had burned most of the ground fog off the landing zone, but there were still patches of it scattered around the ridge like small, furry clouds. The draws on both sides of the ridge, however, still lay hidden under a thick, white blanket.

The pilot turned the ship south and went into a hover at four hundred feet over the larger of the two draws. They were all waiting for something, and it came a few minutes later—a loud roar that split the quiet morning air with the ferocity of a thunderclap. Everyone in the C and C ship looked up at once as two black-and-green-camouflaged Phantom jets exploded from the thick, soupy clouds overhead and rocketed downward, trailing white exhaust fumes, their engines opened up in a full throaty roar. Following closely behind the jets was a much slower twin-propelled OV-10 FAC plane.

Honeycutt was on the horn with the forward air controller as soon as he spotted the plane. "Bilk 34, this is Blackjack."

"Roger, Blackjack."

"What have you got for me, Bilk?"

"I've got some 250-high-drags, napalm, and 20 mike-mike."

"Okay, Bilk, I want you to give me a pass from northwest to southeast. Start out with the HE and napalm."

"That's a roger. Okay, baby, set your ass in. We're comin' down."

"Okay, gunfighters," the FAC pilot said, talking to the jet pilots now, "if you're in position, I'll mark the target."

"Roger that, Bilk."

The FAC plane turned back to the field and began a sliding, quick descent.

Wham!

A white phosphorous rocket shot from a rack under the plane's right wing and, trailing a small thin plume of smoke, streaked toward the ground, exploding in a geyser of white fire directly in the center of the field.

"Can you see my mark?"

"Can see."

"Make your first run fifty meters to the north of the marking round."

One of the fighter-bombers pulled away from the other and went into a steep, growling, angry dive. At five hundred feet, he leveled off and cut loose two 250-pounders. They looked like large darts as they streaked in, at first parallel to the ground and then in a gradually tilting plane. Each hit on a different side of the marking round, hit with a red-orange flash and a roiling ball of thick, brown smoke. The sound came a fraction of a second later, a twin crumpcrump.

The smoke was still funneling upward when the second fighter-bomber made his run, diving, leveling off, and finally releasing two fat-bodied, silver, napalm canisters. Unlike the HE bombs, the canisters moved parallel to the ground for just a few short seconds, then plummeted straight down, exploding in a sheet of red flames that rushed forward across the ground like a huge wave, spewing out thick tendrils of fiery jelly which skipped and rolled and splashed forward through the thick elephant grass. In seconds the thick mat of elephant grass for fifty yards was burned and flattened into a residue of smoldering cinders, and the few stunted trees turned into flaming grotesque shapes. The LZ prep had begun. The scenario was being repeated on the four other LZs and would last a total of fifty minutes.

0620 Hours Firebase Blaze

Twenty kilometers to the southeast, the nearly eighteen hundred men who would make today's combat assaults on the northern A Shau were already waiting on the edge of their pickup zone, listening to the exploding bombs. The sound of the explosions was muted by the distance, muffled, like the rumbling sound of distant thunder.

The PZ was about one thousand meters long and five hundred wide. It lay in the flat bottom of a small valley near the juncture of three small rivers. The five battalions of men were spaced out evenly across it, with the three battalions from the 101st Airborne Division—the 1/506th, 3/187th, and 2/501st—on the east end of the PZ and the two South Vietnamese battalions—the 4/1 and 2/1 ARVN—on the west side. Most of the men had spent the night in the low hills above the valley, right outside the protective guns of Firebase Blaze, which was the staging area for Operation Apache Snow.

For most of the assembled men, there was little to do now but wait. Some of the men spent these last moments walking around the area talking with friends, smoking cigarettes, their helmets off, OD green towels around their necks to catch the sweat running off their faces or over their heads like turbans as protection against the morning sun. Others lay sprawled on the ground, using their helmets or bulging rucksacks as pillows, trying to catch a quick catnap. But most of the men spent these last moments just sitting quietly, listening to the LZ prep, writing a last letter home, paging desultorily through a tattered magazine or dog-eared paperback novel, making final adjustments on equipment or cleaning their weapons. There was still a lot of activity around them, though. Officers and NCOs were rushing about, holding final conferences and briefings, checking and rechecking map coordinates, yelling out orders, holding hurried radio conversations.

Overhead two camouflaged fighter-bombers, their wings loaded with bombs, rocketed by, heading west toward the A Shau. They were followed a moment later by another pair, and then another, all leaving the sky filled with thin white trails of jet exhaust. Finally a FAC plane appeared. At the sight of the assembled men, the pilot dropped into the narrow valley and buzzed the PZ, coming in fifty feet off the ground. Both the pilot and copilot waved as they went by and dipped their left wing in salute to the men. A cheer went up across the field, and hundreds of men waved back.

On the edge of the PZ, a Huey UH-ID landed, and a colonel, surrounded by a bevy of aides, jumped out. A group of officers, who had been standing on the edge of the PZ, rushed forward to meet them. They met in the center of the field and carried on an excited, hurried conversation. One of his aides held a map, and the colonel pointed at various spots on it and delivered a lecture to the other officers, who nodded their understanding. When the lecture was over, the colonel and his aides jumped back into the Huey, which took off and headed west toward the A Shau. Minutes later, another helicopter landed, this time a giant CH47 Chinook. The moment it touched down, the rear ramp dropped and disgorged five men carrying the baseplate, tube, and legs for an 81mm mortar. They were followed by a man with a 90mm recoilless rifle over his shoulder and another ten to fifteen men lugging boxes of recoilless-rifle rounds and cans of machine-gun ammo.

Around the PZ, most of the men just sat and listened, listened and watched. Most of them tried to feign a look of unconcern, a look of disinterest, but it was a false look. Inside, most were anxious and tense, filled with foreboding over the coming combat assault.

Sp.4 Jerry Hoffman, a rifleman with Bravo 1/506th, was one of them. Although he had not been in-country long nor had much specific knowledge about the valley, the little he had heard so far—most of it vague rumors—had given him cause for worry.

Not long after Jerry and the rest of the men in Bravo Company were briefed about Apache Snow at Camp Evans on May 8, an incident took place that made the young soldier realize that, all rumors aside, he had reason to be worried.

Right after the briefing, a group of men from Bravo Company was standing around discussing Apache Snow when Minh, the company Kit

Carson Scout, had walked up and openly announced that he did not intend to go along on the operation.

"Why not?" a soldier had asked.

"A Shau number-one bad place," Minh had said. "Bad, bad place! Me no go A Shau."

Jerry had not personally heard Minh make his pronouncement, but had heard about it from a number of men. Like them, he was stunned by the words. During the four months the former–North Vietnamese soldier had been scouting for the company, he had led them through a number of bad fights and tough situations and never once shown a hint of cowardice. Still, Jerry, like most other men in his squad, had considered Minh's words to be little more than an idle threat, typical soldier bravado. He did, that is, until the next morning when he discovered that the scout had gotten himself arrested for carrying a rucksack full of marijuana through the checkpoint leading into Camp Evans and was now sitting safely in the stockade.

The incident had been upsetting, but what followed had not been much better. For the last two days, Jerry had been forced to listen to the veterans in his platoon tell endless stories about the A Shau Valley. One man told of how mile-long convoys of trucks moved down the center of the valley on Highway 548 with total impunity. Another that the valley floor was covered with enemy division-size base camps, and that they were protected, in turn, by hundreds of tanks, antiaircraft guns, and heavy artillery. One sergeant, who seemed to know his facts, read a litany of every unit, including the legendary 1st Cav, which had invaded the valley over the years and, as he phrased it, gotten their butts kicked.

Jerry had no idea which of the stories were true and which were part of the mystique that had grown up around the valley. If only a small part of it were true, he and the rest of the men in Bravo Company had reason to worry.

Nearby, Lt. Charles Denholm, a platoon leader with Bravo 3/187th, did not have to wonder what awaited him and his platoon when they CA'd into the valley. He knew exactly what awaited them—trouble. Only two weeks before, Denholm, along with the rest of the 3/187th had been in a hard fight with a large NVA unit for control of Dong Ngai, a towering mountain that overlooked the eastern side of the valley floor. The NVA had been firmly entrenched on Dong Ngai, and it had taken the 3/187th over a week to push them off.

One night, while near the peak of Dong Ngai, and with fighting still going on all around him, Denholm looked down into the heart of the A Shau five thousand feet below and saw what he estimated to be a convoy of at least forty trucks, all with their lights on, moving right down the center of the valley. When he got over the initial shock of the sight, the lieutenant called in artillery fire on the convoy, but the trucks quickly turned off their lights and pulled off the road. For a number of nights afterwards, Denholm spotted similar large convoys and each time called in artillery on them, though he doubted if he was causing any damage. One night he and another officer even saw the lights of what they were sure was a giant Russian helicopter flying back and forth from one end of the valley to the other. The sight of the helicopter chilled the lieutenant's blood, and he thought: If they've got trucks and helicopters down there, what in the hell else do they have. He had hoped he would never have to find out.

In still another area of the PZ, the coming CA was the subject of a conversation between Lt. George Bennitt, a platoon leader with Alpha 3/187th, his RTO, and a young sergeant.

"What in the fuck are we going in there for?" the young sergeant asked.

"I don't know," Bennitt said. The lieutenant considered his answer honest, for he really did not know. He personally thought the entire operation smacked of lunacy. Every allied unit that had gone into the A Shau in the last four years had met disaster there, and he was sure it likewise awaited the 101st Airborne Division.

"We oughta just let the NVA have the goddamn A Shau," the sergeant continued, "and just concentrate on defending the plains around Hue."

"You won't get any argument out of me," Bennitt said.

"Yeah," the RTO said, "just let 'em have the goddamn place, and forget about it. Just pretend it doesn't exist."

It all made perfect sense to Lieutenant Bennitt.

0650 Hours

At precisely 0649 the Tac-Air prep of the five LZs stopped, and the FAC planes and fighter-bombers pulled away, lifted up over the mountains, and headed back to the coast. For a long tense minute or two, there was quiet over the LZs, though the prep fire was far from over. On Firebases Bradley, Airborne, Currahee, Cannon, and Berchtesgaden, strung out along the mountaintops of the eastern A Shau, the crews of ten artillery batteries waited by their guns. Most had been waiting for almost an hour and already had dozens of rounds ready to fire and their guns laid in on their targets.

At 0650, the signal to fire was given on each of the five firebases, and sixty howitzers lashed out at once. In a fraction of a second sixty high-explosive rounds were sent hurtling across the valley, and a second later sixty more. On each gun it was the same story. As fast as the loaders fed the rounds into the breach, the gunners pulled the lanyard and sent them hurtling toward the LZs. They fired so quickly that there were hundreds of rounds in the air at the same time, and they struck the LZs in an ever-rising crescendo of noise, a thunderous explosion that ripped apart trees and blew gaping holes in the seas of elephant grass and thick patches of bamboo.

0700 Hours

"Saddle up!"

The words rolled down through the five battalions like an echo. One after another, the eighteen hundred men began slipping on their rucksacks and falling into lines. A minute or so later, they heard the sound they had been expecting, a low thapthapthapthap that came out of the east and grew louder and louder with each passing second. The lift-ships appeared shortly, coming in just above the foothills to the east, then dropping down into the river valley and rocketing forward just above the ground.

There were sixteen ships in the first squadron. Guided by Pathfinders, they settled on the PZ in a roar of noise and flying debris. The men nearest the ships had to hold onto their helmets to keep from having them knocked off by the fierce pull of the ship's rotors and to cover their faces with towels to keep from choking on the dust swirling through the air.

The first squadron of sixteen was quickly followed by another, then at regular intervals by a third and fourth, until eventually the entire PZ was covered with lift-ships and a tornado of sound.

There were sixty-five ships in all, though to Lt. Frank Boccia, a platoon leader for Bravo 3/187th, who stood with the rest of his company on the far south side of the PZ, it seemed like every Huey UH-ID helicopter in Vietnam had arrived to take part in the combat assault. Boccia had read accounts of D-day in World War II in which men were awestruck by the sight of all the ships supporting the invasion, and that is exactly how he felt now—awestruck! My God! he thought, realizing his entire body had broken out in goose bumps, they must be bringing in the entire Army here.

Down from where Boccia stood, Pfc. Michael Smith of Delta 3/187th had also watched the sixty-five lift-ships settle onto the PZ, only not in awe. He had watched instead in stunned silence, more concerned with a rumor that was circulating through Delta Company than with anything else around him. According to the rumor, Delta's LZ was going to be hot. Michael had been in Vietnam only a few weeks and had never been on a CA before, let alone one into a hot LZ. In training, though, he had learned from veterans that there was nothing in Vietnam quite as terrifying as CA'ing into an area the NVA had surrounded and on which they had zeroed in their weapons. Michael had thought that a 50-minute Tac-Air and a 20-minute artillery prep would have been enough to destroy any enemy units dug in around the 3/187th's landing zone, but apparently he was wrong.

"There's some bad shit out there," a man behind Michael said. "Real bad!"

"We'll probably make the news before the day is over," another man added. "That's one thing you can count on when you go into the A Shau."

Make the news! Michael did not know much about Vietnam as yet, but he did know that only the biggest and bloodiest battles were written up in the newspapers. Making the news was certainly not something he was looking forward to.

The rumor of the hot LZ had also filtered down through the ranks of nearby Charlie 3/187th and had spread like a brush fire. When Sp.4's John Comerford, Leonel Mata, and Ron Swanson heard the rumor, however, they ignored it. All veterans of the company and close personal friends, they had been on a number of CAs before and had long ago quit putting credence in rumors. Each had learned early after arriving in Vietnam that fear was contagious and that a man who gave in to it was a man out of control, a man befuddled and confused and a danger to everyone around him, but especially to himself. To survive in Vietnam, you had to be cool and calculating and clearheaded. But most of all, as each believed, you had to have an infinite faith in the idea that you were going to survive the war and make it home. And it was a faith all three possessed in abundance.

0708 Hours

Nearly four hundred men were scheduled to go out in the first lift. When the order was given, they started running across the open field toward their respective ships. The men ran hunched over, holding their helmets on with one hand, their weapons in the other, squinting their eyes against the maelstrom of dust and debris turned up by all the whirling, sucking rotors. They boarded six to a ship, with two men sitting back to back in the center of the floor and two men on each side, their legs hanging into space. As soon as everyone was settled, the signal to start the operation was given. Lift off!

At the signal, the sixteen ships in the first squadron went into a hover, and then one after the other began nosing over and accelerating forward, their powerful jet engines roaring, scudding crablike only a few feet off the ground. As they roared forward, they rapidly picked up speed and altitude until they reached the river juncture, then banked sharply to the left and started out of the small river valley, climbing all the time.

The first squadron was followed quickly by the lift-off of the second, and then, at regular intervals by the third and fourth, so that by 0730, all sixty-five ships—and the lead companies for the 1/506th and 3/187th—were in the air and roaring forward at sixty knots toward the heart of the valley. The long-awaited allied invasion of the northern A Shau was only minutes away.

CHAPTER 2

PARADISE LOST

Although it would play a major role in the Vietnam War, the A Shau Valley is not mentioned in the recorded history of Vietnam. A slash in the mountains on the far western edge of Thua Thien Province, the valley lies at the heart of the Chaine Annamitique, a southern spur of mountains more than eleven hundred kilometers long that begins in China, curls like a snake down through Laos and three-quarters of the way through Vietnam before turning inland and stopping abruptly only sixty kilometers from Saigon.

The valley itself is more than forty-five kilometers long, mostly a flat stretch of land, covered with matted elephant grass and small trees, varying in width from three hundred meters near the eastern tip of Dong So Ridge to more than three kilometers at Ta Bat.

The Rao Lao, which begins in the deep rain forests of Laos, runs through the heart of the valley, a wide, muddy river with a rocky bottom, overshadowed on both sides by towering rugged mountains whose peaks in places lie hidden in thick cumulus clouds.

Because of its rugged terrain, only the Pacohs—one of thirty-three Montagnard tribes that inhabited the mountains of South Vietnam—lived in the valley. Like their cousins to the north, the Bru, the Pacohs were a dark-skinned people with short, muscular legs, whose men wore loincloths and women colorful wraparound skirts and a plethora of bracelets, necklaces, and amulets.

There is no record to indicate how long the Pacohs had inhabited the A Shau, but they had managed to stay isolated from the cultural influences, invasions, migrations, and dynastic struggles that ebbed and flowed out of India and China and across Vietnam for a thousand years before the coming of the first Europeans.

Like the Bru, the Pacohs were a shy, passive people who detested violence and lived in a magical, animistic world of spirits, myths, and supernaturalism. And like them, also, their isolated mountain valley kept them safe from the human turmoil on the coastal plains only twenty kilometers away.

To outsiders, the jungled mountains of the northern A Shau were a hostile environment, a dangerous maze of impassable terrain and wild animals. But to the Pacohs, it was a lush paradise, filled with everything they needed for a full and happy life.

Practicing a slash-and-burn agriculture, they cleared tracts of jungle, then planted and harvested a cornucopia of squash, sweet potatoes, corn, rice, cucumbers, manioc, and numerous other vegetables. Around their more permanent villages, they planted orchards of bananas and oranges and small patches of tobacco.

In the forests, using spears and crossbows, the men hunted an endless supply of deer and wild pigs, and in the countless clear mountain streams trapped trout as big as salmon. In these same forests, the women gathered mint and saffron, wild fruit and nuts, berries, and bamboo shoots. And both surrounded all their efforts at food gathering with a continual cycle of festivals, feasts, and celebrations.

The tribe had lived like this for a thousand years, maybe five thousand. And though they had no written language or history, their oral traditions were filled with vivid stories. One in particular, like the biblical tale of Noah, told of a great flood covering the entire earth and of a single woman and a dog who survive. It was from this woman that the Pacohs believed they had descended.

During their entire history, the Pacohs had gone to war only once, and then only to avenge a woman killed by some Phuong traders. It was a war that lasted only a few hours, and when it ended only two people lay dead. Nonetheless, their isolation in the valley was slowly, almost imperceptibly, coming to an end. While the French had controlled Vietnam since the 1880s, they had never shown more than a passing interest in the Pacohs. Occasionally colonial officials would forcibly take young Pacoh boys off to be educated in French schools in Hue or Saigon, but other than that had little interest or contact with the tribe. The beginning of the First Indochina War between the French and Ho Chi Minh's communist army, however, brought an immediate end to the A Shau's isolation. It ended with a single statement by Gen. Vo Nguyen Giap, Ho's commander in chief and the eventual architect of the massive French defeat at Dien Bien Phu. "To seize and control the highlands," Giap said, "is to solve the whole problem of Vietnam." Giap's simple, somewhat enigmatic statement would for the first time draw the Pacohs and their valley into the 5,000-year-old struggle to control Indochina.

Soon after the outbreak of hostilities between the French and the communists, both sides, realizing the value of the Montagnards as guides, food providers, porters, and guerilla fighters, began trying to win them over as allies. The violent tug-of-war for their allegiance that ensued quickly produced a tragic situation. For a variety of reasons, some tribes sided with the French and others with the communists. Many neighboring tribes with conflicting loyalties—tribes that had lived in peace for hundreds of years—soon found themselves at war with each other.

Since most of the fighting in the First Indochina War took place in northern Vietnam, the Pacohs managed to avoid getting drawn into it, though once when the French were defeated in a battle near the valley, the Pacohs helped to carry their wounded to safety in Laos.

Their immunity from the war was short-lived, however. With the end of hostilities in 1954 and the signing of the Geneva Accords partitioning Vietnam at the 17th parallel, the struggle for the allegiance of the Montagnards only intensified.

In the communist north, Ho Chi Minh managed to pacify the tribes by offering them self-government in certain autonomous zones and some representation in the National Assembly. It was a different story in the south. Now under the control of the fiercely anticommunist government of President Ngo Dinh Diem, a new battle was already brewing for their control.

The Viet Cong, the communist guerilla group in South Vietnam, kept undercover for four years after the signing of the Geneva Accords, but in 1959, under specific instructions from North Vietnam's Politburo, they began dispatching political cadre into the highlands in order to proselytize the tribes with communist ideology.

In that same year, fearing the loss of the tribes to the Viet Cong, President Diem sent out a proclamation ordering all the Montagnards in the provinces of northern I Corps to abandon their villages and move to the lowlands. There, Diem told them, the South Vietnamese government could better protect them.

Like all the tribes in I Corps, the Pacohs were dumbstruck by the government edict. Although most tribesmen had never left the A Shau, they had heard enough tales from Montagnards who had lived in the lowlands to dread such a move. Why would they want to leave their beautiful mountains and bountiful farms to live in rat-infested shantytowns on the outskirts of Hue and Phu Bai? they reasoned. Why give up hunting their meat with crossbows in the lush rain forests to accept starvation wages working on the docks of Da Nang? There were about twelve hundred Pacohs living in the A Shau at that time, spread out among forty large villages and a number of small settlements. Not one, however, obeyed the government edict.

The South Vietnamese responded to the rebuff with more edicts, but when those edicts likewise failed to get any results, they turned to deceit. They sent delegations into the valley and, with trickery, convinced most of the village headmen to come down to Hue for what they described as a ''short training course.'' They told the men not to bring many personal belongings for they would be returning home shortly. Once the headmen arrived in Hue, though, the government had them imprisoned, then sent word back to the Pacohs that their leaders would remain in jail until the entire tribe had moved to the lowlands.

The Pacohs could not even begin to comprehend this act of treachery by the South Vietnamese. It was so alien to their simple moral code that many were forced to assume that all South Vietnamese had two livers, which filled them with an inordinate amount of bile. The Pacohs grieved for their imprisoned leaders, but still refused to leave their valley.

After this second rebuff, the South Vietnamese became furious. They returned to the mountains this time not with edicts, but with troops, intending to round the people up like cattle and drive them down to the lowlands. At the sight of the soldiers, however, most of the Pacohs fled into the forests. There they huddled in silence while the soldiers burned down their homes and crops and went on a rampage of destruction.

When the soldiers finally left two or three days later, the Pacohs came out of hiding and began rebuilding their homes and replanting their crops, unaware that the cycle of peace they had known for hundreds of years had been broken for good.

No sooner had the soldiers left the villages than the Viet Cong arrived. In a number of villages, they abruptly rounded up all the able-bodied men, then marched them off like slaves to work as porters on the nearby Ho Chi Minh Trail. Those who resisted conscription were shot on the spot. In one large prosperous village, the communists ordered the chief and his young daughter to go with them into the Laotian mountains for reeducation. When the chief refused, he was beheaded and his daughter forcibly carried off.

Fearing the Pacohs were beginning to side with the Viet Cong, the South Vietnamese once again returned to the A Shau and began arresting suspected communist sympathizers. Back at Hue, these men were tortured and forced to sign confessions admitting to being VC. Other Pacohs were rounded up by government troops and, with their arms bound, paraded through the streets of Hue and Phu Bai as captured Viet Cong.

Caught in this violent struggle, Pacoh tribal life began fracturing and then disintegrating completely. Still unwilling to take sides in the war, entire villages began making the ignominious trip down to the lowlands. There, as they had always suspected, they were crammed into muddy, fetid resettlement camps, surrounded by concertina wire and bunkers. Other Pacohs, unable to leave their mountains, packed their few simple belongings and moved into the Laotian mountains only a few miles away, where they hid in deep caves and subsisted on roots and small game. The exodus continued steadily for the next two years, so that by 1963 there were only a few dozen Pacohs still living in the A Shau.

The Viet Cong had had considerable success in the highlands, but it was obvious to their North Vietnamese surrogates that they were far too weak to gain full control of them and, by extension, to win the war. In late 1963, the Central Committee of the Vietnamese Worker's Party met in Hanoi and passed a resolution calling for an escalation of the war in the south "in order to create a basic change in the balance of forces between the enemy and us in South Vietnam." This somewhat cryptic statement meant basically that the North Vietnamese had decided to win the war, and to win it with North Vietnamese troops. While their first infiltrators were political cadre, before long, companies, battalions, and finally even regiments of North Vietnamese Army regulars were making the long trip south down the Ho Chi Minh Trail. With these troops, the communists began dramatically escalating the fight for control of the mountains, their first step toward the eventual conquest of the entire south.

The Americans were hardly ignorant of the North Vietnamese intentions and, like Giap, more than aware of the strategic importance of the highlands. Special Forces troops, popularly called Green Berets, already had a number of outposts strung across the entire length of the South Vietnamese highlands. Faced with North Vietnamese troops now, they began dramatically increasing both their numbers and strength. Manned by a mixed bag of American and South Vietnamese Special Forces troops and Montagnard irregulars, these camps were placed strategically both to blunt any communist attempt to gain control of the highlands and to stop them from infiltrating men and supplies down to the coastal plains.

The scenario that followed the construction of these camps was the same in the A Shau as in a dozen other places in the highlands, although the stakes were considerably higher. Because of the valley's length, it was a natural conduit down which the enemy moved the troops and supplies needed to launch attacks against Hue and the surrounding coastal regions of Thua Thien and Quang Nam provinces.

Hue was not so much militarily important as symbolically. The Center of Hue, called the Citadel, had been built to resemble China's Imperial City at Peking, and was considered one of the most beautiful places in Vietnam. About two miles square, the Citadel sat on the banks of the languid Perfume River and was surrounded by a wall that was from sixty to two hundred feet thick. Among its many impressive buildings was the Imperial Palace, which had served as the residence for generations of Annamese emperors. Thousands of Vietnamese tourists and religious pilgrims visited the Citadel each year, and its loss to the communists would have dealt the country a serious psychological blow and sent the government reeling in confusion. The communists knew this also, and by 1964 began moving troops into the A Shau and developing the logistical system in the valley that they would need for an eventual attack on Hue.

In an attempt to counter this new enemy move, the Americans and their South Vietnamese allies began the immediate construction of what was to be a chain of Special Forces camps in the A Shau. Within a year, they managed to complete a camp at Ta Bat in the central valley near an abandoned French airstrip, another at A Loui in the northern valley, and a final one in the southern valley near A Shau, an abandoned Pacoh village and namesake for the entire valley.

With these camps as bases, American and South Vietnamese Special Forces troops, aided by various civilian irregulars and Nung tribesmen, began monitoring and attacking enemy troops and supply columns in the valley. In the beginning all three camps met with some limited success, and it seemed for a time as if the allies might be able to break the stranglehold the communists were developing on the valley.

It was to the camp at A Shau that the last Pacohs in the valley—their number having now dwindled to twenty-two—came for protection. Frightened by the steady stream of North Vietnamese pouring into the valley, but still unwilling to leave their ancestral lands, the twenty-two thought they might find a modicum of safety within the camp's perimeter.

The Pacohs instead found themselves in the center of yet another nightmare. It did not take the North Vietnamese long to respond to the threat the camps posed to their logistical system in the valley. Since they did not have the forces in the valley at the time to attempt an all-out attack on the camps, they opted instead to start an ever-escalating campaign of harassment against them.

Forced to live near the camp's perimeter in corrugated-metal lean-tos, the Pacohs frequently had to run to their bunkers to avoid mortar attacks and infantry probes. They tried growing their own food on a few small fields near the camp, but the defoliants used by the Americans to clear field-of-fire destroyed their crops before they could be harvested. A few even tried hunting in the surrounding jungle, but the incessant bombing and artillery had driven most of the game from the area. In the end, most were forced to subsist on the garbage left by the camp's defenders.

Hearing of the plight of these last twenty-two, Richard Watson, a linguist who had studied the Pacoh language and written extensively about the tribe, visited the camp in April 1965 in order to make arrangements for their removal to a farm outside of Hue. Watson arrived with a young Pacoh friend, who became very distressed at the sight of his people dressed in rags and wandering through the camp like beggars. While Watson watched in silence, his friend turned away in disgust and stared off mutely at the Laotian mountains to the west.

Tearfully, the young man pointed to one of the taller mountains, "Do you see that?"

Watson soon located two or three small trails of smoke coming from an area near the top of a 5,000-foot-high peak right on the edge of the border. The smoke, Watson knew, was coming from small cooking fires, likely those of Pacohs who had fled the A Shau.

"Do you see them?" the young man asked again.

"Yes, I see them."

"Those little wisps of smoke are the last of my people."

CHAPTER 3

FALL OF A SHAU

About the time the last Pacohs departed the A Shau with Richard Watson, the communists decided drastically to increase the scale of their attacks on the three allied camps. A good portion of the 325th NVA Division had recently come south, and most of its battalions were either bivouacked in the A Shau or scattered in camps in the huge communist Base Area 611 just across the border. While the 325th had been earmarked for eventual attacks against the coastal regions, it was first given the assignment of destroying the three Special Forces camps and ridding the valley of all allied forces.

Units from the 325th moved in quickly and established positions around all three camps, cordoning them off as you might a city under siege. The camps soon found themselves subject to nightly mortar attacks and periodic small, but savage, infantry assaults. Any force larger than a few men that ventured outside the wire of any camp was almost certain of being ambushed, and large platoon- and company-size units that attempted to launch operations into the valley faced almost certain destruction. After a while, the allies rather than the communists were forced into a defensive role, with the camps becoming not as they were intended, springboards for aggressive offensive operations, but little more than muddy, fetid, besieged enclaves.

On December 25, 1965, fatigued by the incessant attacks and realizing that they were eventually going to be overrun, the South Vietnamese who controlled the camps at A Loui and Ta Bat abandoned them and fled the valley. They reasoned correctly that their few infantry companies would be no match for a determined reinforced NVA regiment.

The Americans, who controlled the A Shau camp, decided to stay. Their decision was the beginning of a long chain of causality which would end four and a half years later in one of the bloodiest and most controversial battles of the Vietnam War.

Triangular shaped, surrounded by minefields and rows of razor-sharp concertina wire, and defended, in turn, by 17 American Green Berets, and 210 South Vietnamese civilian irregulars, the camp at A Shau, while the last in the valley, was still a formidable obstacle to NVA hegemony in the A Shau. Although far from impregnable, to take it would require a major effort on the enemy's part and a huge loss of life. It was a price they were more than willing to pay, however.

In early March, the camp commander, Capt. John D. Blair IV, received an intelligence report pointing to the arrival of the 325th's 95th Regiment to the area. Although Blair could not be certain what the 95th's intentions were, he assumed they meant to attack the camp. His assumption was substantiated two days later with the capture of an NVA soldier from the 95th in the act of scouting the camp. Under interrogation the man admitted that on two other occasions, in order to test the camp defenses, he had actually penetrated one layer of its concertina wire. If Blair needed any further proof, two days later, two other enemy soldiers from the 95th surrendered and told him that the camp was going to be attacked on March 11 or 12.

Armed with these facts, and realizing he had nothing close to the manpower he would need to take on a 1,500-man North Vietnamese regiment, Blair immediately sent in a request to the South Vietnamese I Corps commander for reinforcements. The I Corps commander, however, refused to send help, saying that he was already understrength and that the defense of Hue was a higher priority.

Blair next called the 5th Special Forces Group, and they dispatched 143 Nung tribesmen. The Nungs were Vietnam-born Chinese who hated both the Vietnamese and the communists. Though mercenaries, they were noted for being savage fighters and incredibly brave. With these additions, Capt. Blair now had a total of 434 men under arms.

The first warning of the impending attack came in the early morning hours of March 9 when guards on the camp's perimeter heard digging just outside the wire. Thinking the enemy might be digging assault trenches, the guards opened fire with their M79 grenade launchers, then adjusted 81mm mortar fire on the suspected enemy positions.

The digging stopped, but a few hours later, the NVA responded with mortar fire of their own. At first they hit the camp with just a few rounds, but after adjusting their fire, they opened up with every gun they had. A plethora of enemy 60mm, 82mm, and even the giant Russian 120mm mortars hit the camp with salvo after salvo, a torrent of fire that drove the camp's defenders into their bunkers.

They assumed the mortar attack would last only a few minutes, but an hour later the rounds were still falling, and half the camp lay in shambles. The shelling had destroyed the water tower, reduced the team house to rubble, and set a number of other structures on fire, and still the rounds continued falling.

In the camp, the men braced for the inevitable, knowing that the NVA would not put out such intense firepower just to knock out the camp's water supply or destroy its team house.

More than two hours after the shelling started and with mortar rounds still falling on the center of the camp, two companies of NVA infantry, led by sappers carrying Bangalore torpedoes, broke from the surrounding treeline and started heading for the camp's south wall. The sappers were either completely naked or wore loincloths. The enemy infantrymen wore pith helmets, green fatigues, tire-track sandals and carried AK47 assault rifles with 30-round banana-clips.

The men on the wall braced for the attack and met the enemy infantry with a torrent of heavy machine-gun and rifle fire. In the center of the camp, mortarmen cranked the barrels of their mortars up until they were nearly perpendicular with the ground and began dropping rounds right into the center of the charging enemy. The enemy companies buckled under the heavy fire, retreated momentarily, then regrouped and charged once more, but were again chopped to pieces by mortar, machine-gun, and small-arms fire.

Sullenly, angrily, the NVA pulled back from the wire, collected their wounded and moved back into prepared trenches in the treeline. They left nearly fifty of their dead dangling in the wire around the camp or splayed out across the open field.

The NVA commander was furious over the setback and ordered the camp shelled again. For the next two hours, the enemy mortars pounded the camp with hardly a pause. When they finished, everything in the camp was flattened and fifty men inside lay wounded.

The camp needed help, but it was not to be forthcoming. The 3d

Marine Amphibious Force at Da Nang had operational control over the camp, but there was little they could do to help. The A Shau was beyond the range of any artillery they had, and because of a thick ground fog and 100-foot cloud ceilings, their fighter-bombers could not make bomb and strafing runs around the camp's perimeter.

The camp was on its own, and all night long its defenders huddled in their bunkers, enduring an endless rain of mortar rounds, bracing themselves for the final human-wave assault they knew the NVA would eventually throw against them. Their only hope was that the clouds would lift in the morning and that the sun would come out and burn off the ground fog. If that happened, the fighter-bombers would come with napalm and cluster bombs and clear the surrounding jungle of NVA infantry.

But in the morning the low cloud ceiling did not lift, and the defenders of A Shau found themselves staring out at a perimeter half-hidden in soupy gray mist.

The mortar barrage had stopped for two or three hours during the night, but with first light the NVA opened up again, and this time not only with their mortars, but with a number of recoilless rifles they had brought up during the night and positioned all around the camp.

The fire was again relentless, and inside the camp the numbers of dead and wounded began adding up. To try to suppress some of the enemy gun positions, an Air Force AC47 gunship was called in. Nicknamed "Puff," after a popular song of the time, this fixed-wing plane was fitted out with six miniguns and was capable of saturating an area the size of a football field with fire in just a few seconds. Unfortunately, the pilot could not see below the cloud ceiling to make his gun runs, but instead had to come in right above the jungle. The ship was just getting ready to make its first run on some enemy positions north of the camp when a number of enemy heavy machine guns found it first. With everyone in the camp watching, the ship was riddled with machine-gun fire and sent flaming into the jungle. Half of the gunship's crew members were rescued, but the loss of the ship dealt a demoralizing blow to the camp's defenders.

Two Skyraiders arrived minutes later to make bombing and strafing runs around the camp, but likewise had to fly so low to avoid the cloud ceiling that they began getting hit with flak by enemy 37mm antiaircraft guns dug in at the top of the mountains east of the camp. The enemy guns were so high up that they actually fired down on the Skyraiders.

One of the planes, piloted by Marine 1st Lt. Augusto Xavier, ignored the flak and went right at a cluster of enemy gun positions north of the camp with 250-pound bombs and 20mm cannon fire. Xavier made two successful passes against the enemy positions, but on the third was hit and crashed into the side of a mountain east of the camp.

Two Air Force A-1E Skyraiders arrived a short time later and likewise began making bomb and strafing runs on the enemy positions. After the third or fourth run, one of the planes, piloted by Maj. Stafford Myers, was hit and forced to crash-land on the airstrip on the western edge of the camp. Upon stopping, Stafford jumped out of the burning plane and scrambled into a nearby trench. Enemy infantrymen spotted Stafford and poured out of the jungle after him. Myers's wingman, Maj. Bernard Fischer, like an avenging angel, flew back and forth above the airstrip, cutting down groups of enemy soldiers with cannon fire every time they tried to get at Myers. After his fifth or sixth strafing run, Major Fischer, in a daring move, landed his plane on the airstrip. Under a hail of machine-gun fire, Fischer taxied down the runway, flipped open his cockpit, and pulled Myers in. Then, with his engine opened to full throttle, he roared down the runway and took off to safety.

Fischer and Myers were lucky. Four medevac helicopters that had tried to land in the camp at the same time Fischer and Myers were making their escape, lay beside the same airstrip, destroyed. The NVA had, in fact, so tightened their cordon around the camp that they were shooting down more than half the helicopters that tried to land.

That night the camp was once again pounded unmercifully with mortar and recoilless-rifle fire, though there were no buildings left standing in the camp and half the camp's 434 defenders were either dead or wounded.

At four in the morning, the NVA launched another assault, this time with two battalions, three times the number of troops they had thrown against the wire the first time. A thousand strong, they charged across the airfield, then right through the minefield. Dozens of enemy soldiers were shredded by the mines and lay screaming in the open field. The infantry behind them, though, ran over the top of their bodies and right into a hail of fire from the camp. Scores more enemy soldiers went down to claymore blasts and small-arms fire, but still others came on. In the middle of the NVA platoons and companies, political cadre urged the men on. And behind them came their commanders, screaming orders. Last came the porters carrying ammunition, and stretcher bearers policing up the broken bodies from the battlefield.

There was no stopping the NVA this time. They swarmed through holes in the wire that sappers had blown on the south side, then leaped over the dirt berm and into the camp.

On the south wall, part of the South Vietnamese 141st CIDG Company, led by Lt. Chung Wei, suddenly stopped fighting and joined the communist troops pouring into the camp.

When he witnessed this act of betrayal, Capt. Blair was furious, but not surprised. He had never completely trusted the CIDG companies, which were made up mostly of South Vietnamese hoodlums and thugs from the waterfront districts around Da Nang and Saigon.

Rather than be overrun by the swarming enemy troops, Blair ordered the rest of his men, the Nungs, and the few loyal South Vietnamese troops to retreat to the north side of the camp. There, centered around a concrete communications bunker, Blair formed another defensive perimeter.

They were no sooner in position than the enemy, reinforced by Lieutenant Wei's troops, launched another attack. The enemy charged across the middle of the camp, their AKs blazing away, but Blair and his men drove them back with a fusillade of small-arms fire, killing another fifteen of them.

During the attack, Blair placed an emergency radio call to the Marines. "Need reinforcements," he said simply. "Without them, kiss us good-bye."

A short time after he made the call, the cloud ceiling lifted over the camp. Blair wasted no time in honking up two Skyraiders. He told them to drop their bombs right on top of the camp, then strafe it from end to end. Blair had all his men get under cover while the planes worked over the camp. When they finished their runs, he and the surviving twelve Green Berets led a counterattack in an attempt to regain the south wall. Blair and his men made it about halfway across the camp, but were soon driven back to the communications bunker.

By now there were only about 200 men left of the original 434-man garrison, and most of them were wounded. With their backs to the wall, however, they continued to fight on. Time after time during the rest of the morning, they drove back repeated enemy attempts to overwhelm them.

At Da Nang later that afternoon, Gen. Lew Walt, the commander of the 3d MAF, held an emergency meeting to discuss the deteriorating situation in the camp. Attending the meeting were most of Walt's senior officers, along with Lt. Gen. John A. Heintges, the deputy commander of USMACV and General Westmoreland's personal representative, and General Chuan, the Vietnamese I Corps representative.

The problem the men faced was monumental, and the meeting was tense. Only a month before, they had learned from intelligence sources that the Military Affairs Committee in Hanoi had transferred the control of Quang Tri and Thua Thien provinces from their Region Five Headquarters in the Central Highlands to their Region Four, the area just north of the demilitarized zone. Region Four was under the direct command of the legendary General Giap. Although they had no way of knowing for sure, it was suspected by allied intelligence officers that this transfer was a preliminary step for an all-out invasion of both provinces. Once under their control, it was believed the communists would then use the provinces as bargaining chips in any future negotiations. Of course, this was only one of a number of possible scenarios, but every commander at this meeting knew that if the camp at A Shau fell, the communists would have carte blanche in the valley and an open road to Hue.

But what could be done to save the camp? Even if they could get reinforcements into the camp, which they seriously doubted, would they not be sending them into a death trap? The men discussed this question at length, then called in Marine Corps Gen. Marion E. Carl, who had earlier flown over the camp in a gunship, and asked him if he thought it could be reinforced. Carl bluntly told them what they already suspected—that the camp was doomed and would have to be evacuated.

When one of the officers present asked Carl, in turn, what he thought the losses in helicopters would be during such a rescue attempt, Carl was again blunt. "One in four," he said.

Some of the officers seemed stunned by the pronouncement, but Carl was not exaggerating. He had flown right through the enemy fire around the camp and knew that, if anything, his prediction might even be optimistic. Another Marine Corps officer who had flown through the same fire had told Carl before the meeting that he thought a rescue force could lose as many as half its ships. That officer, in fact, had recommended against making any air rescue, which he feared would turn into an even worse debacle than the camp was already in. He had suggested instead that the men in the camp try to break through the enemy cordon and attempt to escape into the jungle.

That, of course, was an option General Carl had refused to even consider, and he pleaded with the assembled generals not to consider it either. "I don't think we can abandon those people in there," he told them. "We'd never live it down."

After a hurried discussion, the men decided to follow Carl's advice, and the rescue was set in motion right after the meeting adjourned. Picked to lead it was Lt. Col. Charles House. Shortly before six that evening, House led sixteen UH-34s (helicopters), supported by six UH-1E gunships and two fighter-bombers, into the valley.

Once over the camp, the gunships and Skyraiders began strafing the enemy positions, after which House, piloting his own ship, led six others down through a sky filled with green enemy tracer rounds toward an LZ on the north side of the camp. House went in first. As he was descending the last few hundred feet toward the LZ, his ship was peppered with machine-gun fire. He veered away from the fire, but as he approached the LZ was shocked to see an apocalyptic scene below. At the sight of the approaching helicopters, South Vietnamese soldiers stampeded over the dirt berm and surged like a crazed mob toward the LZ, trampling their wounded, pushing, and shoving each other to be the first aboard.

When House set down his ship, the men swarmed all over it. This first ship had been reserved for the wounded, and the twelve surviving Green Berets rushed forward and began pulling off the South Vietnamese troops. When this did not deter them, the Americans began clubbing the men. The South Vietnamese, however, preferred the blows to facing the North Vietnamese regulars and still did not dismount from the ship. Finally, in frustration the Green Berets flipped their M16s on automatic and fired right into the frightened men.

The fire killed a number of South Vietnamese troops and drove the rest back across the berm. The melee on the LZ, however, had cost House the few seconds he needed for a quick exit. The NVA zeroed in on the LZ and began pummelling it with RPGs. The Green Berets nonetheless loaded the ship with wounded, and House gunned his engine and started up. He managed to travel only one hundred meters, though, before an enemy recoilless-rifle round ripped off the ship's tail section. The ship crashed, and House and his crew had to drag the wounded back into the camp. A few minutes later, House's wingman, Lt. William Gregory, also had his ship shot down.

Six ships did manage to get down and take out sixty-nine men, most of them wounded, but three others that attempted to land were heavily damaged and driven off. In addition, four Marine fighter-bombers and two gunships were damaged.

With night approaching, the Marines halted the evacuation, and House was ordered to attempt a breakout. House led his ragtag group—which included Nung tribesmen, South Vietnamese irregulars, Green Berets, and helicopter pilots and their crews—out the northwest side of the camp and into the jungle. All night they moved through the jungle, fighting rear-guard actions every foot of the way against enemy patrols trying to finish them off. After covering three thousand meters, early the next morning House and his group were spotted by some rescue helicopters circling the valley. As the ships approached, the South Vietnamese again panicked and stampeded forward. The Green Berets once again opened fire into the surging mob and killed thirteen of the men. When the rescue ships finally landed, only sixty men boarded out of the one hundred who had attempted the breakout.

Another thirty-four survivors, who had broken out separately from Colonel House, were spotted the next morning, but again there was an ugly incident. As South Vietnamese soldiers rushed to get aboard one of the ships, someone threw a grenade in their midst and killed ten of them.

In the end, only 180, including 12 Green Berets, out of the original 434-man garrison made it out of the A Shau camp alive. The rest were either dead or prisoners of the NVA.

The loss of the camp was a bitter pill for the allies to swallow, and especially bitter because of the ignominious way it took place. It was news they would have preferred to have kept hidden from the press. Not long after his return to Phu Bai, however, Lieutenant Colonel House was interviewed on national television by CBS correspondent John Laurence. During the interview, House spoke out angrily against both the wisdom and futility of the mission and the cowardly behavior of the South Vietnamese CIDG troops. House's sentiments were echoed later in an interview that Captain Blair, the A Shau camp commander, gave to syndicated columnist, Jim Lucas, a good portion of which appeared in Lucas's March 14 column.

Furious over these disclosures, the Marines gave House a letter of reprimand. The Office of the Secretary of Defense, in turn, ordered both MACV and the 3d MAF to initiate an immediate investigation into the "unfavorable TV and press releases" of the story in the United States.

Both their investigations, however, were far too late. The damage was already done, and the subsequent rash of stories about the fall of the camp that appeared in newspapers across the country during the following week were a profound embarrassment for the U.S. government.

What the media did not uncover, however, and what could have been just as embarrassing for the allied command, was a rift that was developing between the Army and the Marine Corps. Some Marine officers began privately to express doubts about the efficiency and competency of Special Forces troops, which they variously described as colorful, lazy, and unmilitary. Many Green Berets, in turn, believed that the Marines had bungled the rescue attempt and that they were not competent to handle similar operations.

Whatever the truth, the fall of the A Shau camp left a deep wound in the psyche of the allied command and, according to noted Vietnam War historian Shelby Stanton, not only "had a major impact on the future course of the war," but led to "the ghastly battle of Ap Bia Mountain," which the soldiers who fought there would call Hamburger Hill.

CHAPTER 4

THE ENEMY TAKES OVER

Like General Giap, his main adversary, Gen. William Westmoreland, the commander of USMACV, considered the control of the highlands to be one of his highest priorities. By 1964, when he assumed control of MACV, the communists not only controlled a large portion of the highlands, but seemed on the verge of severing them from the rest of South Vietnam. Although many military experts would be critical of his highland policy, Westmoreland reacted strongly to the enemy threat, and would for the rest of the war. "You can ring a bell and General Westmoreland will come out of the ring like a *pug*," one of Westmoreland's aides, Marine Corps Gen. John Chaisson would say, "And two of the bells you can ring that get this reaction are the A Shau . . . and the highlands."

Westmoreland had closely followed the fight for the A Shau camp and was disturbed by its fall. Although he had earlier rejected a plan calling for the reinforcement of the camp, he left open the option of a large search-and-destroy operation somewhere else in the valley, to be followed immediately by the construction of another Special Forces camp.

The South Vietnamese I Corps commander, General Nguyen Van Chuan, also supported this last plan. He, in fact, encouraged Westmoreland to move troops back into the valley before the communists consolidated their power there. Chuan, however, did not want to use his own troops, which he had reserved for the defense of strategic coastal installations and cities. He wanted to use the U.S. Marines.

The Marines did not take kindly to Chuan's suggestion. They, likewise, wanted nothing to do with the valley. They had watched the South Vietnamese bug out of A Loui and Ta Bat, and, after participating in the debacle at the A Shau, they no longer had any illusions about the possibility of launching a successful operation in the valley. For a time during the A Shau battle, the 1st Battalion of the 4th Marine Regiment had been earmarked by 3d MAF for a possible counterattack on the valley. Colonel Sullivan, the 1st's commander, even flew over the besieged camp to do a preliminary reconnaissance for the counterattack. After seeing at first hand the intensity of the enemy fire, though, and after a long talk with Colonel House the next day, Sullivan strongly recommended against the Marines' launching an assault on the valley.

To Sullivan, the A Shau was nothing but "a place for disasters to occur," and he reasoned that to return would require at least two battalions, with a regiment in reserve, which was nearly every troop the Marines had at Phu Bai, the northernmost of their three base areas. Sullivan's recommendation was unanimously endorsed by his superiors and passed on to Westmoreland. For the general this left only the Army, but they likewise were incapable of providing enough manpower for a sustained presence in the A Shau. Although they had 126,000 troops in Vietnam at this point in the war—nearly five times the number of Marines— nearly 23,000 of them were Special Forces personnel manning dozens of camps and outposts in the mountains, and the rest were spread out thinly through the other three corps areas. Westmoreland was faced finally with the choice of either establishing another Special Forces camp in the A Shau, and facing a possible future debacle, or conceding control of the valley to the communists. He chose the latter, though having to make the decision would rankle him for the next two years.

With the last allied soldier out of the valley, the communists wasted no time in beginning the work needed to turn the A Shau into a giant logistical base and staging area to support attacks against the nearby coastal regions of Thua Thien and Quang Nam provinces. It was an ambitious project, but they had more than enough manpower and knowhow to do it.

The construction of a road system through the mountains on the southwestern side of the northern valley became one of their first priorities. Unlike the mountains on the northern end of the valley, which form a solid chain, the mountains on the southwestern side are more individual, distinct formations and are separated from one another by long, narrow river valleys.

Around the bases of these mountains and through these narrow valleys snaked a myriad of small Montagnard trails. Using hundreds of workers and a number of bulldozers, North Vietnamese engineering detachments began widening most of the trails for bicycle and cart traffic and widening and hardening a few, like Route 922, for use by heavy trucks. Once completed, this network of trails and roads was then tied to the west with the huge Base Area 611 and the Laotian section of the Ho Chi Minh Trail and to the east with Highway 548, which ran beside the Rao Lao River through the heart of the A Shau. Finally they went to work improving the entire 27-kilometer length of Highway 548 and tying it in with Highway 547 and a number of large trails which weaved their way down from the central valley to the coastal plains around Hue. Off 548, they also bulldozed a number of short branch lines leading to giant truck parks and maintenance areas, carefully hidden under the jungle canopy, and to large, deep caves, which they turned into warehouses for their growing stockpiles of weapons, ammunition, and food.

To protect this massive network of trails and roads and the ever-growing supply depots, the communists built large base camps and bivouacked troops all across the valley. Many of the mountains were turned into small fortresses, protected by concentric rows of deep bunkers and trench lines, their peaks and ridges bristling with antiaircraft guns and mortars.

General Westmoreland gave little consideration to a return to the A Shau during the rest of 1966. For the time being, he had more immediate problems to worry about. North Vietnamese troops were now infiltrating South Vietnam at the rate of five thousand per month, and Hue and Da Nang were the scenes of increasingly vociferous student and Buddhist protests against the government. To exploit this instability, on June 6, the North Vietnamese 324B Division moved across the demilitarized zone and into Quang Tri Province. Realizing that an enemy move on the northern provinces, coupled with large political disturbances in Hue and Da Nang, might not cause only the loss of these provinces, but might even conceivably topple the South Vietnamese government, Westmoreland ordered General Walt and his Marines to stop the 324B.

On July 7, in what was being called Operation Hastings-Deckhouse II, five Marine and four ARVN battalions moved quickly into staging positions below the DMZ and attacked the 324B, starting the first round of a hard-fought battle that would continue almost nonstop for the next three weeks. The engagement was the biggest of its kind up to this point in the war. When it ended on August 3, nine hundred NVA soldiers lay dead and the 324B was so savaged that its survivors fled in disarray back across the DMZ.

The Marines, though, had little time to gloat over their victory. Within a week more large enemy units were detected crossing the border, and Walt had to rush troops forward to stop them. In another running battle toward the end of September, the Marines killed an additional one thousand NVA, thwarting yet another attempt by the enemy to make a move on the northern provinces.

Even though they were stymied in Quang Tri Province, in the A Shau, the enemy, still untouched, continued daily to grow stronger. By the end of 1966, convoys of North Vietnamese trucks, loaded with ammunition and supplies, moved openly day and night down Highway 548, oblivious to any allied attempt to stop them.

They were right. The allies could not stop them. Westmoreland was now convinced that an invasion of the northern provinces would come across the DMZ, and it was there that he decided to concentrate his forces. He was bothered by the situation developing in the A Shau, but he simply did not have troops in I Corps to deal with the enemy threat simultaneously in Quang Tri and the valley.

Toward the end of 1967, the North Vietnamese finally made the big move in Quang Tri that Westmoreland had been expecting for over a year. Whether it was meant to presage an invasion of Thua Thien and Quang Nam provinces is not certain, but in early September, the communists launched an all-out attack on Con Thien, a Marine base camp only a few miles from the DMZ. Using long-range artillery and 122mm rockets, communist gunners pounded the base for eight straight days with more than three thousand shells, then began moving assault troops into position around the Marine perimeter.

The firepower the communists used to soften up Con Thien was unprecedented, and so was Westmoreland's response. As the NVA troops moved up, he hit them repeatedly with B52 strikes, massed artillery fire, tac-air strikes, even naval gunfire. The B52s alone dropped more than twenty-two thousand tons of bombs on the NVA lines. During one strike, an entire enemy infantry company was wiped out in a matter of seconds and large numbers of other NVA staggered away from their positions in shock. When the battle for Con Thien ended in late September, the North Vietnamese had lost over two thousand men killed to the Marines' forty-nine. Those not killed, again retreated across the DMZ.

The situation at Con Thien was repeated numerous times during the rest of 1967 as communist units in ever-increasing numbers flung themselves against the Americans in open battle and were deluged by torrents of bombs and shells. At Loc Ninh, in a two-day battle near a rubber plantation, the 9th Viet Cong Division lost more than two thousand men assaulting a Special Forces camp, and a month later four NVA regiments lost another twelve hundred men after a fierce four-day battle near Dak To with elements from the U.S. 4th Infantry Division, 1st Cavalry Division, and 173d Airborne Brigade.

Nineteen sixty-seven had been a good year for Westmoreland. By conservative estimates, the communists had lost over ninety thousand men killed during the year and suffered untold wounded, losses they were increasingly unable to replace. But more important, from the general's point of view, he was getting the steady influx of troops he needed to increase the scope and intensity of his operations. Before long he would have enough troops to make a strong move against the highlands.

By the end of 1967, in fact, Westmoreland started drawing up the preliminary plans for a series of four operations, code-named York, which would be his boldest, most aggressive strike yet against the enemy. Besides an invasion of North Vietnam just above the DMZ and another of the Laotian panhandle, York called for a multidivision sweep across the provinces of I Corps, to be coupled with a renewed assault on the A Shau.

While plans were being drawn up for the A Shau assault, Westmoreland's attention was suddenly diverted by a steady series of intelligence reports pouring into his MACV headquarters, all indicating that the communists were about to launch a huge countrywide offensive in the next couple of months. Although the general had no idea of the scope of the coming attack, the reports worried him enough so that he scrapped York and started preparing his forces to meet this assault, if and when it came.

Unknown to Westmoreland, for the past six months an angry debate had been raging in the Politburo in Hanoi between two factions over what direction the war in the south should take in the coming years. Led by General Giap, one faction wanted to launch a massive countrywide offensive in South Vietnam with the purpose of causing a popular uprising and the collapse of the South Vietnamese government. The other faction, led by Truong Chinh, one of the original founders, with Ho Chi Minh, of the Indochinese Communist Party, wanted instead to gear the war down and return to the guerilla tactics that the People's Army of Vietnam had used so successfully in the first few years of the war with the French. Chinh had seen enough casualty reports and felt North Vietnam's army was finished as it continued trying to wage a big-unit war against American firepower.

Giap had seen the same casualty reports, but he interpreted them quite differently. Giap was frightened by a number of ominous signs coming out of the war. For one thing, his army was being soundly defeated on the battlefield and losing troops, as Westmoreland suspected, faster than he could replace them. Equally disheartening for the general was the situation he saw developing in Saigon. There, the South Vietnamese government, while still unbelievably corrupt, was beginning to slowly solidify its control over the country. There had not been a coup attempt in over two years, and there were even signs that a burgeoning democracy was beginning to take shape in the newly elected general assembly.

There were also a number of positive signs coming out of the war, oddly, though, not in Vietnam, but in America. There, Giap could take heart from an ever more vigorous antiwar movement, which slowly but surely was eroding the will of the American people to continue the war. A big communist victory in the south, he reasoned, might finally crack this will and send the American diplomats scrambling to the peace table. It had happened that way in France after their monumental defeat at Dien Bien Phu during the First Indochina War, and Giap was confident the scenario could be repeated.

With Ho Chi Minh's support, Giap's plan was accepted by the Politburo, and sometime around June 1967, the first order for what would come to be called the Tet Offensive was issued. Besides being desperate, the plan was grandiose. It called for simultaneous assaults on thirty-six South Vietnamese provincial capitals, five of their autonomous cities, sixty-four district capitals, and fifty hamlets. Leading the attack would be eighty-four thousand Viet Cong, with a sprinkling of North Vietnamese cadre.

One of the cities targeted for attack was Hue. A little after midnight on January 30, nearly a division of Viet Cong and North Vietnamese troops—which had been bivouacked and supplied in the A Shau—struck the city from three different directions. After some initial sharp fighting with some small American and South Vietnamese units, enemy troops managed to take control of the entire city except for the 1st Vietnamese Army Division Headquarters in the Citadel and the U.S. Military Assistance Command compound.

With control of the city, the communists then went on an orgy of destruction. Working from lists prepared months in advance by communist agents in the city, squads of enemy soldiers and political cadre moved methodically from house to house rounding up anyone with the slightest connection to the South Vietnamese government. Anyone was fair game for these roving squads—schoolteachers, businessmen, Christian missionaries, students, clerks, and, of course, political leaders—and few on the lists escaped the roundup. Some of the people were killed on the spot, but most—thinking they were being taken away for reeducation—were marched into isolated rural areas and either clubbed to death or buried alive in mass graves. It is not known exactly how many people the communists murdered, but teams of searchers continued to find mass graves for months after the battle. Though almost thirty-five hundred bodies were eventually uncovered, it is thought by some that the communists killed twice that number.

While these murder squads were busy with their gruesome work, eleven ARVN and three U.S. Marine battalions launched a counterattack to retake the city. Because Hue was such an important cultural center, General Westmoreland at first forbade the attacking units the use of tanks, artillery, and air support. But as his casualties mounted and it became obvious the enemy soldiers intended on fighting to the death, he instructed his commanders to use whatever force was necessary to destroy them.

What followed was a battle many older veterans would compare with the worst city fighting in World War II. With tanks, recoilless rifles, multibarreled Ontos, supported by a steady stream of fighter-bombers and gunships, the Marines and ARVN started a steamroller attack that moved methodically through the city, house by house, street by street, until every enemy soldier in Hue was either dead, wounded, or on the run back across the coastal plains toward the mountains around the A Shau Valley.

The first fight lasted twenty-three days. When it ended on February 25, Hue lay devastated. Fortunately the palace and a majority of the other buildings of the imperial court were only slightly damaged, but much of the rest of Hue had been leveled. Only seven thousand of seventeen thousand houses were still standing, and many of them were no more than burnt-out shells. But the human damage was even more terrible. Nearly 8,000 civilians were dead and another 18,000 wounded. To hold the city, the communists sacrificed 5,000 troops, and to take it 384 ARVN and 142 Marines were killed.

The story of the communist defeat at Hue was to be repeated in a hundred other villages, hamlets, and cities all across South Vietnam. Instead of the popular uprising the communists had expected, they suffered the worst military defeat in their history. Their losses were staggering. Of the more than eighty thousand troops who had participated in the attack, nearly half had been killed and the rest so demoralized as to be ineffective. After Tet, in fact, the Viet Cong would never again be a serious factor in the war, forcing the North Vietnamese to take over the bulk of the fighting.

These were reassuring statistics for the allies, but they were quickly negated by the press reports of the Tet Offensive. Shocked by the massive destruction in cities like Saigon and Hue, and stunned by some early enemy successes during the battle, the press portrayed Tet to the American people not as an allied triumph, but as a communist victory. Their faulty and sensationalized accounts of the battle shocked and demoralized the American people, the very result ironically that General Giap had thought he could achieve only with a battlefield victory.

CHAPTER 5

BACK INTO THE A SHAU

General Westmoreland was angry over the way the press reported the Tet Offensive, but he had little time to concern himself with the issue. Much of South Vietnam lay in ruins; countrywide, the fighting had destroyed more than one hundred seventy thousand houses and buildings, and the refugee camps, already overburdened, had to contend with an additional six hundred thousand homeless people.

The Viet Cong had been destroyed as a fighting force, but most North Vietnamese units, secure in their jungle base camps along the Cambodian and Laotian borders, remained untouched. It was from these same base camps that the Viet Cong had drawn the weapons and ammunition they used for their Tet attacks, and Westmoreland and his MACV staff began targeting them for destruction.

One base area the general particularly wanted hit was the A Shau. Stunned by the extensive damage Hue had suffered and the large number of civilian casualties, and armed with numerous intelligence reports pinpointing the A Shau as the main enemy staging area for the attack, Westmoreland became convinced that the valley had to be hit—and hit hard. He simply could not afford another battle like Hue.

It was a decision he could not have considered a few months before, but with the threat of Tet out of the way and fifty thousand new troops in I Corps, he now felt he could finally begin the mobile operations along the border that he had wanted to get under way since 1965.

The heads of both the Marines and Air Force this time were vehemently opposed to such large, mobile, search-and-destroy operations, wanting instead a kind of modified version of the enclave strategy first proposed by Gen. James Gavin, under which the allies would more or less concede the mountains to the enemy and concentrate on protecting the lowlands and coastal regions. Westmoreland, however, rejected this strategy out of hand. He believed passionately that the war had to be taken to the enemy, rather than waiting around for him to attack, and that it was better to do battle in the mountains than in the congested cities of the coastal plains. Gen. Earle Wheeler, the Army Chief of Staff and the head of the Joint Chiefs, also supported this tactical concept, and as a result, search-and-destroy operations became an integral part of allied tactics for the remainder of the war.

As in 1966, after the fall of the A Shau camp, the Marines were the first considered for the job of leading the initial assaults back into the A Shau. They seemed a logical choice, especially considering their history as shock troops and their recognized ability to open beachheads. Unfortunately, the A Shau was not an island, but a fortified valley, and the Marines again, as they had two years before, wanted nothing to do with leading an attack on it.

Part of their reluctance to go into the valley was based on a legitimate fear that they might find themselves mired in some monumental disaster, but a lot more was based on the simple fact that they did not have the logistical capabilities to launch such an assault. As General Chaisson warned at a MACV planning session right after Tet, for the Marines to go into the A Shau would require not only every helicopter they had in Vietnam, but a complete cessation of all their other operations, including the removal of their crucial blocking forces on the DMZ, something no one desired. Chaisson recommended instead that the 1st Cavalry Division be given the job, and it subsequently was.

It was a wise choice. Considered by many military professionals as the best division in Vietnam, "the Cav," as it was nicknamed, was also the best equipped. With nearly five hundred helicopters, they had five times the number of any other American division in Vietnam. And they knew how to use them. At Fort Benning before the war, they had been the first division to develop the new airmobility tactics, and once in Vietnam had honed, refined, and perfected them. The Marines liked to joke that every soldier in the Cav had his own personal helicopter, and while that was an exaggeration, it was true that the division disdained plodding group operations, preferring instead to go everywhere by air. With their helicopters they were capable of a mobility one hundred times greater than any other army in history. As they had proven conclusively at the Battle of the Ia Drang Valley in 1965—during which they had frustrated General Giap's attempt to seize Pleiku and thereby chop South Vietnam in half—they were the masters of the lightninglike assault and the sudden decisive maneuver.

The Cav had spent most of its four years in Vietnam operating in II Corps. In January 1968, General Westmoreland, feeling the enemy was going to launch a massive attack on the northern provinces, moved the Cav from its AO in Quang Ngai and Binh Dinh provinces north to Thua Thien Province. It was a move the general would later consider one of his soundest tactical decisions of the war.

Since its arrival in I Corps, the Cav had been on a roll. During the Tet Offensive, it had successfully blocked and then put on the run three enemy regiments trying to reinforce and resupply their comrades in Hue. Then with hardly a pause or a rest, they had hurried north and staged at Quang Tri City. From there—in what strategists would later call a classic example of fire and maneuver—they launched a lightning attack west, reopening Highway 9 and shattering the enemy forces laying siege to the Marine base at Khe Sanh.

After Hue and Khe Sanh, anyone who had any doubts about the Cav quickly put them to rest. They were quite simply the best. When Westmoreland chose the Cav to lead Operation Delaware, the first assault on the A Shau in over four years, he could have had little doubt that if anyone could break the enemy stranglehold on the valley, it was the Cav.

Gen. Jack Tolson, the division commander, had no doubts either. A hard-nosed, no-nonsense leader, Tolson had been impressed with how smoothly and professionally his division had operated at Khe Sanh and Hue and was looking forward to the even bigger challenge the A Shau presented.

Tolson found out quickly, however, that there was a considerable difference between fighting an enemy on the open plains around Hue and air-assaulting into the heart of a valley where he has had four years to prepare his defenses.

Tolson's aerial rifle teams were the first to make this discovery. In Huey helicopters, they entered the valley on April 14, four days before the scheduled assault, with the mission of pinpointing enemy antiaircraft positions and then targeting them for destruction by B52s, fighter-bombers, and gunships. From the moment they entered the valley, though, they found that it was they who were marked for destruction.

Intelligence estimates had predicted a heavy concentration of antiaircraft fire over the valley, though nothing as heavy as what the aerial rifle teams ran into. The NVA had nearly every mountain on both sides of the valley floor defended by antiaircraft guns. Most were the 12.7mm heavy machine guns, but they also had a large number of 37mm flak guns. On wheels and with seven-man crews, the 37mm was capable of blowing a helicopter or jet from the sky at twenty-five thousand feet. As the aerial rifle teams roared down the center of the valley, they had to run a gauntlet of flak and machine-gun fire. They did not have any trouble finding targets because they were everywhere. Hitting them proved to be much more difficult. For six days they called in repeated B52 strikes, fighter-bombers, and gunships on the enemy positions, and the valley shuddered under a fire storm of fragmentation bombs, napalm, and rockets. In all, the B52s flew almost two hundred sorties and Air Force and Marine fighter-bombers another three hundred. And it was all for naught. Most of the enemy positions were dug in so deeply that the bombs and rockets had little effect on them, and the enemy quickly replaced the few that were knocked out.

Tolson had planned to kick off Operation Delaware on April 19 with a combat assault by the 3d Brigade's 1st Battalion into an LZ near the abandoned South Vietnamese Special Forces camp and airstrip at A Loui. At the last minute, however, he was forced to cancel it because of intense flak and machine-gun fire over the central valley. He picked a new LZ astride a large North Vietnamese road connecting the northern valley with Laos. Although the first lift-ships managed to land safely beside the road, subsequent ones were hit by heavy antiaircraft fire. In a matter of hours, enemy gunners severely damaged twenty-three helicopters and shot down ten others.

Most of the 1st Battalion of 7th Cav managed to get on the ground, but ran into overwhelming problems trying to fulfill their mission. They had been ordered to begin the immediate construction of a firebase to support a cross-country attack toward A Loui. They found themselves instead pinned down by enemy fire coming from positions all over the surrounding mountains, burdened with a large number of dead and wounded, and surrounded everywhere by the burnt-out hulks of helicopters, their rotors twisted in grotesque shapes, their plexiglass windshields shattered, and their interiors splattered with blood.

While the 1/7th fought back against the enemy entrenched above them, nearby at Tiger Mountain, the 5th Battalion, 7th Cav, also began coming in. Like the 1st, they also had to land under fire, and once on the ground they dug in quickly to avoid a rain of mortar rounds coming in from enemy guns just across the border in Laos.

After a few hours, the 1st Battalion consolidated its position enough so that it could begin once again to try to carve a firebase out of the valley floor. Engineers with chain saws worked frantically cutting down trees, and infantrymen with machetes hacked away at strands of bamboo and elephant grass, clearing fields-of-fire. About an hour later, a bevy of giant Chinook helicopters arrived, each carrying a 105 howitzer in a giant sling under its belly. Others came bearing huge pallets of ammo, and still others with the artillerymen. In a blind rush, the artillerymen laid their guns in and minutes later began firing back at the NVA gun positions on the mountains above. The NVA, in turn, answered with a rain of mortar rounds.

In the morning, both the 1/7th and the 5/7th went on the attack, the 1st southeast toward the A Loui airstrip and the 5th down the highway toward Laos. The 1st battalion ran into stiff resistance. Every foot of the way across the valley floor, they had to deal with small groups of enemy soldiers fighting rear-guard actions, soldiers who slashed at the column with rifle and machine-gun fire and then melted into the jungle. And, as always, there were snipers. Perched at the top of hundred-foot-high trees or hidden in caves or behind huge rocks, they also pecked away at the Americans, dropping soldier after soldier with well-aimed shots, then likewise fading into the jungle or into deep caves. To deal with the wounded and dead, a steady stream of medevacs moved in and out of the valley. Many of the medevacs, already loaded with wounded, became casualties themselves, either getting shot out of the sky or being so riddled with bullets that they were forced to crash-land.

To compound the problem, the weather also began turning against Tolson's skytroopers. On the morning of April 21, they awoke to fog and cloud ceiling so low they could not see the tops of the mountains above them. And then, about the third day of the operation, it began raining. It was not the light afternoon drizzles they expected this time of the year, but a violent monsoon thunderstorm with wild crackling bursts of lightning and rain that fell from the sky in sheets. After days of rain, the valley floor turned into a quagmire, and operations slowed to a crawl.

To keep the troops on the ground resupplied, helicopter pilots had to fly missions that even Tolson would describe as "sheer terror." With the valley completely shrouded in fog, they had both to land and take off using only their instruments. Ordinarily the trip from Camp Evans to the valley took about twenty minutes, but with the fog and rain, it took most pilots almost four times that long. Even with their instruments, many pilots either brought their loads down in the wrong places or, worse, flew around in circles over the valley, not knowing where they were.

Still, the Cav made some progress. At the original LZ in the northern valley, the 3d Brigade continued bringing in supplies and the artillerymen kept their guns hot lobbing shells up at the enemy gun positions on the mountains. At the same time, the 1st Battalion kept slogging steadily forward through the ankle-deep mud toward A Loui.

In order to widen the operation, Tolson knew he was going to have to bring in bigger and bigger loads of ammunition and equipment, and to do that he was going to have to reopen the A Loui airstrip. Helicopters simply could not supply the 3d Brigade with enough material to hold the valley. For that he needed the U.S. Air Force's giant C130 cargo planes.

Around April 21, it stopped raining, and the sun came out and quickly dried out the valley. Tolson moved quickly to take advantage of his good luck. When the 1/7th finally fought their way to A Loui, Tolson ordered them to secure an LZ, then CA'd in the 2d Battalion of the 3d Brigade. Together these two battalions routed a small enemy force around A Loui and secured the airstrip. Engineering detachments arrived within hours and, working night and day, started getting the old French airstrip ready to accept cargo planes.

They completed the job on the morning of April 26, and by early afternoon C130s finally began landing with the first of the hundreds of tons of material it was going to take to continue the attack on the valley. Resupplied, elements of the 1st Brigade started RIFs to the south and west of A Loui. Enemy troops retreated before their advances, and 1st Brigade troopers began uncovering huge arms and food caches. In one cache, they discovered ten 37mm flak guns and hundreds of thousands of rounds of ammo, in another a small fleet of trucks.

Other Cav units joined the search of the valley floor, but the enemy units confronting them likewise retreated, some moving higher up into the mountains and others farther south toward Ta Bat. The troopers of the Cav were looking for the big fight where they could bring their massive firepower to bear, but the enemy seemed unwilling to give it to them.

Two or three days after the start of the push, it started raining again, a sporadic, drizzling rain which again slowed the infantry RIF of the valley floor. With the rain came a 300-foot cloud ceiling and a soupy fog. Coming down through the clouds and fog had been difficult for helicopters, but it was treacherous for the lumbering C130s. Unlike helicopters, they could not drop suddenly through the clouds and fog, but had to come in under them instead, then coast for miles just above the ground before they landed. As they made their runs, enemy gunners fired down on them the entire way. On the second day the airstrip was operational, a number of C130s were not only badly damaged but forced into near crashes on the runway bringing a temporary halt to the airlift into A Loui. Then the rain, coming down once again in monsoon torrents, stopped it completely.

Hoping to wait out the rain, Tolson halted operations in the valley, and his troops hunkered down under any cover they could find. But instead of slowing, the rain fell only harder, and slowly the A Loui airstrip began washing away. The engineers worked frantically to keep the strip open, but it was an impossible job.

On May 11, after another day of rain, Tolson decided to halt operations in the valley and ordered a withdrawal. Although the general would later call Operation Delaware a success, the actual results were less than satisfactory. While 1st and 3d brigade troops did uncover a large amount of enemy ammunition and supplies, it still represented only a small fraction of the North Vietnamese logistical capability in the valley. At the same time, the Cav lost, along with the C130, a large number of helicopters and had little to show for the loss except a bruised ego.

General Westmoreland likewise would call Operation Delaware an unmitigated success, though it seems obvious that he must have been less than satisfied with the meager results it produced. It is also obvious that, given the general's strong feelings about the valley, he would have soon launched another attack against it. On June 11, however, he was replaced as MACV commander by Gen. Creighton Abrams and assigned to a new job as the Army's Chief of Staff.

Although Abrams was not as obsessed with the A Shau as Westmoreland, he still considered its neutralization one of his main priorities. In July 1969, less than two months after taking command of MACV, he ordered another assault on the valley, this time by the 101st Airborne Division. Although recently removed from jump status, the 101st, like the 1st Cav, was an elite unit. Its tenacious defense of Bastogne during World War II—made especially memorable by Gen. Anthony C. McAuliffe's legendary reply of "Nuts!" to a German surrender demand—had given the 101st instant fame and a solid reputation. In the four years since the division had deployed to Vietnam from Fort Campbell, Kentucky, it had steadily built on that reputation following a number of major operations and battles. If the 1st Cav was the best division in Vietnam, the 101st was running a close second.

Unfortunately, the 101st, like the Cav before it, was soon to discover that its reputation meant little when placed up against the A Shau Valley. Called Somerset Plains, the 101st's assault on the valley was in many ways a replay of the Cav's. Planned for August 1, the operation had to be postponed when the valley was socked in by drifting fog and intermittent rain showers. When the rain quit and the fog lifted on August 4, the 2/327th CA'd into an LZ near the Ta Bat airstrip and the 2/502d near A Loui, kicking off the first official airmobile operation of the 101st. While both battalions managed to get down without the loss of a single lift-ship, enemy gunners quickly shot down six Cobra gunships, a light observation helicopter, and a Phantom jet.

On the ground it was the same story. As the two battalions broke out from their LZs and started riffing (reconnaissance-in-force) south down the valley, small enemy units harassed them every foot of the way. In a number of sharp, bloody firefights, ninety-three NVA soldiers were killed, but the Cav had nineteen KIAs of their own, over one hundred wounded, and even two MIAs. The larger enemy units, however, refused to become engaged. As before, they either fled south down the valley or moved up into the mountains. The 101st had intended reopening the airstrip at Ta Bat, but heavy rains hit the valley before they could even chopper in the engineering detachment. They instead had to rely exclusively on helicopters for resupply. Two ARVN battalions eventually joined the operation, but had no better luck. In a few small firefights, they killed eighty-eight NVA, but had nearly eighty total casualties of their own.

On August 18 and 19, all four maneuver battalions were withdrawn from the A Shau. They left without even the consolation of having uncovered a single large enemy cache. In fact, the total haul for their frustrating fifteen days in the valley was a few AK47 assault rifles and three 15-year-old French mines. As could be expected, the After Action Reports that division historians wrote about Somerset Plains described it as a great success. In reality, it was even more of a failure than Operation Delaware. It would leave many staff officers, from MACV down, shaking their heads with consternation, wondering what it was going to take to crack the A Shau. It was a question no one seemed able to answer.

CHAPTER 6

THE MARINES CROSS THE BORDER

What it was going to take to crack the A Shau was a road. That was what Gen. Richard Stilwell decided shortly after he took over as commander of XXIV Corps, which had been activated on August 12, 1968, and given control over all ground tactical units in I Corps. Stilwell reasoned correctly that in order to cut the North Vietnamese Army's ability to move supplies in and out of the valley on a sustained basis, a permanent allied presence there would be required. Raids on the valley, like Operations Delaware and Somerset Plains, were simply not going to do the job. While they might temporarily disrupt enemy logistics, that was about all they could do. Still, the problem was not one of simply constructing and manning large camps in the valley or of initiating large search-and-destroy operations, but of keeping both resupplied. While the heavy enemy antiaircraft fire in the valley was a problem and would have to be dealt with eventually, the most difficult problem the allies faced in the A Shau was the weather. To hold the valley permanently, General Stilwell had concluded, would require a large steady stream of supplies. And to insure that would, in turn, require the construction of an all-weather road from the 101st Airborne Division's base camp at Camp Eagle, across the coastal plains, through the mountains, and right into the heart of the valley. To build such a road would be an ambitious undertaking, but it was the only choice the allies had short of abandoning the valley to the North Vietnamese.

Strangely, the road—which the engineers had to cut through triple-canopy jungle and often along the edge of towering mountains or steep cliffs—was the easiest part of the job of reopening the A Shau. If Americans are good at any one thing, it's the building of roads. In less than three months, using gargantuan 15,000-ton bulldozers and fleets of road graders and dump trucks, engineers from the 101st had a hardened two-lane road stretching the nearly twenty miles from Camp Eagle to the eastern side of the A Shau Valley. It was an incredible accomplishment in such a short time and through such rugged terrain, but the road was still seven miles from completion—and those were seven miles through the heart of enemy-held territory. Before it could be completed, the valley would first have to be attacked and secured.

As Marine Corps Colonel Sullivan had noted back in 1966 following the fall of the camp at A Shau, to neutralize enemy activities in the valley was going to take more than an occasional foray by a couple of battalions or even a couple of brigades. The failure of all such operations in the past could not be attributed to a lack of tactical expertise by the allied units, but to a lack of troops, logistics, and firepower. What it was going to take to crack the valley was not a brief raid or large reconnaissance-in-force, but an all-out World War II–type invasion. In early January 1969, the staff at XXIV Corps formulated just such a plan. Broken down into four separate operations, the plan called for a single attack against Base Area 611 and three against the valley.

The Marines were scheduled to kick things off on January 20 with Operation Dewey Canyon, which called for a regimental assault over land from their Vandergrift Combat Base south through the Da Krong Valley and into the heart of the enemy's giant Base Area 611. Sprawling as it did on both sides of the Laotian–South Vietnamese border, 611 had for years been a thorn in the side of the allies. Supplies moving down the Ho Chi Minh Trail were first stored there, then transshipped either farther down the trail or, as was more common, down Highway 922 in the A Shau. While always a hotbed of logistical activity, during the last month, truck sighting around 611 had doubled to around one thousand per day. It was a staggering figure, and when added to the fact that four NVA regiments had been spotted in the area recently, it meant only one thing to allied intelligence experts: the enemy was building up the supplies and troops needed for another attack on Hue. Although they had no way of certifying this assumption, it gave Operation Dewey Canyon, which had been in the planning stages for a number of weeks, a greater sense of urgency.

The attack against 611 was led by three battalions—the 1st, 2d, and 3d—of the Marine 3d Regiment. They pushed out of the Vandergrift Combat Base in the early morning hours of January 20 in three columns and, with artillery rounds walking ahead of them, started an aggressive RIF right into the heart of the Da Krong. As the Marines had expected, the enemy had no intention of giving up their huge supply depots and arms caches in the valley without a fight, and all three battalions soon found themselves in bloody little battles with platoon-sized groups of enemy soldiers.

The Marines, however, built firebases as they moved forward so that every inch of their advance was covered by an umbrella of artillery fire. Whenever they encountered an enemy position, they massed artillery fire on it, then sent the infantry in to overrun it. The fights were all small, but by the end of the first week in the Da Krong, the Marines had killed more than four hundred enemy soldiers and sent many hundreds more fleeing toward Base Area 611 or the A Shau.

As the Marines neared the border, the NVA struck back with their own artillery, the giant 122mm field cannons. A favorite weapon of the Russians in World War II, these wheeled guns had a greater range and a much bigger impact than the standard Marine 105. The NVA had them positioned in deep caves on the Laotian side of the border, and their gunners were expertly trained. Rather than going after the more fluid infantry columns, they turned the fire of the big guns on the firebases, pounding them incessantly night and day. On one firebase a direct hit on a command bunker killed five Marines, and on another an entire 105 crew was either killed or wounded by a direct hit. Marine gunners tried to knock out the 122, but they were so well protected by the caves that it was impossible to hit them.

Instead, the Marines continued their three-column push toward the border. The fighting got more intense and two days later, all three battalions closed with the border and entered a part of Base Area 611 on South Vietnam's side of the border. There they stopped, though many men, angry over the continuous 122 fire, were eager to launch a cross-border raid to knock out the guns. A request for permission to launch the raid was passed up the Marine chain of command and finally reached

General Abrams at MACV headquarters. The request in hand, Abrams was like a man holding a hot potato. While he sympathized with the Marines' frustration with the 122s, there was nothing he could do. U.S. policy clearly stated that line companies were not to cross the border except under the most critical situations. Rather than grant the request, Abrams told the Marines he would study the question and get back to them later.

The Marines, however, could not wait for an answer. On February 20, a company from the 2d Battalion on top of a mountain overlooking Highway 922 spotted a large convoy of trucks moving slowly along the Laotian side of the border. Artillery fire was called in on the convoy, but the fire dissipated in the thick jungle canopy, and the convoy hurried out of sight. For the Marines of 2d Battalion, this was the last straw. Having to sit helplessly and watch the enemy moving supplies just a few hundred yards away infuriated them, and they begged their commanders for permission to launch a quick raid on Highway 922. Although he knew he was violating U.S. policy, Colonel Barrow, the 1st Battalion's CO, granted permission for the raid. That night, the men of H Company slipped across the border, set up an ambush position above 922, and the next afternoon shot up a large enemy truck convoy. Fearful that a longer stay in Laos might lead to a conflict with MACV, the company then slipped back across the border. Once back in South Vietnam, however, they discovered that General Abrams, after a long debate with his staff over the situation, had given the Marines permission to launch a battalion-size raid across the border with the purpose of knocking out the 122s.

With hardly a pause, Company H linked up with the rest of 2d Battalion and slipped back across the border. Although they never did knock out the 122s, in a number of initial sharp firefights they killed dozens of NVA soldiers and routed the units guarding the sprawling base area. With the last enemy resistance gone, the Marines moved about at will and began uncovering some of the largest enemy caches of the war.

When Dewey Canyon finally ended in late February, the final totals of captured materials were staggering: seventy-three antiaircraft guns, sixteen 122mm field cannons, nearly a thousand AK47s, hundreds of grenades and rockets, over a million rounds of small-arms and machine-gun rounds, and a quarter of a million pounds of rice. The enemy's most serious losses, however, were in manpower. Nearly 1,700 of their best troops lay dead, and three times that number were wounded. These were losses they would never be able to completely replace. With 130 KIAs of their own and more than 900 wounded, the Marine losses during Dewey Canyon were minuscule by comparison.

It would be an understatement to say that there was joy in the allied camp after Dewey Canyon, but it was a hesitant joy. Commanders from General Abrams on down knew only too well that the enemy, like the mythic bird the Phoenix, had an uncanny ability to rise time after time from the ashes of defeat and restore himself. As they had learned only too well in past operations, it was one thing to drive the enemy from a base area and quite another to keep him out.

CHAPTER 7

BLOODY RIDGE: PREMONITION OF THINGS TO COME

Three days after the Marines moved back across the border, aerial recon-naissance photos showed that the NVA were indeed moving back into Base Area 611; and, although still a trickle, trucks were once more heading down Highway 922 toward the A Shau. Worse, they also showed that three NVA regiments, which had fled deep into Laos during Dewey Canyon, were not only back in 611, but were also en route to the valley.

As could be expected, they were moving toward what they thought would be a haven. In reality they were about to run head-on into three of the biggest allied operations of the Vietnam War and a battle that would rage up and down the A Shau for the next 167 days. In the coming months, two of the enemy regiments—the 6th and the 9th—would suffer terrible casualties, and the third—the 29th—on its way to a bivouac on a small nondescript mountain called Dong Ap Bia, would be almost wiped out.

The battle for control of the A Shau was one the allies intended on winning this time. If Dewey Canyon had sent the enemy reeling, the next three operations—Massachusetts Striker, Apache Snow, and Mont-gomery Rendezvous—each targeted against a different area of the A Shau, were designed to deliver the knockout blow.

And it was to be a big knockout blow. General Stilwell, the XXIV Corps Commander, had marshaled most of the forces of two infantry divisions and a plethora of supporting units for the coming battle and then backed them, in turn, with a veritable armada of helicopters, gunships, fighter-bombers, and B52s.

The first of the three operations scheduled was Massachusetts Striker. Aimed specifically at the southern valley, the 2d Brigade kicked it off on March 1 with the insertion of an engineering detachment at Dong Tre Gong. Under the protection of the 2/17 Cav, they started construction of Firebase Whip. When completed, Whip was to be used as both the staging area for operations into the southern A Shau and the nearby Rao Nai River Valley and as a forward base camp for the 2d Brigade.

As he readied his battalions for their insertion into Whip, Col. John Hoefling, the 2d Brigade commander, told them, "We are in for some tough fighting ahead, but I feel we have never before been more capable of success than now. The NVA we are going to meet out there will be highly trained, well-equipped, hard-core troops who will stand and fight, especially when we get close to his base camps and supply depots."

Although his speech would eventually prove to be truly prophetic, it was a bit premature. The only nemesis of the valley, the weather, quickly began complicating the schedule for Massachusetts Striker. On Dong Tre Gong, the engineers had hardly started clearing the bamboo, elephant grass, and trees off the top of the mountain when they were deluged by an early monsoon rain. Rain fell intermittently for the next two days, slowing work to a crawl, and on the third day a thick fog settled over the mountain, reducing visibility to zero.

After ten days of waiting on the rain to stop and the fog to lift, Colonel Hoefling had no choice but to shift his staging area from Dong Tre Gong to a mountain on the edge of the central valley. Firebase Veghel had once dominated this mountain, but the position had been abandoned a year earlier. Hoefling ordered Lt. Col. Donald Davis to combat-assault his 1/502d into an area near Veghel, reopen the firebase, and rif the surrounding area. Intelligence reports had not indicated any enemy units in the area around Veghel, so the RIF was supposed to be a routine operation, a way for 1/502 to keep occupied until the fog lifted over the southern A Shau.

It proved to be anything but routine. Lieutenant Colonel Davis, after an aerial reconnaissance of the area, ordered his Charlie Company in first, with the job of securing an LZ for the rest of the battalion.

Charlie Company arrived in three lifts of six helicopters each, certain, like everyone else in the battalion, that they were headed for a cold LZ and a routine RIF. On the ground, though, a reinforced company from the NVA's 816th Battalion lay in wait for them.

The NVA, as always, had been diligent and thorough with the preparations for the ambush. Not only did they have infantrymen completely surrounding the LZ, but also they had rigged it with rows of claymore mines pointing skyward and wired to be detonated simultaneously.

As the first six helicopters, bearing thirty men of Charlie's 2d Platoon descended toward their LZ, the NVA exploded the rows of claymores. They went off with a blinding, ear-splitting crash and sent hundreds of steel pellets into the six ships, shattering their plexiglass windshields, peppering their thin steel hulls, rupturing fuel lines, and wounding about ten men. Although a number of pilots were also wounded, they all managed to bring their helicopters down, and with the infantrymen scurried to the cover of some bomb craters in the area, dragging their wounded with them. There the Americans formed a hasty perimeter and hunkered down as the NVA hit them with a fusillade of rocket-propelled grenades and rifle and machine-gun fire.

The Americans responded with rifle and machine-gun fire of their own, and the NVA, in turn, with the shower of RPGs. Overhead, the second lift, carrying Charlie's 3d Platoon, approached the LZ, but seeing the disaster on the ground, pulled back and began circling a short distance away.

Not content with a standoff, NVA infantrymen formed a rough line, broke out of the treeline, and charged the Americans, firing from the hip as they moved forward. The Americans met them with rifle and machine-gun fire and a shower of grenades, stopping the attack cold. The NVA responded angrily with a torrent of RPGs and 60mm mortar rounds, wounding five or six more members of the 2d Platoon. A few moments later they charged the American perimeter a second time, but again were driven back into the treelines.

By now there were dead NVA lying in heaps all around the perimeter, but it was no consolation to the men of the 2d Platoon. More than half of the men in the platoon were now wounded, and it was obvious they could not take another enemy charge. Seeing the enemy preparing for another assault, they called in a napalm strike only seventy-five meters from their positions. Two of the bombs landed so close to the platoon's perimeter that a number of GIs had their hair singed by the heat, but they did manage to stop the enemy from launching a third assault. Stunned by the napalm, the enemy soldiers pulled back momentarily, dragging away their dead and wounded, and tried to regroup.

In the pause, six more helicopters managed to land with most of the 3d Platoon. While some of these fresh troops rushed forward to strengthen the perimeter, others hustled the wounded aboard the helicopters. The helicopters managed to get away with only minor damage, but they were to be the last that day.

Before the lift carrying the rest of Charlie Company could land, fog settled over Veghel, and a short time later it began to rain. In this nether world, with visibility limited to three or four feet, the battle went on. Crawling forward through the rain and fog, NVA infantrymen threw satchel charges and grenades at the American perimeter. The Americans answered with grenades and M79 canister rounds. Night fell, but the battle went on. At times during the night, there were small, bloody, two- and three-man fights all across the perimeter, as GIs and NVA soldiers blazed away at each other. At other times, the mountain was silent as both sides sought cover against a sudden burst of rain.

At daybreak, the fight was still going on. Fortunately for the Americans, the fog lifted about midmorning. Colonel Hoefling immediately ordered in gunships and fighter-bombers and had them pound the enemy positions. While they were working over the enemy, he CA'd in the rest of the battalion.

Seeing the reinforcements, the NVA troops abandoned their fortified bunkers and trenches and fled down a wide, heavily-travelled trail leading straight west toward the A Shau. They left behind twelve of their dead around 2d and 3d platoon's perimeter and carried another eight with them, burying them finally in a mass grave along their route.

Colonel Hoefling decided not to let the enemy force escape and immediately ordered Lieutenant Colonel Davis to lead his battalion cross-country to overtake them. It was a bold plan, but it fit in well with the expectations of Massachusetts Striker.

The 1/502d moved out at a vengeful pace from Veghel and, with its three companies moving on separate axes, started out on the trail of the enemy company thinking they were chasing a single company, but realized after a while that they were up against the entire 816th Battalion. Unlike past battles in the A Shau, however, the NVA had no intention of fighting a permanent holding action. On April 14, thirty-three days after their retreat from Veghel, the 816th Battalion stopped at a small mountain called Dong A Tay and decided to make a stand. As always, the Americans were looking for a big, decisive battle, and the NVA were now ready to give it to them—more ready, in fact, than the Americans could have possibly imagined.

Around eight hundred meters above sea level, Dong A Tay was a round squat hill with a large razorback ridge flowing out of it to the north. Just below the crests of both the main body of the hill and this large ridge, the NVA had built a system of deep, spacious bunkers, all interconnected by tunnels and trenches and looking down on carefully cut fields-of-fire. In these bunkers from three hundred to five hundred men of the 816th hunkered down and waited for the arrival of the 1/502d.

Colonel Davis suspected the presence of enemy troops on Dong A Tay, but had no idea of their number. He gave Alpha Company the job of finding out. Expecting to encounter some sniper fire and possibly a squad or two of enemy soldiers, Alpha started up the ridge just after first light on April 17. Instead of trail watchers, they ran head-on into a hailstorm of small-arms and machine-gun fire. In a few minutes, Alpha's lead platoon had a dozen killed and a similar number wounded, and was sent reeling back down the mountain. They called in airstrikes and artillery on the enemy positions for over an hour, and then started an on-line assault by one platoon up the ridge. The platoon managed to advance about halfway up the ridge this time, but was finally thrown off by an enemy counterattack.

Realizing now that he was up against a large force, Lieutenant Colonel Davis ordered Charlie Company to set up a blocking position on the south side of the main hill and Bravo to launch another assault up the opposite side of the ridge. Unfortunately, Bravo's scenario was as grim as Alpha's. After advancing only a few meters from their assault positions, they took ten casualties and quickly withdrew.

Bombs and shells rained down on the hill for two hours this time, but a follow-up assault by Alpha and Bravo was quickly repulsed. All three companies dug in around the hill, and the rest of the day and all that night, 105 and 155 howitzers from four nearby firebases blazed away at the enemy positions above. While the howitzer shells did not knock out any of the enemy bunkers, they opened up the jungle and exposed them.

In the morning, armed with 90mm recoilless rifles that had been flown in during the night, both Alpha and Charlie again attacked up opposite sides of the main ridge. In sharp fighting, both companies pushed up to the top of the north end of the ridge, where the recoilless-rifle teams proceeded to knock out four or five enemy bunkers. As the companies consolidated their positions on the ridge and prepared to start an attack toward the main body of the mountain, the NVA launched a strong counterattack and pushed them back down the ridge.

Both companies medevacked their wounded, then dug in below the mountain. The NVA launched repeated ground attacks and probes against the American positions during the night, then withdrew just before first light.

In the morning, Alpha and Bravo's grunts found twenty dead NVA around their perimeters, but it was little consolation for their own losses. Since the fighting had started three days earlier, both companies had suffered nearly 50 percent casualties, and the enemy was still firmly entrenched on Dong A Tay—or what the grunts were now calling Bloody Ridge.

In the morning, the Air Force, realizing that their bombing so far seemed to be having little effect on the enemy bunkers on both sides of the ridge, decided to try something new—1,000-pound bombs with delayed-action fuses. They suspected that there was a long tunnel running down the center of the ridge and that the bunkers were all connected to it. They reasoned that if they could collapse this tunnel, the bunkers would likewise cave in. It was a difficult job hitting the top of the razorback ridge, but the Air Force finally managed to place about two dozen bombs squarely on it. Their theory proved correct. The 1,000-pounders caused the whole top of the ridge to cave in. In two or three spots, huge secondary explosions ripped gaping holes in the top of the ridge.

As soon as the last bomb hit, the men of Alpha and Bravo got on-line and started back up the ridge. It was believed that the NVA, with their bunkers knocked out, would desert the position and flee toward the A Shau, and a number did. But more than one hundred NVA decided to stay and fight until the end.

Raymond Harshberger, who went up Bloody Ridge that day as a member of Alpha Company, would later describe what followed as a "truly terrifying experience. Even now when I think of it seventeen years later, I get goose bumps on my arms, and the hair on the back of my neck stands up."

What followed was one of the hardest and bloodiest single days of combat in the history of the 101st Airborne Division. Enemy soldiers were everywhere on the ridge—under fallen trees, behind rocks, in spider holes, and in the rubble of the collapsed tunnel and bunkers—and they fought back suicidally, refusing to give ground. Three times that morning, Alpha and Bravo fought their way up the ridge and were repulsed. Finally, in the early afternoon, after the ridge had been pounded for nearly an hour with the massed fire of four artillery batteries, both companies managed to get a toehold on the north end of the ridge and start an on-line sweep toward the main mountain. Flanked, their position now untenable, the surviving NVA still refused to retreat. Instead, like the Japanese defenders of Iwo Jima during World War II, they stayed at their positions until they were killed.

It took until later in the afternoon to finally clear the ridge and hill. In the rubble and torn-up earth, GIs counted the bodies of 86 enemy soldiers. Later that day they discovered an enemy hospital on the south side of the mountain and a list of patients who had been treated there. According to the list, over half of the nearly 700-man battalion had been either killed or wounded in the 33-day running fight with the 1/502d. On the floor of the hospital, the GIs discovered another list, the sight of which shocked and dismayed some of them and caused others to fly into a rage. This list was of medicines that had been shipped to the hospital, followed by the words: ''Donated by your friends at the University of California at Berkeley.''

Taking Bloody Ridge, the Americans lost thirty-five killed and more than one hundred wounded, a staggering figure for such an insignificant piece of real estate. As much as the casualties, the new tactics the NVA employed on Dong A Tay sent a shock wave through the 2d Brigade command. Intelligence officers made particular note of the fight in the division After Action Report and sought to analyze in detail the meaning of the suicidal defense of the mountain. Although not specifically stated, the question their inquiry sought to answer was simple enough: Was Dong A Tay an isolated incident, or a premonition of worse things to come? The answer to the question was less than a month away.

Not all units involved in Massachusetts Striker had it as rough as the 1/502d. For some, like the 1st Brigade's 2/327th, the operation was a cakewalk. After the 1/502d became heavily engaged at Veghel, the 2/327th was put under the operational control of the 2d Brigade and given the mission of invading the southern valley. With almost no enemy resistance, they entered the southern valley on March 22 and quickly secured the airstrip near the abandoned Special Forces camp. When recon patrols spotted some large enemy forces to the west, the battalion started off across the valley floor on three different axes. The enemy units, however, did not want to get engaged and slipped into Laos.

Unable to follow them into Laos, Lt. Col. Charles Dyke, the battalion commander, instead ordered his men to retrace their steps back across the valley and thoroughly search the area. It was a wise decision. As Dyke's troops swept back east, they began uncovering larger and larger caches of enemy supplies and munitions. Their biggest find, though, was a large hardened road which enemy engineers were building from the southern valley to Quang Nam Province. Hidden beside the road was a fleet of twenty Russian trucks, two bulldozers, and a fully equipped maintenance garage.

After mopping up around Dong A Tay and getting a short rest and a number of replacements, the 1/502d also got into what was becoming a giant treasure hunt in the southern valley. On April 17, they were inserted astride Highway 614, another enemy-built supply route, which connected the southern A Shau with northern Quang Nam Province. Because of the always-heavy enemy traffic on 614, soldiers had nicknamed it the Yellow Brick Road after the mythic road in the movie *The Wizard of Oz*.

There was no Land of Oz at the end of this road, but the 1/502d did uncover a large enemy hospital complex; ten Russian trucks; six hundred SKS rifles; and thousands of recoilless-rifle, mortar, and howitzer rounds. They also constructed Firebase Lash astride Highway 614 and cut the numerous enemy supply routes moving in and out of the southern valley.

The contact the 2d Brigade had hoped to make with a large enemy unit in the southern valley, however, did not materialize. Units from the 9th NVA Regiment that were known to be in the area, rather than fighting, abandoned their base camps, caches, trucks, and supply routes and retreated north.

Unknowingly these retreating troops were heading right into an area that Gen. Richard Stilwell, the XXIV Corps commander, was preparing to invade with ten battalions. Spearheading his attack would be three battalions for the 101st Airborne Division—the 1/506th, 3/187th, and 2/501st—and two ARVN battalions from the South Vietnamese 1st Division.

Although they would not be participating in the initial combat assault on the northern A Shau, the 3/5 Cav, the 9th Marine Regiment, and two other ARVN battalions were poised to play supporting roles in the operation. Stilwell had tasked the 3/5 Cav with the mission of clearing Highway 547, so the hardened road could be completed through the eastern mountains and pushed into the heart of the valley, and the 9th Marines with reentering the Da Krong Valley and blunting any enemy attempts to reinforce the northern valley.

The coming invasion of the northern A Shau was being called Operation Apache Snow and labeled a reconnaissance in force. In reality it was being launched as a direct challenge to the North Vietnamese troops bivouacked there. The challenge was simple: the NVA could either abandon their arms caches, roads, and base camps—as they already had in the southern valley—and flee into Laos, or they could defend them and face destruction. Their decision to stand and fight for the northern valley set the stage for what many military men would call the toughest single battle of the entire Vietnam War.

CHAPTER 8

APACHE SNOW—CONTINUED

At 0710 the artillery prep of the LZs stopped. A few minutes later a pair of Cobra gunships appeared over each LZ and started the final prep. While one Cobra hovered off to the side, the other rolled in and unleashed barrage after barrage of HE rockets in the LZ and the surrounding jungle, then hosed the area down further with whirring, crackling blasts of minigun fire. When one gunship expended its ordnance, the other rolled in and repeated the routine.

The squadrons of lift-ships were only seconds behind. As each squadron neared its LZ, the lead Cobra moved ahead slightly from the formation and gave the LZ yet another long dose of minigun fire, then hammered it further with blasts from its 40mm automatic grenade launcher and a salvo or two of flechette rockets. At the same time, the four Cobras guarding the flanks of each formation moved off to the sides and raked over the area around the LZ with even more minigun fire, then blasted it with flechette rockets and automatic grenade fire.

The softening up of the LZs had gone on continuously for seventy-four minutes. At precisely 0710, it stopped, and the gunships pulled off and went into a hover off to the side, ready if needed to suppress any ground fire.

Still in their V formation, the squadrons, which had been hovering nearby during the final gunship prep, began their runs in. All five LZs were too small for the sixteen ships in a squadron to land at once, so the ships went into the LZs one and two at a time. Because of the blasted, cratered terrain, they did not attempt to land, but instead went into a hover five to ten feet off the ground while the door gunners fired up the area around the LZs one last time with furious bursts of machine-gun fire. While the ships hovered, the soldiers, weighted down with their 60-pound rucksacks, leaped to the ground and scattered quickly around the LZs to set up circular perimeters. With the drop of each new group, the perimeters were expanded, and more troops brought in.

Strangely, almost ominously, the landing went nearly uncontested. The 4/1 ARVN received some sniper fire as they secured their LZ on top of Tran Lay Mountain, and a company of the 2/1 ARVN lost a Chinook helicopter to ground fire as they started the construction of Firebase Tiger on Ka Lou Mountain. But all three U.S. battalions landed without making contact, and by midmorning had secured their respective LZs and were preparing either to push out or had already pushed out. The basic mission of all five battalions was the same, which was to run simultaneous RIFs both west toward the Laotian border and east toward the valley floor.

Three of the five had also been tasked with more-specific missions. In the far north the 2/1 ARVN had orders to cut Highway 548 and block any enemy attempts to withdraw from the valley, and in the south the 1/506th had orders to interdict Highway 923 from the Laotian border to its juncture with 548. In between, the 3/187th was given the task of securing Dong Ap Bia, which both the brigade and division intel shops believed was being used as a way station for the transshipment of supplies between the nearby enemy Base Area 611 and the myriad of high-speed trails on the valley floor.

The fact that the landing went so easily was not lost on Lt. Col. Weldon Honeycutt, the commander of the 3/187th. He, like many others, had expected to enter the valley with guns blazing. He had led the attack on Dong Ngai only two weeks earlier, and during the initial CA had lost three lift-ships to ground fire and had had a number of others damaged. He likewise expected heavy fire today and was amazed when the assault went so easily.

It went too easily, in fact. At 0801, led by Capt. Luther Sanders, Delta Company was the first down, followed by Alpha and Charlie companies. While Charlie secured the perimeter around the LZ, Delta and Alpha started riffing in opposite directions along the large ridge the LZ sat on, Alpha northwest toward the Laotian border, and Delta southeast toward the top of Dong Ap Bia.

Honeycutt himself landed with his staff at 0930, relieved Charlie Company of its security duties on the LZ, and ordered Capt. Dean Johnson to start his company on yet another company-size reconnaissance-in-force down the large draw to the southwest, heading, like Alpha, toward the Laotian border. Then with his staff and 81mm mortar platoon in tow, the colonel started up the ridge to the southwest, trailing behind Delta Company.

A profane, outspoken, fiercely competitive man, Honeycutt was the prototype of the hard-nosed commander. Born in 1931 in the mill town Greensboro, North Carolina, Honeycutt had lied, at sixteen with only a sixth-grade education, about his age and enlisted in the Army. Although at five feet eight, he lacked what officers called command presence, he had applied himself to the military life with a religious passion and quickly began a meteoric rise through the ranks.

In five short years he moved from private to captain and with the start of the Korean War was commanding a company with the 187th Regimental Combat Team, then under the command of Gen. William Westmoreland. When two other companies in the 187th had failed to take a key hill from the Chinese during fighting along the DMZ, Honeycutt had led a third assault, overrun the hill, and driven off the Chinese. Westmoreland had been so impressed with his young captain's aggressiveness that he had nicknamed him "Tiger." The name had stuck, and thereafter most of Honeycutt's Army superiors had called him simply Tiger Honeycutt.

The Korean War was the beginning of both a long professional relationship and a personal friendship between Honeycutt and Westmoreland. It would be an understatement to say that Westmoreland thought highly of Honeycutt. But his was not a universal feeling within the Army establishment. Always a controversial figure, the colonel was considered by some fellow officers as one of the best young commanders in the Army and by others as nothing more than a hothead and egomaniac. In a way, Honeycutt seemed to thrive on controversy and revel in the strong feelings others had about him. Regardless, he made little attempt to temper the impressions people had of him.

Honeycutt had a lot of strong feelings of his own, and one was for the 3/187th, which had evolved from the same 187th Regimental Combat Team that he had served with in Korea. He had been given the battalion in January, and it had taken him nearly a month to put it into the kind of fighting shape he wanted.

It had been a difficult job. The colonel had discovered upon taking command that many of his officers were not in the field with their men; instead they were hanging around Camp Evans, looking for the slightest excuse to stay in the rear. Except for the most essential people, he immediately ordered every officer into the field, where he announced to them, "From now on this battalion is gonna fight. This battalion is gonna go out and find the enemy and kill him. This bullshit of running around and hiding is over."

A short time later, when an officer had been hesitant about leading a patrol into an enemy-controlled area, Honeycutt had called him "a sniveling coward" and threatened him with a court-martial. When another officer, upon being assigned to the battalion, expressed his opposition to the Vietnam War and refused to go into the field, Honeycutt dragged him bodily out of the battalion headquarters building and threw him headfirst into the street. When the headquarters company commander, Capt. James Ogle, hearing the commotion, appeared, Honeycutt screamed at him, "Get this miserable fucking traitor out of my sight, Captain. Cut orders and send his ass to Laos."

Such actions were inflammatory, but they got the results the colonel wanted. Within a month after taking over the 3/187th, Honeycutt had honed the unit down into the trim, hard, spartan battalion he felt he needed for the hard fighting he was certain lay ahead.

He felt his methods proved themselves a month later during the Leach Island Battle, where he thought his men had performed magnificently. After the fight for Dong Ngai in late April, for which the 3/187th was awarded the prestigious Valorous Unit Award, Honeycutt became convinced that the Rakkasans were not only the best battalion in the 3d Brigade, but in the entire 101st Airborne Division.

Honeycutt linked up with Captain Sanders and Delta Company at noon about one thousand meters from the top of Dong Ap Bia. There he put everyone to work preparing an LZ and a battalion CP. The next day the colonel planned on installing a more permanent CP on top of Dong Ap Bia, but for now he needed to be close enough to control Alpha and Charlie companies' combined RIF toward the Laotian border.

On the narrow ridge, Honeycutt's men worked quickly to prepare an oblong-shaped position. On the northwest end of the position, engineers with chain saws knocked down a dozen 100-foot-high trees and a number of smaller ones and built a one-ship LZ. In the center of the position, other engineers opened a hole in the jungle canopy so the 81mm mortars could fire, then on the southeast end hacked away a thick stand of bamboo with machetes for the battalion CP area. While the engineers struggled in the 100-degree heat, the ninety-four grunts of Delta Company surrounded the position with fighting holes, set out trip flares and claymore mines, and started running small RIFs into the surrounding ravines and draws to make sure it was clear of enemy soldiers.

Events were moving rapidly all over the northern A Shau. Although both Alpha and Charlie companies had moved only a few hundred meters from the original LZ, they had discovered enemy huts and bunkers all along both their lines of advance. Some of the huts were large enough to accommodate an entire platoon of men, with large, carefully tended gardens in the rear and deep, spacious bunkers. Charlie's discovery of a still-smoldering fire in one hut made it obvious that enemy soldiers had left the area only minutes before their arrival.

Overhead, the pilots of light observation helicopters, flying at treetop level so they could peer down holes into the jungle canopy, were likewise sighting huts and bunkers all over the area around Dong Ap Bia.

Around 1400, one of these LOHs, part of a Hunter-Killer Team with two Cobras, had the first contact of the day. While hovering over a patch of jungle, two thousand meters west of Dong Ap Bia, the pilot of the LOH, while using his prop wash to blow an opening in the canopy, spotted five or six North Vietnamese soldiers run out of a hut and make a mad dash down a nearby trail. The pilot called in the Cobra gunships, which were circling in the area, and they began raking the trail with minigun fire. One of the gunships managed to drop two of the enemy soldiers, but the others escaped into the deep jungle.

A few minutes later, a FAC plane, while circling an area to the east of Dong Ap Bia, was taken under fire by a 12.7mm antiaircraft gun. After nearly getting shot down, the FAC pilot likewise called for help. Two fighter-bombers responded, and after the position was marked by the FAC, went in with four 500-pound bombs. One of the bombs landed right on the position, and the FAC pilot saw parts of the antiaircraft gun blown thirty feet into the air.

When he heard of these two incidents and balanced them with the ever-increasing signs of the enemy that Alpha and Bravo were uncovering, Colonel Honeycutt had no choice but to conclude that his battalion had set down in the center of some kind of enemy base area. He still could only guess at how extensive the base might be or how many troops might be bivouacked there, but he knew that at any time the North Vietnamese might decide to defend it.

And that was what worried him. If the NVA did decide to put up a fight for the area, Honeycutt knew, as on Dong Ngai two weeks earlier, he might be forced to bring in reinforcements, and bring them into a hot LZ. He reasoned further that it would be far better to bring them in now while the LZ was still cold than in the middle of a wild firefight.

Since his own Bravo Company was being held in 3d Brigade reserve back on Firebase Blaze, Honeycutt honked up Col. Joseph Conmy, the 3d Brigade commander, explained his reasoning, and asked for release of the company. Without hesitation, Conmy agreed to release Bravo Company, and by 1400 hours the entire company was on lift-ships and heading for the A Shau.

Things did not go as smoothly for Bravo Company as they had for the rest of the battalion. Fifteen of the sixteen lift-ships carrying the company managed to get to the LZ without difficulty, but the last ship, carrying Lt. Charles Denholm and his CP group, caught fire, forcing the pilot to auto-rotate it down to the valley floor. Another lift-ship arrived minutes later to pick up everyone, but it likewise ran into difficulty. As the ship climbed out of the valley, heading west toward Dong Ap Bia, it was taken under fire by a number of flak guns, firing from the mouth of caves on the western side of the A Shau. Two or three of the proximity shells exploded near the tail of the lift-ship and sent it reeling crazily for a few horrifying seconds before the pilot finally brought it under control.

When Lieutenant Denholm and his CP group finally got on the ground, they joined up with the rest of Bravo Company and started the 800-meter hike up the ridge toward the battalion CP. When they arrived an hour later, Honeycutt pulled Captain Littnan aside and with a grease pencil and acetate-covered map sketched out the route he wanted him to take from the battalion CP up the large ridge to the top of Dong Ap Bia.

"I doubt if you make it tonight," Honeycutt explained, "but sometime late tomorrow morning I want to move the CP up there."

"That shouldn't be any problem."

"And be careful."

"Don't worry, Colonel."

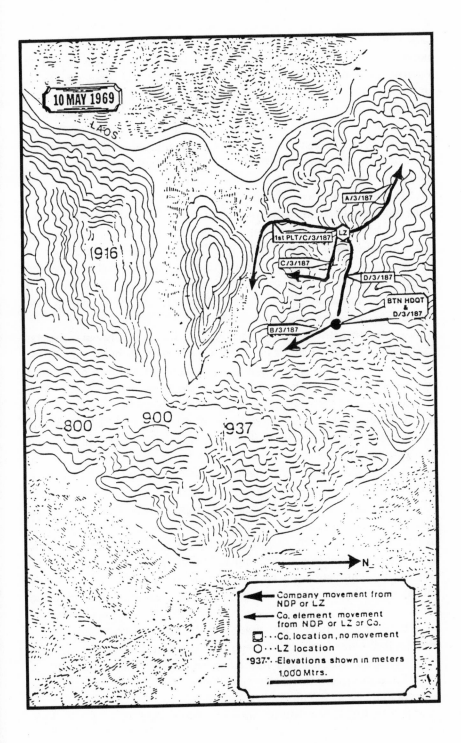

10 MAY 1969

LAOS

916

A/3/187

1st PLT/C/3/187

LZ

C/3/187

D/3/187

BTN HDQT
&
D/3/187

B/3/187

800   900   937

N

Company movement from
NDP or LZ

Co. element movement
from NDP or LZ or Co.

▣···Co. location, no movement

O···LZ location

"937"··Elevations shown in meters

1,000 Mtrs.

Captain Littnan was unconcerned about the mission of securing the mountain. The 29-year-old career officer had already spent a year in Vietnam humping with an 81mm mortar platoon and three months of his present tour leading Bravo Company, and in all that time he had carried out dozens of similar missions with little problem. Although he knew that just being in the A Shau would require extra caution on everyone's part, he had yet to feel any unusual premonitions of danger. To Littnan, he and his men were about to start out on what the grunts called "just another walk in the sun."

Littnan's feeling was shared by most men in the company. As news of the mission passed down the column, men began joking and congratulating each other on their sudden good fortune. Most had expected to spend the next week or two humping a 60-pound rucksack up and down the steep mountains of the northern A Shau, risking ambush and sudden death at every turn in the trail, but instead they would be spending it guarding the battalion CP. It was duty they sarcastically called "palace guard."

"After the hard fight on Dong Ngai," Lt. Frank Boccia, the 1st Platoon leader, would say later, "the job of securing that mountain for a battalion CP would be like going on R and R. Like everyone else, I was really looking forward to a nice easy week up there."

Regardless of their optimism, the men still had one thousand meters to cover before they reached the top of the mountain, one thousand meters up a narrow, steep trail strewn with fallen trees and choked with bamboo and vines.

They started out at 1620, with Lt. Marshall Edward, 2d Platoon, in the lead, followed by 1st Platoon, the company CP, and 4th Platoon. Edward, in turn, put his 2d Squad up front and Sp.4 Ron Storm on point and Sp.4 James Rocker on slack. Storm started up the trail slowly and cautiously, his every step deliberate, his eyes scanning the jungle from side to side, ready to respond to the slightest movement. He had his M16 on automatic, and he kept it pointed forward, ready to let fly with an entire 20-round magazine in the flash of a second. Rocker followed ten meters behind, as silent as a cat, stepping slowly over rocks and logs, moving gracefully under vines and low-hanging branches.

The trail wound forward through the deep jungle like a tunnel. Palm fronds reached over the trail like large hands. Overhead a labyrinth of vines filled the trees. Because of the thickness of the canopy, the light was gray and wan, the air dank and fetid.

Storm pushed forward one hundred meters, and then two hundred.

They were soon off the small plateau the battalion CP sat on and into a small low saddle, then out of it and on flat ground again. Three hundred meters later, Storm came to the edge of another saddle. This one, however, was much deeper than the first. While Rocker covered him, he scrambled down into it about twenty meters, then motioned Rocker to bring the rest of the company forward.

Storm moved across the bottom of the saddle, then up the other side. Most of 2d Squad was out of the saddle and moving up the side of the mountain when an RPG whooshed from a spot on the trail ahead and exploded with a deafening boom against a tree to Storm's left. The concussion lifted him off his feet and knocked him off the trail, sprawling down the steep side of the ridge on the right side. He passed out for just a few seconds, then came to to the familiar crackcrackcrack sound of AK47 rifle fire. Storm looked up over the ridge to see confusion on the trail. Three men were down, and one of them was screaming over and over again, "I'm hit!" A number of other men were crawling forward trying to help the wounded while rifle fire ripped through the trees overhead.

At that same moment an enemy rifleman spotted Storm and opened up on him with his rifle. Storm went flat to the ground to avoid the bullets, and a second later an RPG exploded in the trees over his head, showering him with leaves and bark. He peeked over the top of the ridge for a second trying to locate the position where the RPG had come from and saw instead three or four enemy riflemen manning a position on the left side of the ridge about twenty-five meters away. He yelled down the trail for the men in his fire team to move up, and Sp.4 James Rocker and Pfc.'s Anthony Tolle, Alan Bork, and James Prefundo came at a run. Storm then led the group forward about thirty meters, until they were just opposite and slightly to the rear of the enemy position.

Storm took another quick look and thought he saw four or five enemy soldiers on the other side. They were behind a large tree and partially hidden by some low-hanging branches and palm fronds. He first thought to try to shoot them, but they were so well protected that it would have been difficult. He instead suggested to the men in his fire team that they grenade the position, and they all agreed. On a signal from Storm, all five men pulled the pins from their grenades and threw them all at once, then ducked for cover as the left side of the trail was rocked by a huge explosion.

We got 'em, Storm thought as he looked up over the top of the gaping hole in the jungle where the enemy position had been. To make sure, however, they all grenaded the position one more time, and again the left side of the trail was rocked by a huge explosion.

The men had little time to celebrate, though, for they soon found themselves receiving heavy fire from another enemy position farther up the trail. When an RPG exploded over their heads, Storm ordered the men to start backing down the side of the ridge. When they reached the rest of the men, they found that medics were tending to the three wounded men off to the side of the trail while the rest of the men in the squad fired wildly at the enemy positions up ahead.

"They're gonna call in an airstrike," Storm heard someone scream. "We gotta get out of here."

Storm and the rest of the men in the squad followed the company back down through the saddle and up the other side. There, 2d Platoon formed a quick perimeter on both sides of the trail.

The request for the airstrike was passed up the chain of command and approved by Honeycutt. About five minutes later, a FAC plane appeared, escorting two propeller-driven A-1 Skyraiders. Rather than marking his forward position with a smoke grenade, Captain Littnan instructed the FAC pilot to have the Skyraiders make their runs along the same line as the ridge and to start their bombing and strafing runs on the south side of the saddle, moving them gradually up the mountain.

One of the Skyraiders made a dry run to make sure Littnan approved of the approach, and then the other, given the go, zoomed in at treetop level and started up the ridge, his 20mm cannons blazing. The first Skyraider came in a few seconds behind him with more cannon fire, and the second returned with a pair of 500-pound high-drag bombs.

It took both planes about fifteen minutes to expend all their ordnance. They pulled away at 1900, leaving the trail for one hundred meters above the south side of the saddle smashed and smoking. The bombs had knocked over a number of 100-foot-high trees, blown gaping holes through the jungle canopy, and flattened thick stands of bamboo for twenty meters on both sides of the trail.

Honeycutt had wanted to send a patrol back up the trail to check the damage, but had to scratch the idea because of approaching darkness. Instead, he ordered Captain Littnan to form a night defensive position on the north side of the saddle and to continue the RIF toward Dong Ap Bia in the morning.

After digging fighting holes on both sides of the ridge and putting out listening posts and perimeter guards, the 107 men of Bravo Company settled down for what would be for most an uneasy night's sleep. In their minds, most of the soldiers tried to balance the optimism they had had as they started up the trail with the shock of this brief but bloody firefight. Was this an isolated incident or a presage of far worse things to come? It was a question that a lot of men asked themselves that night.

CHAPTER 9

FIRST RIF*

Colonel Honeycutt had placed no special significance on this first brief skirmish. Although he had no way of knowing for certain, he assumed that the NVA troops Bravo had run into were part of a large party of trail watchers. Honeycutt figured that the NVA soldiers, having seen the lift-ship coming in, decided to sneak down the mountain and recon the LZ. Instead, they ran head-on into Bravo's lead platoon. It was only a theory, but he had no reason to assume anything else. Either way, he still wanted his CP on Dong Ap Bia by early afternoon and radioed Captain Littnan to continue the RIF up the ridge.

Captain Littnan moved his company out about an hour and a half after first light, putting Lt. Frank Boccia's 1st Platoon in the lead this time, followed by the 4th Platoon, the company CP, and the 2d Platoon. Pfc. Terry Gann took the point for 1st Platoon, and Boccia himself the third position back. At 0747 Gann moved back down the saddle and up the other side. He got down on his hands and knees and started creeping forward. The trail ahead was littered with debris—splintered trees, pieces of bamboo, palm fronds, and tangled vines—and the gagging smell of cordite still lingered in the air.

Gann crept slowly through the debris. There were a number of large holes in the canopy now, and the morning sun poured through them like spotlights. Gann crawled about fifty meters, but was finally stopped

* Reconnaissance in Force

75

by a huge stand of bamboo that the bombs had blown over the trail. He pushed some of the debris aside and noticed that the bamboo had fallen in such a way as to create a tunnel down the center of the trail. He looked into the opening of the tunnel then looked back at Lieutenant Boccia. "What do you want me to do?"

Boccia moved up beside the slackman. "Nothing you can do but check it out."

Gann went in on his hands and knees and a moment later called out, "We've got some bodies in here."

Boccia called forward six men and had them move forward and guard both sides of the trail, then crept in after Gann.

There were three dead NVA soldiers about five meters into the bamboo tunnel and another one just a short distance past them. All were young men in brand-new uniforms, though without any unit identification, with short, boot-camp-like haircuts. Lying near them were two rifles, an RPG launcher, and six rocket grenades.

Boccia closely inspected the bodies. He assumed the men had not been in the jungle long because none of the bodies had any jungle sores or bamboo cuts. All had been hit in the back by 20mm shells, and it seemed obvious to Boccia that they had been trying to run back up the ridge when the first Skyraider raked it with cannon fire.

In the shirt pocket of one of the men, who seemed to be an officer, Boccia found a picture of the man and his wife and a packet of documents. In the rucksack of another man he discovered a package of unposted letters. They were obviously letters home, and Boccia was filled with a tremendous sadness knowing that the man's family would never get them. For a second he toyed with the idea of keeping the letters and someday trying to mail them, but he eventually bundled them up with the rest of the documents and sent them back to the battalion CP.

After a short break, Boccia put Sp.4 Phil Nelson on point and Pfc. Nate Hyde on slack. Gann was a good pointman, but Nelson and Hyde were his two most experienced trackers. Both had grown up in rural areas, Nelson in Virginia and Hyde in Louisiana, and both had proven in the past to have an uncanny ability to see things in the jungle no one else could.

Nelson pushed out at 0913 up the 25-degree slope of the ridge. A short distance from the bombed area, he discovered a number of blood trails, all leading up the trail toward the mountain. A little farther, he discovered a pile of bloody bandages lying in the center of the trail, then a set of footprints, and, finally, even farther up, another pile of bandages.

Nelson and Hyde stopped to inspect the bandages, and Boccia crept up to join them.

"Look at this shit, Lieutenant," Hyde said. "Look at this! Shit, they might as well of laid out a fuckin' road map for us. Christ, there's shit all over this trail."

"Something's wrong here, Lieutenant," Nelson added. "Something's real wrong."

They were right, Boccia thought. Something was wrong. He had seen the NVA hit many times before, and even if they were dragging a lot of dead and wounded, never once had they left a hint of a trail, not so much as a drop of blood or a broken twig.

While Boccia was inspecting the bandages, his RTO motioned him to come to the radio. It was Captain Littnan. "Why aren't you moving any faster?" he asked.

"We're movin' as fast as we can, sir."

"You don't seem to be making any progress."

"We're movin' slow, captain. We're takin' our time. I think there's something up here."

"Look, Blackjack's on my ass. He wants to know why you are not movin' any faster."

"I can't move any faster than I am, Captain. I'm doin' the best I can."

"I know that. I know what you're saying. If you've got something ahead you're not sure of, take your time. But I just wanted to let you know that the man's on my case. You hear what I'm saying?"

"Yes, sir."

"Good."

Nelson again moved out at a creep, and once more started inching his way up the narrow jungle-choked trail. It took him an hour to cover one hundred meters. At the edge of a small knoll, he halted the column once again and motioned Boccia forward. There was a small clearing on top of the knoll, and right in the center of it, Nelson found a rucksack filled with rice balls, a brand-new AK47 in a leather carrying case, a pile of banana-clips for the rifle, and two Chicom grenades.

Boccia looked the stuff over and once again was forced to pose the question: Why did the NVA, always so careful with their equipment, just leave this stuff behind? Boccia almost feared contemplating a possible answer.

While Boccia inspected the NVA equipment, back at the battalion CP, Honeycutt and Capt. Charles Addison, the S-2, were kneeling on the ground near the battalion radios, going over the documents found on the dead NVA soldier.

Honeycutt had sent for Vinh, the battalion Kit Carson Scout, and when he appeared he handed them over to him. "See what you can make of this stuff," Honeycutt said, and Vinh went down on his hands and knees and started reading the documents.

Honeycutt did not like Vinh or the policy of using former North Vietnamese soldiers as scouts. As far as he was concerned, a man who would turn against his own country would turn against anyone. As a result, he referred to Vinh simply as FT, which was short for "fucking traitor." Still, he wanted to have some idea of what was in the documents before he sent them on to brigade, and Vinh was the only one who could tell him.

Vinh started reading the documents slowly, his lips forming some of the words. When he was about halfway through the first page, his eyes opened wide with shock. By the second page he was talking out loud to himself in Vietnamese, and by the third he was babbling excitedly at Honeycutt and Addison.

"What's he sayin', Chuck?"

Addison used the little Vietnamese he knew to question Vinh, but the scout seemed unresponsive. His face ashen with fear, he ignored Addison and kept babbling in Vietnamese, all the time shaking his head back and forth.

"Chuck, what the fuck is he saying?"

"I don't know."

"Find out. Calm him down."

Addison again questioned Vinh and at the same time tried to settle him down. When he finally did and Vinh started talking, it was in a combination of English and Vietnamese.

Addison quickly translated. "He says those men we killed were members of the 29th NVA Regiment. It's called The Pride of Ho Chi Minh. Supposedly they're one of the best regiments in the entire North Vietnamese Army. He says also that 'they're big American killers' and that we had better clear out of this area because the entire regiment is somewhere around here. 'Many, many soldiers everywhere. Hundreds of soldiers.' ''

"Tell the little sonofabitch that's great," Honeycutt said. "Tell him I'm glad to know they're around here. Tell him that's why we came here—to kill North Vietnamese soldiers—and if they are around, they'll just be doin' us a favor."

When Addison translated Honeycutt's message, Vinh looked at the colonel incredulously, pointed to the documents, and again started babbling out his warning.

Up the trail, Captain Littnan had stopped the company for a quick 15-minute lunch break, and then was forced to hold them another 15 minutes to wait out a sudden rainstorm. At 1220, however, the company started moving again, with Hyde once more on point. As he led the company higher up the mountain, the country started gradually changing. The bamboo which had hugged the sides of the trail most of the way up gradually disappeared. So likewise did most of the secondary growth. Giant teak trees, many well over 100 feet high, began appearing everywhere. The trees had huge, gnarled, buttressed trunks and tops that merged over the top of the trail, forming a vaulted ceiling. Visibility before had been limited to only a few feet in any direction. Now, in many places Hyde could see more than fifty meters down the trail.

Hyde kept up the creeping, snaillike pace, nonetheless, for with the trail opening up it was now more important than ever to be cautious. Still bothered by the slow pace, Captain Littnan finally radioed Boccia and told him to halt the column. Accompanied by Lieutenant Denholm, Littnan rushed forward up the trail until he was up with Boccia.

"Frank, you've got to pick up the pace," Littnan said. "Do you hear me? You've got to move faster."

"Sir, like I said, I know I'm taking a long time. But you've seen the trail for yourself. You've seen the shit we're finding. I just don't feel comfortable moving any faster."

"I don't care what you feel, Frank," Littnan said, his anger barely concealed. "You've got to move faster. It's as simple as that. Blackjack's on my ass, and he says we've got to be on this mountain by 1530. Did you hear what I said?"

"Yes, sir."

"Then move it out."

At Littnan's command, Boccia's RTO, who had been sitting down and resting against a tree, jumped up and picked up his radio. As he was slipping it on, however, one of the straps broke, and the radio crashed to the ground. Littnan watched impatiently as the radio operator tried futilely to repair the strap, then turned abruptly on Boccia, "Frank, we can't wait on you any longer." Littnan turned to Lieutenant Denholm, "Charlie, move your people up and take over point."

The switch took place quickly. While Boccia held his position on the trail, Denholm double-timed his men forward. The two platoons passed each other in silence.

Denholm put Pfc. Bill Stevens on point and Sp.4 Aaron Rosenstreich on slack, followed by Sp.4 John McCarrell. The lieutenant took the fourth position in the column. Although it was Stevens's turn to walk point, Denholm had hesitated putting him there. The kid lived in a perpetual state of fear and worry and at times during past firefights had been barely able to function. To complicate things, Denholm had received a letter from Stevens's mother only a few days before, one line of which still stuck in his mind. "Please don't let my son get hurt," she had written. "Please, please, take care of him. He's all I have."

Denholm realized he should not let sentiment get in the way of his command responsibilities, but he could not help but be affected by the woman's letter. Still, in fairness to the other men in the platoon, he had no choice but to make Stevens take his turn on point.

It was a decision he regretted almost instantly. Stevens moved out stiffly and hesitantly, and after covering about ten meters stopped cold in the trail. He looked back at Denholm, his face riveted with fear, but the lieutenant waved him forward. Stevens crept forward another five to ten meters and then dropped to one knee and once again froze. This time he did not look back.

Denholm moved up behind him. "What's the problem?"

"I'm scared," Stevens mumbled.

"Just take your time," Denholm said, putting his hand on Stevens's shoulder. "We're in no hurry. This is no big deal." Denholm gave him a gentle shove forward. "Let's go. We've got to keep moving."

Denholm moved back down the line, and Stevens, now on his hands and knees, started crawling forward. He had not covered more than a few meters, however, before a sniper somewhere up ahead opened up on the front of the column. Three or four bullets ripped through the trees overhead, and everyone dived off the trail and went flat.

Both Rosenstreich and McCarrell were the first to recover from the shock of the sniper fire. A few seconds after the last shot, both moved back into the center of the trail and with their M16s on automatic raked the trees up ahead. They both caught just a glimpse of the sniper as he abandoned his position behind a log and dashed up the trail toward the mountain.

Denholm radioed the report to Littnan and got a simple reply: "Keep moving!"

Stevens, though, once again balked when told to move out. "I can't do it," he said, his hands shaking, his breath coming in spasms.

"You've got to," Denholm snapped. "You don't have any choice in the matter. Let's go!"

Stevens got a hurt look on his face and seemed for a second as if he were going to start crying, but eventually he turned around and started forward yet a third time. The sniper let him take only a step or two this time before he cut loose.

Stevens jumped off the trail and huddled behind a log, while Rosenstreich and McCarrell lashed the trees with rifle fire. The sniper fire stopped instantly.

Denholm crawled forward and prodded the huddling Stevens. "Let's go, Billy."

"I'm not going any farther," Stevens said. "I'm too scared . . . I just can't . . ."

Rosenstreich listened to Stevens, then turned to Denholm. "Look, I'll take the goddamn point."

"Okay, Rosey," Denholm said. He looked Stevens in the eye long and hard, trying to decide what to do with him, and finally said angrily, "Go on back to the rear."

The kid scampered away like a whipped dog, and Denholm put his hand on Rosenstreich's shoulder. "Be careful, Rosey."

"Don't worry about me, Lieutenant, I know what the fuck I'm doing."

"I know."

And indeed he did know what he was doing. Denholm knew that if anyone could handle point in a tough situation like this, it was Rosey. And if anyone could handle slack, it was McCarrell. They were, in fact, two of his best men. But this was not what worried him. Although officers were not encouraged to fraternize with enlisted men, Denholm had become good friends with both men, and he did not think he could bear the fact of either of them getting hurt. Both he and Rosenstreich had studied art in college, and their mutual interest in painting had not only been the subject of many long conversations, but the beginning of a friendship that Denholm was sure would survive the war. Although he did not have a lot in common with McCarrell, he liked him a lot also. McCarrell was the company "flower child," a former hippie who opposed the war, wore peace beads around his neck, and was openly contemptuous of the military. His attitude had nearly put him in the stockade a number of times, and he had been transferred in and out of two companies and three different platoons during his three months in Vietnam. When Denholm finally got him, he decided not to push the kid any further, but to allow him his individualism and to show him respect. The approach had worked, and McCarrell, while still maintaining a passionate hatred of the military, had finally started soldiering. In the last month Denholm not only had not had any trouble with McCarrell, but had come to consider him one of his better soldiers.

Rosenstreich started the column moving again at 1300. He alternated between crawling and walking and in thirty minutes covered one hundred meters. Near a large teak tree he finally stopped and raised his hand for the column to halt. He slipped off the side of the trail, felt around with his hand in a patch of bamboo and vines until he touched something, then motioned McCarrell and Denholm to move forward.

"Look at this," said Rosenstreich, holding up a thick insulated wire, "they got fuckin' commo wire running up here. I wonder what the fuck they got up there? Must be important, though, to string wire up to it."

Denholm moved closer to inspect the wire. He lifted it free from the bamboo and saw that it was neatly attached to a small tree with an insulator. He followed it with his eyes as far as he could southeast toward the top of Dong Ap Bia and straight west down into the large draw to the right of the trail and toward Laos. Denholm got on the horn to Littnan and asked him what he should do about the wire, and Littnan told him to hold in place, that he was coming forward to have a look at it.

While Littnan was moving up the trail to check the wire, Colonel Honeycutt was standing on the edge of the LZ waiting for Captain Fredericks, the brigade intelligence officer, to arrive with a full translation of the captured documents. When the captain's ship landed, Honeycutt pulled him aside, and they knelt down on the edge of the LZ to go over the translations.

"What'd you find out, Captain?" Honeycutt asked.

"Colonel," Fredericks said, "there's a lot of gooks somewhere in this area—and I mean a helluva lot!"

"That's what I figured too. But where in the hell are they located?"

"I don't know. The documents don't say. All they say is that the unit operating in this area is the 29th NVA Regiment."

"That's what Vinh said."

"From our intelligence, we estimate their strength at between twelve hundred and eighteen hundred men, reinforced with heavy weapons. According to the documents, they left Hanoi recently and they have explicit orders to kick the shit out of some American unit in these mountains. Following that they are supposed to infiltrate down to the plains and attack Hue. The documents don't say where or when they are supposed to do all this, but one thing they make real clear is that they are definitely looking for a big fight."

"Good," Honeycutt replied. "That's what we are lookin' for too— a big fight!"

While Bravo Company riffed its way southeast toward the top of Dong Ap Bia, Alpha Company had been following the same ridge in the opposite direction, northwest toward the Laotian border and the Trung Pham River. When the ridge dropped sharply down toward the Trung Pham River Valley, Alpha split into platoons and started pushing toward the border on three different axes. Leading one of these smaller RIFs was Lt. Frank McGreevy and his 1st Platoon. They had started down toward the river valley at 0800, and from the beginning the going had been rough. Fearing ambush, the 24-year-old McGreevy had been forced to avoid the trails and move the platoon cross-country, with the pointman cutting trail with a machete. Because of this, it had taken them about four hours to cover the one thousand meters from the ridge to the river valley. There the lieutenant had turned the platoon north and started cross-country again down the heart of the valley.

The platoon moved for about three hours without incident, until about 1400, when the pointman, cutting and chopping his way through a tangle of vines, pushed his way through a thick stand of bamboo and right into the center of a large North Vietnamese road.

Lieutenant McGreevy came forward and with the point and slackman inspected the road. The grunts called it a "superhighway," and though the lieutenant had heard of such roads in his eleven months in Vietnam, he had never seen one. The surface of the road was packed hard and

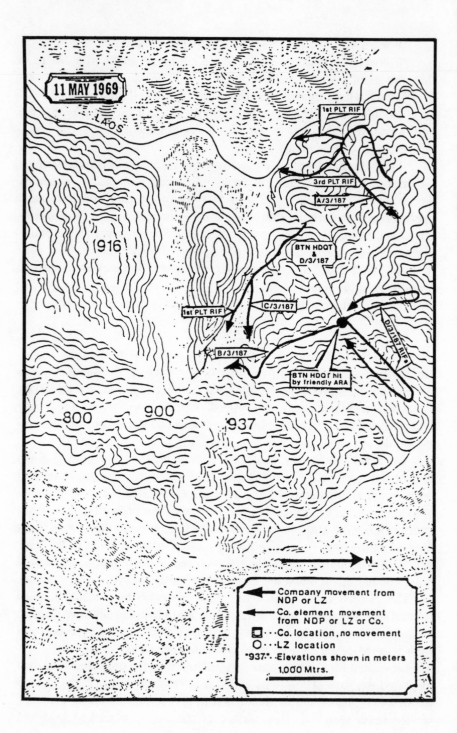

11 MAY 1969

LAOS

1st PLT RIF

3rd PLT RIF

A/3/187

1916

BTN HDQT
&
D/3/187

1st PLT RIF   C/3/187

D/3/187 RIF

B/3/187

BTN HDQT hit
by friendly ARA

800   900   937

N

Company movement from
NDP or LZ

Co. element movement
from NDP or LZ or Co.

⬛··Co. location, no movement

〇···LZ location

"937"··Elevations shown in meters

1,000 Mtrs.

was wide enough to accommodate a truck. Over the top of it, the jungle had been woven together to form a solid canopy, making it completely invisible from the air.

As he looked at the superhighway, McGreevy felt a chill of fear creeping up his back, and he thought: We're definitely in their country now. They must have a lot of people in this area to construct a road like this. One helluva lot of people!

When they checked the road out further, they discovered that it pointed straight west toward the Trung Pham River and east toward the northern edge of Dong Ap Bia. McGreevy put a squad on each side of the superhighway and another on the road surface itself and started his platoon moving west toward the river. The road led right to a cluster of huts. In the area behind the huts, his men discovered a bunker filled with live chickens and an assortment of clothing and ammunition. A fire that was still burning made it obvious that whoever was occupying the huts had left in a hurry.

Led by Lt. Daniel Bresnahan, Alpha Company's 3d Platoon had also riffed its way down to the Trung Pham River, only farther south. While McGreevy was searching the superhighway, the 3d Platoon was moving north down a trail parallel to the river. Like McGreevy, they were also more than conscious of the fact that they were in the heart of an enemy base area. Although they had not made contact yet, there were signs of the enemy everywhere.

Around 1420, the platoon turned west and started heading directly for the river. Sp.4 James Maynard was on point, with Sp.4 Michael Vallone on slack. About fifty meters after they made their turn toward the river, Maynard suddenly yelled "gook," and a burst of machine-gun fire slashed through the bamboo and elephant grass on both sides of the column.

Everyone in the platoon went flat to the ground except the slackman, Vallone. Instead, he crawled frantically to the right about twenty meters in an attempt to flank whoever was firing. When he looked up over the top of some bamboo, he saw an enemy soldier carefully bringing an RPG up to his shoulder. Vallone brought his M16 up at the same moment and fired. Shot, the enemy soldier fell forward and triggered the rocket grenade into the ground at his feet. There followed a blinding explosion, and Vallone watched in shock as parts of the soldier were scattered all over the area.

At the same moment, Maynard and two other men leaped up and charged the enemy ambush position farther up the trail. Two NVA soldiers leaped from their positions and tried to run. Maynard brought them down with a burst of M16 fire, but one of the men got up again and crawled into the jungle. The platoon followed the blood trail for about five minutes, but, fearing another ambush, finally stopped and backtracked to the main trail.

A few minutes later, Lieutenant Bresnahan turned the platoon down another trail, and they again started a RIF toward the river. Maynard and Vallone this time moved to the rear of the column; Vallone's nerves were rattled by the sudden shoot-out, and he thought bringing up the rear would give him time to settle down. He was wrong. The column had moved barely one hundred meters when he looked to his left down a shallow draw and saw a North Vietnamese soldier about twenty meters away. The man was on one knee and carefully inserting an RPG round into his launcher. Vallone had more time to sight now. Taking careful aim, he squeezed off a five- to seven-round burst. The bullets hit the man's chest pouch and set off two or three RPG rounds at once. There was an even larger explosion this time, and Vallone again watched as the enemy soldier literally disintegrated.

Half an hour later, 3d Platoon reached the river. Like 1st Platoon, they discovered a cluster of huts and what must have been a way station, but the enemy had likewise hastily deserted it.

On the mountain, Captain Littnan had checked out the commo wire and sent a squad from 2d Platoon to follow it down the draw to see where it led. At 1400 Rosenstreich started up the mountain again. He moved cautiously. Unlike Stevens, he was a professional. He was afraid, but he had learned how to master his fear. He moved a step at a time, a slow creep, checking out every rock, every palm frond, every low-hanging branch, every twig and rotting log. Occasionally he stopped to call McCarrell or Denholm forward to look something over with him and to get their advice, but then he started moving again.

At 1500 the sniper opened up again. The shots were again high, and Rosenstreich responded by emptying a magazine into the trees ahead. Then he reloaded and started reconning by fire. With his rifle on semiautomatic, he walked slowly forward and snapped off shots at likely ambush positions—at bushes, stands of bamboo, and small patches of elephant grass, at anything that might conceal a man.

As Rosenstreich was firing, a North Vietnamese soldier suddenly popped out of a spider hole in the center of the trail and, with his AK47 on automatic, shot the pointman right in the chest. The burst lifted Rosenstreich in the air slightly and flung him back down the trail. At that same instant another enemy soldier popped out of a bunker farther up the trail and fired an RPG. The rocket grenade hit McCarrell in the chest, exploded, and set off a claymore mine the slackman was carrying over his shoulder in a canvas pouch. The explosion blew McCarrell into pieces all over the trail and blew Denholm ten feet into the air. His ears ringing, passing in and out of consciousness, the lieutenant stumbled to his feet and crawled forward. He knew his body was peppered with shrapnel, but he felt no pain, only the sense that he had somehow stepped right into the center of a nightmare. Instinctively, he screamed, "Get the sixty up! Lay down some fire."

On hands and knees, Denholm crawled forward, thinking, I have got to do something. Something. Anything. His ears still rang, and he felt as though he had been hit in the head with a ball bat. Machine-gun fire lashed through the trees overhead, and RPGs were impacting everywhere. Everything was noise and wild movement and madness. He crawled past what was left of McCarrell and then up to Rosenstreich. His friend was slumped against a large tree on the left side of the trail. He was gasping for breath, slowly dying. Denholm tried to pull the rucksack off Rosenstreich's back so he could lay him down, but he couldn't get it off. Instead, he pulled out a large bowie knife he carried and cut it off. He laid his friend down behind the tree, only to have him die a few seconds later. The lieutenant put his hand on Rosenstreich's head and thought angrily: They killed my boys! The bastards killed my boys!

His last seconds with Rosenstreich were like a moment out of time. He turned back to a maelstrom of wild shooting and explosions. He screamed again, "Get the sixty up! Put out fire!"

As if heeding the order, Sp.4 Terry Larson rushed forward up the center of the trail, fired off a few rounds up the trail, then pitched forward face first in the trail, shot in the head. Sp.4 Donald Mills, a machine gunner, followed right behind. He was holding the gun at his hip and pouring a torrent of fire up the trail. Ten meters away, the same NVA soldier who had shot Rosenstreich popped out of his spider hole and shot Mills in the chest before he could bring the machine gun around. Mills fell down behind a log, lay there for a few seconds, then leaped to his feet filled with the rage of a bull. "That sonofabitch shot me," he screamed at the top of his voice. "The goddamn-sonofabitch-bastard shot me!" Mills picked up his M60, but discovered that the firing mechanism had been crushed by a bullet. Still raging and cursing, he picked Larson's M16 up off the trail and then, with blood pouring from half a dozen chest wounds, staggered over to the spider hole and emptied what was left of the 20-round magazine into the NVA in it. "You slimy bastard," he screamed as he fired. "You little piece of shit." When the magazine was empty, he flung the rifle aside and stumbled back down the trail.

Behind the tree near Rosenstreich, Denholm had a bag of grenades and as fast as he could pull the pins was pitching them up at the enemy positions. He could not tell for sure, but the fire seemed to be coming from an area on the trail about twenty-five feet away, between two low knolls. He could not tell, however, whether the enemy soldiers were firing from bunkers or spider holes, or even from trenches. Down the trail, he could see the company first sergeant, William Murtiff, and the 4th Platoon Sergeant, Louis Garza, trying to move forward with a group of men up the right side of the ridge. The men were firing and maneuvering forward slowly. On the right side of the trail, there were two or three wounded lying off the side of the ridge. While Denholm watched, a medic rushed forward to help the wounded, but was hit himself. Thinking he might be able to help some of the wounded, Denholm dashed across the center of the trail and hit the ground. He was crawling forward toward one of the wounded men when an enemy soldier popped suddenly from a spider hole on the right side of the trail. Denholm froze in place, and for a fraction of a second he and the NVA rifleman locked eyes.

Brppp! The soldier fired a quick burst from his AK47 then dropped out of sight. One of the bullets ricocheted off the lieutenant's helmet, and another tore off his glasses. Denholm moved quickly to his right and into some. tall grass. He thought he could see the spider hole and threw a grenade at it, but it exploded harmlessly on the ground. He threw another, but it likewise went off on the ground.

Where was the hole?

His mind racing and his heart still fluttering from his near miss with death, Denholm crawled forward up the side of the ridge, searching frantically for the spider hole.

Where was the sonofabitch? Where . . . ?

Two feet away, partially hidden by a clump of elephant grass, the enemy soldier popped out of the spider hole again. The man was looking down the trail for a target, his rifle pointed forward, finger on the trigger. Denholm was going to shoot the man, then realized he had left his rifle somewhere below. He reached down at his side for his bowie knife and discovered it was already in his hand. Then in a spasm of fear and frustration, he thrust his knife out as hard as he could and buried it in the NVA soldier's throat. The man gasped and turned slightly toward Denholm. Once again their eyes met for a fraction of a second, and then the enemy soldier, the knife still in his throat, slipped down into the spider hole. With his mind teetering on the edge of shock, Denholm rolled away and started crawling back toward his men below, completely oblivious to the torrent of enemy rifle and machine-gun fire hitting all around him.

Down the trail fifty meters, Captain Littnan was standing next to his RTO, the handset held to his ear. For five minutes he had been listening to the clatter of fire up ahead without any idea of what was happening. He was keying the handset, trying to get through to Denholm, when he looked up the trail and saw a short, stocky kid with glasses clutching his rifle in one hand, tearing down the trail toward the company CP. Littnan could not believe what he was seeing. The kid was in a complete panic, absolutely terror-stricken. As the kid went by, Littnan tried to grab him, but missed and screamed, "Somebody stop that man!"

A short distance away, two men jumped into the center of the trail and tackled the kid then wrestled him to the ground. The kid was hysterical. He started screaming at the top of his voice, then tried to squirm free of the men holding him.

"What's wrong here?" Littnan asked. "What happened?"

The kid gave up struggling. He looked up at Littnan and seemed about to say something, then started crying furiously, his chest heaving, his breath coming in short pistonlike gasps. Littnan looked down at the crying soldier and thought: Jesus, what in the hell did we run into up there?

It was only much later that Littnan would find out why the kid was crying. It turned out he had been standing only a few feet away when the RPG hit McCarrell in the chest and blew him into pieces for ten meters up and down the trail.

* * *

On the trail 4th Platoon was in the process of withdrawing. Garza took charge of the platoon from the rear. First he sent a squad up to join Denholm on the right side of the trail, then had another move up on the left. With both these squads pouring suppressive fire on the enemy positions above the trail, he had groups of two and three men rush forward and start pulling the three dead and seven wounded men from the center of the trail.

It was a difficult job. The NVA showed excellent fire discipline, and as the two squads increased their volume of fire, the enemy also increased theirs. The men retrieving the dead and wounded had to run a hail of fire, but by 1645 had them all down in the saddle.

Lieutenant Boccia, whose platoon was second in the column, had stood in the center of the trail and listened to the entire firefight without the slightest idea of what was going on. Now he watched as the first walking wounded moved by on their way to the battalion CP. Behind them came the stretcher bearers, and not far behind them Lieutenant Denholm.

The sight of his friend shocked Boccia into speechlessness. Denholm was covered with blood and was stumbling forward on rubbery legs like a drunk. His arms hung limply at his side, and his eyes had a distant, hard look.

"Chuck . . . what happened?"

Denholm looked at Boccia blankly and muttered, "Where's Rosey? Where's McCarrell and Larson . . . ?"

Boccia did not know how to respond. He made a gesture to help his friend, but Denholm pulled away and staggered past him down the trail.

With 4th Platoon down off the trail, Bravo Company's forward observer crawled far enough up the trail to pinpoint the enemy positions, then called in artillery on them. For fifteen minutes artillery pounded the area. When they finished, the FO crawled forward and marked his position with a smoke grenade, then called on two Cobra gunships to hit the enemy positions further with HE rockets.

What happened next would never be fully explained. At the battalion CP, Honeycutt was unaware of the request for the gunships. As they went into a hover over the mountain, the colonel turned to Captain Addison, "Chuck, what in the fuck are those guys doin' up there? For

Christ's sake, they're flying right through the artillery arc. Are they both crazy?''

As Honeycutt spoke, the gunships, which had seemed to be heading for the top of Dong Ap Bia, suddenly did a quick turn and lined up on the battalion CP. "Oh, Jesus!" Honeycutt screamed. "Those clowns are gonna fire us up!''

Honeycutt picked up the handset of one of his radios and tried desperately to reach the ships over the fire channel. It was a wasted gesture, for one of them had already banked and cut loose with a barrage of rockets.

"Get down!" Honeycutt yelled at the nearly fifty men standing around the battalion CP. "Incoming! Incoming!''

The rockets burst in the treetops, and shrapnel rained down over a 30-meter area. Some men fell in clumps, and others scattered wildly for cover on the edge of the position. Honeycutt himself was hit in the back by a piece of shrapnel as big as his thumb. It knocked him down, and when he got to his feet, he found both his legs going numb. He limped over to his radio and grabbed the handset again. As he was keying it, the second gunship also volleyed. Four or five more rockets burst in the treetops, and shrapnel again tore through the CP area like a giant scythe, knocking down men two and three at a time.

Honeycutt screamed into the handset, "Stop firing! You're shooting friendlies! Stop, for Christ's sake!''

When the gunship pilots finally realized their mistake, they tried to offer an apology, but the colonel refused to accept it. "Get your asses out of this area," he screamed. "Do you hear me? Clear the area, or we'll shoot you down.''

The piece of shrapnel in his back had pinched a nerve, and Honeycutt now could barely walk. He limped around his shattered CP and tried to gauge his losses. It seemed total. The rockets had killed two men, wounded thirty-five others, and completely halted the functioning of his command post. His sergeant major, Bernie Meehan; artillery liaison officer, James Deleathe; and ten other men who had played key roles in the operation of the CP were wounded seriously enough to require immediate evacuation. The CP area looked like a medical aid station after a large battle. Men were sprawled about everywhere, and the few available medics were running about trying to save those near death.

As if to compound things, an NVA 120mm heavy mortar, hidden somewhere across the Laotian border, suddenly opened up on the CP area. Within seconds, five or six of these gargantuan rounds impacted, forcing men already hit once again to crawl for cover.

At nearly the same moment, while mortar rounds were still falling, five enemy soldiers burst out of the draw south of the CP and, with their AKs blazing, charged the position. Captain Addison reacted angrily to this new threat. Grabbing his M16, he charged out of the perimeter right at the five. A long burst of M16 fire dropped three of the soldiers, and two others retreated back into the draw. Addison went after them firing wild bursts into the jungle, but after a while turned back and returned to the CP.

On another radio, Honeycutt called brigade and got through to the operations officer, Maj. Kenneth Montgomery. Although he had wanted to control himself, the colonel's anger over the gunship incident boiled over.

"You tell the division artillery commander to get his ass out here, and when you get done, call the battalion artillery officer and tell him to get his ass out here. And you can also tell division that the next one of their goddamn gunships shows up out here that I haven't personally called for, if he makes any threatening move—anything at all!—we're gonna blow his ass out of the sky. Do you hear me, Major. And if none of these people believe me, tell 'em to send one out right now and see what we do. But we're not gonna take another forty casualties because of their fucked up way of doing things. You got that, Major?"

"Yes, sir. I'll see what I can do."

"You better because this bullshit is gonna end right now."

His anger vented somewhat, Honeycutt proceeded to try to come up with a solution to Bravo's predicament. Initially he had wanted to pull back only temporarily in order to soften up the enemy position with a good, hard dose of artillery, gunships, and airstrikes. After softening it up, he had then wanted Captain Littnan to quickly punch another platoon in and—while the NVA were still reeling from the shock of the bombardment—quickly overrun the bunkers and spider holes around the two small knolls.

With his CP shot to hell, though, he realized there was simply no way he could control such an attack. If Bravo ran into an even bigger fight than they had just pulled out of, there was simply no way he could either send them reinforcements or coordinate artillery or air support they might need. It was with the greatest reluctance that he called Captain Littnan and told him to pull his entire company back another one hundred meters and dig in for the night.

As he knelt there by his bank of radios—all around him medics worked over the wounded—he was forced to some quick and sobering conclusions. He had at first suspected that Dong Ap Bia was being garrisoned by either a small enemy recon party or possibly by a group of trail watchers. Bravo's discovery of the commo wire, coupled with the hard contact they had, now convinced him that there had to be at least a reinforced platoon on the mountain, and possibly an entire company. He suspected they were from the 29th NVA Regiment, but there was as yet no way to prove it.

Either way he intended to find out exactly what was on Dong Ap Bia—and not with a single company, which could search only a limited area, but with three companies, each going up the mountain from a different direction. If there was more than a platoon on the mountain, he expected to know it within the next couple of days.

With his decision made, Honeycutt honked up Capt. Dean Johnson, Charlie Company's CO, and told him to halt operations along the Trung Pham and start a company-size RIF straight east toward Dong Ap Bia. They were to move up a large ridge that started near the edge of the river and rose gradually in height to an intersection with the mountain between Hills 900 and 937.

Next he called Capt. Gerald Harkins and ordered him likewise to cease his operations near the river and move back up the large ridge to the battalion CP and take over responsibility for its security from Delta Company. Freed up, Delta in the morning was to move down into the large ravine northeast of the battalion CP and start another RIF up the north side of Hill 937. If everything went according to plan, Honeycutt would have three companies in position by the morning of the thirteenth for a concerted push on the mountain.

From their NDP on the south side of the deep saddle, the men of Bravo Company watched a Skyraider growl past overhead and dive at the enemy positions two hundred meters above. The 500-pound bombs separated from the plane's wings and arched down at the jungle. The explosions were sharp, and the men watching were all jolted back by the concussion. Two brown funnels of smoke poured out of the jungle as if from a large smokestack. The Skyraider, the last of four which had been pounding the enemy positions for the last thirty minutes, lifted its nose and headed east toward the coast.

At his CP, shortly after the bombing stopped, Captain Littnan got a call from Honeycutt wanting a situation report on his casualties and equipment. Littnan hesitantly admitted that all his men were accounted for, but that two M60 machine guns had been left on the hill.

"Where are they? Do you know where they're at?"

"We think so. We know the general area they were left in anyway."

"Then you send somebody up there right now," Honeycutt said, "and bring those goddamn weapons back. And I mean right now! We don't leave weapons behind."

Littnan would have had difficulty picking anyone for such a hazardous mission and was glad when Lt. Marshall Eward and two other men from 2d Platoon volunteered. After waiting until dark, the three men, without helmets or rifles, slipped out of Bravo's NDP and on cat's feet started back up the trail.

Littnan waited for them near the edge of the NDP, fearful of the worst. After only a 30-minute wait, however, all three returned, carrying the machine guns, and Littnan was able to breathe a sigh of relief.

The short mission had nonetheless taken an emotional toll on all three men. Breathing heavily and nervously, Eward sat on a log and said, "There's gooks all over up there, Captain. And I mean a lot of them. And they aren't any damn trail watchers. These bastards are NVA regulars. I could hear 'em talking and moving all over up there. Jesus, I don't want to ever do that again."

Eward's discovery was not an isolated one, for the NVA, after nearly forty-eight hours of lying low, were now on the move all over the northern A Shau and ready to go on the attack. It was a fact the 1/506th was also about to discover—and discover in a big way.

Like the 3/187th, they had spent the past two days riffing the northern A Shau. Their particular area of operation lay just north of the abandoned Pacoh village of Bou Aie Ha and east of the Trung Pham. As a hub for his AO, Lt. Col. John Bowers, the CO of the battalion, had established his CP on top of a small hill about five hundred meters east of the Laotian border. From this hill, Bowers's four companies had been running RIFs both toward the border and into the valley floor.

Slated to guard the perimeter on the night of the eleventh was Lt.

Ian Shumaker and the three platoons of Charlie Company. Ordinarily the commander of the 1st Platoon, Shumaker had to take command of the entire company when the regular CO, Capt. William Stymiest, was hurt earlier in the day in a freak accident.

The 22-year-old Shumaker had spent the night of the tenth on ambush patrol near the border and most of the day riffing along the edge of the river, where his platoon had discovered and then torched a large enemy farm. He had not arrived at the battalion CP until late in the afternoon, but was shocked at what he saw. He was shocked initially by the discovery that the battalion was going to spend two nights in a row in the same position, which to the lieutenant was only begging for a mortar attack. By now, in fact, he was sure the NVA gunners had the coordinates of the position plotted and might possibly even have their tubes laid in.

But what shocked Shumaker just as much was the condition of the LZ. The two platoons of grunts who had guarded the position on the tenth had yet to fortify the oblong-shaped perimeter. Only a few men had even bothered to dig fighting holes, and to the lieutenant's dismay those were too shallow. And while there were a few claymore mines scattered around the perimeter, no one had bothered to set out a single trip flare.

The lieutenant spent the rest of the afternoon trying to shape up the position. He ordered every grunt on the perimeter to dig at least a six-foot-deep fighting hole, equipped not only with overhead cover but with a grenade sump. And he ordered them also to set out trip flares all around the position. Although it was far from ideal, within two hours Shumaker's perimeter was in acceptable condition.

There were others, though, who resisted his order to dig in. When he told the men of the mortar platoon to dig in, they balked, claiming they were too busy with fire mission to have time. Shumaker thought of going to Colonel Bowers and having him order the men to dig in, but decided against it. If the mortarmen wanted to get their asses shot off, so be it. He had enough to worry about with his own men anyway.

Shumaker found more resistance when he made the same suggestion to a reporter from the *Stars and Stripes* who had decided to spend the night on the LZ. A short, pudgy man with hair over his shirt collar, he laughed at Shumaker's suggestion.

"What? Dig a hole? You want me to dig a hole?"

"Yeah. I really think you should. We might get mortared tonight."

"If we do, I'll have to take my chances."

When Shumaker persisted, the reporter finally snapped, "Look, Lieutenant, you don't give me orders. Is that clear? You worry about your men, and I'll worry about myself. Okay?"

"Okay."

"Good."

Shumaker walked away enraged. Later he gathered together his three platoon leaders and related the incident with the reporter. "If we get hit tonight—tell all your men this—under no circumstances is anyone to let that asshole in a hole with them. And that's an order."

The mortar attack came just as the lieutenant had expected. Just before dark, while he was standing near his CP in the center of the LZ, he heard a series of bangs from the surrounding hills and turned to see the mortar position bracketed by explosions. In quick succession fifteen to twenty rounds hit the open gun pits, knocking the exposed mortarmen around like bowling pins. In less than a minute, half of the thirty men manning the four guns went down to shrapnel that filled the air like swarming bees. After the first barrage, the enemy gunner stopped firing for just an instant, then started marching the rounds from one end of the positions to the other. In the flash from the round, Shumaker watched more men blown off their feet and scattered around the gun pits. At once a dozen voices were screaming with pain and crying out for a medic. A few of the men who were not wounded managed to get two of the guns turned in the direction of the enemy fire and eventually were firing back, but Shumaker could tell they had no idea of what they were shooting at.

Shumaker turned away and started running around the perimeter checking his men, telling them to be on their toes for a possible ground attack. By now the enemy gunners had shifted their fire from the mortar position and were pounding the entire LZ. As Shumaker moved around the position, he was knocked off his feet twice by explosions. Everywhere he looked mortar rounds were impacting.

After he made a complete circuit of the perimeter and was starting back to his CP, the lieutenant stopped at the sight of a man about ten feet away who was moaning and digging furiously at the ground with his hands. He knelt down beside the man, thinking to help him, and discovered that it was the reporter. The man's clothes were shredded and burned, and he had several shrapnel wounds.

"I've got some bandages," Shumaker said. "Do you want me to try to treat your wounds?"

"No," the man said, still digging. "I don't even wanna know how bad I'm hurt."

Shumaker ran back to his CP and got his entrenching tool and threw it in front of the reporter. "Try this. I think you'll do better."

Without a thank you, the man grabbed the shovel and started wildly scooping dirt.

Shumaker wished he could have found some consolation in the sight of the man digging, but he did not. The situation on the LZ was beyond humor. There were wounded everywhere, and the mortar bombardment, rather than slackening, was increasing.

Shumaker felt he had to do something to stop it and decided to try a trick he had learned from an old sergeant at Fort Benning on how to gauge the direction and distance of an enemy mortar position. Standing in the center of the LZ, he watched two rounds hit then took a compass sighting down the V of each blast. When they both read the same azimuth, he ran across the LZ to the south side and tried to give the information to the FO in the battalion CP. The man, however, did not seem interested in anything but staying in his hole.

"Get back to your company," another officer in the CP group yelled. "You're drawing fire on us."

Angry at the rebuff and feeling somewhat foolish, he started back toward his own CP. Before he had moved five meters he was knocked down twice by mortar blasts, but still was not wounded.

On the way there, he stopped at the mortar position, which was still in total confusion. Only one gun was still firing, and it had fired so many rounds that its base plate was buried a foot in the ground. While he was standing there, a helicopter descended on the position, landing just to the north of the gun pits. It was a C and C ship, and out of the back of it jumped Gen. Jim Smith, the 101st Airborne Division's assistant commander.

While medics started loading Smith's personal ship with wounded, Shumaker tried to apprise the general of the situation. He did not need to. At that moment a flare, fired from a firebase on the eastern side of the valley, burst overhead. Under its light, the general could see for himself. Smith looked blankly at the three mortars lying on their sides, their legs twisted from direct hits, then at the wounded lying everywhere and said, "This is the worse mortar attack I have ever seen." Even as the general spoke, two or three rounds went off near his ship, peppering it with shrapnel.

Fortunately for the LZ, a C47 Spooky gunship arrived overhead at that very instant. It circled the LZ slowly, its two giant engines droning harshly. Shumaker called over his RTO and honked up the pilot, giving him the azimuth he had computed and the range, which he estimated at three thousand meters.

The plane turned north and was soon over the enemy position. Strangely, at the sight of the giant gunship, the enemy gunners did not attempt to flee, but kept steadily dropping rounds in their tubes. It was a big mistake on their part. After less than a minute over the area, the gunship pilot spotted the flashes from the tubes. He swept down on them like an avenging angel, his six miniguns crackling. Tracer rounds flowed down from the ship like molten lead. Twenty seconds after he started his gun run, one of the rounds hit a stack of mortar ammunition, and a huge rippling explosion tore the jungle apart below, obliterating the enemy position and everyone on it.

When he heard the explosion and then spoke with the gunship pilot, Shumaker breathed a sigh of relief. But relief was all he felt. There was certainly nothing to be proud of. The battalion LZ lay in ruins, and it was only too obvious to the young officer that if the NVA had followed up the mortar barrage with a concerted ground attack, they might have been able to kill or wound everyone on the LZ. It was a chilling thought.

CHAPTER 10

SECOND RIF

Before first light on the twelfth, Colonel Honeycutt had himself flown to Firebase Currahee, where in a quick operation the battalion surgeon removed the piece of rocket shrapnel from his back. Bandaged and sore, he was back at his CP by daybreak. With Capt. Gerald Harkins's Alpha Company now guarding the CP, the colonel started his battalion in motion.

At 0700 a pair of Skyraiders appeared over the mountain and once again started bombing and strafing the enemy positions above Bravo Company. Each plane carried six 500-pound high-drag bombs and a full load of 20mm rounds. They went at the mountain for nearly ten minutes, and when they finished, another pair appeared and likewise started bombing and strafing.

While the last pair went at the mountain, Honeycutt called Littnan and gave him some final instructions. "Try and find out what's going on up there. We've got a lot of support available to us, but we can't use any of it unless we know exactly what we're facing up there."

Littnan, in turn, walked up the column until he found Lieutenant Boccia, whose 1st Platoon would have to take the lead today, and passed on the mission.

"What if we get hit?" Boccia asked.

"If you start getting real heavy fire, pull back. I don't want any casualties."

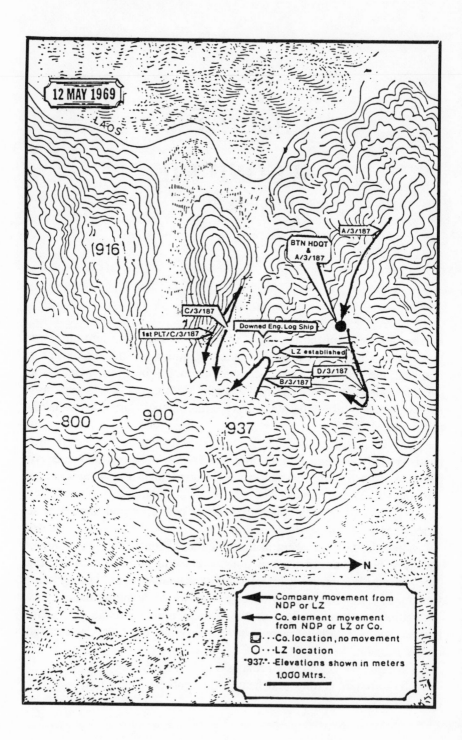

First Platoon moved out at 0820 in two columns. Sp.4 John Snyder took the point for the column on the left and Sgt. John Eden slack. Ten meters behind him trailed Sp.4 Smokey Miller and then Boccia. All the men in the platoon had left their rucksacks at the NDP and, besides their web gear, carried only their personal weapons, grenades, ammo, water, and gas masks.

As the two squads moved up the steep trail, they discovered that there were even more holes in the jungle canopy than there had been the day before and that the bombs and artillery fire had also knocked down numerous long stretches of bamboo and elephant grass. In a few areas all the low growth under the canopy had been reduced to cinders by napalm. Numbers of small trees, their leaves burned away, flanked both sides of the trail.

Again moving cautiously, it took the 1st Platoon about thirty-five minutes to cover the two hundred meters back to the clearing. At the outer edge of it, both columns stopped, and the men started crawling forward on their hands and knees. The ground was steep and got steeper as they inched their way forward.

On the left, Snyder spotted a dead NVA soldier in the center of the trail. He stopped for a few seconds, then, crawling from log to log, moved in for a closer look. He stopped about fifteen meters away and scanned the clearing. The bombing had likewise opened up the jungle there. The small knoll had been hidden by the jungle the day before, but napalm had burned it clean. As his eyes searched the clearing, he spotted an enemy bunker a short distance from the dead soldier. He took a long look into the aperture and thought for sure he spotted two enemy soldiers moving inside.

He backed up a few meters, then passed the word back that he wanted the recoilless rifle up front. A moment later, Sp.4 Phillip Nelson and his assistant gunner crawled forward on their stomachs, dragging the gun between them. In a hushed voice, Snyder told the men what he wanted them to do, then crawled another five meters forward and took up a position on the left behind a large log in order to provide covering fire.

Nelson took up a position behind another large log on the right side of the trail. After he inserted the round, he brought the gun up, rested it on the log, sighted carefully, then pulled the trigger.

Crack boom!

The two sounds came milliseconds apart, and Nelson looked up to see that the round had gone right into the aperture and collapsed part of the bunker's log roof. While brown smoke poured from the bunker, the assistant gunner quickly reloaded the gun, and Nelson brought it up on the log again. He was preparing for the second shot when an enemy soldier popped out of a bunker on the knoll and fired an RPG. The rocket grenade sailed down through the clearing like a toy airplane, its fins wobbling, and hit the log right below the barrel of the recoilless rifle. The explosion blew the gun fifteen feet into the air, wounded both men, and sent them flying down the hill.

The first shot was a signal. NVA soldiers from countless bunkers and spider holes leaped up at the same moment and let off with a volley of RPGs. They went off in the trees above the two advancing squads and showered the men with shrapnel. Before the Americans could respond, the NVA rocketed them again, and then again. The GIs hugged the dirt, crawling for whatever cover they could find.

In a matter of seconds, six men were wounded and the cry of "medic" rose above the noise of impacting rounds. The platoon medic, Sp.4 Francis Muldon, rushed forward to help the wounded, but was himself hit by shrapnel and knocked down.

Along both sides of the trail, men began trying to return the fire, but the NVA again raised the ante. At once, twenty to thirty NVA soldiers rained a torrent of rifle and machine-gun fire down on the Americans. Men tried shooting back, but the enemy fire was so intense that all they could do was keep their heads down.

Lieutenant Boccia had never experienced fire either as heavy or as concentrated in one area as this. It was simply overwhelming. Everywhere he looked bullets were hitting. Tree branches and leaves fell like snowflakes. Machine-gun rounds walked up and down the trail, cutting furrows, throwing up showers of dirt and gravel.

Captain Littnan radioed Boccia, wanting a situation report, and the lieutenant screamed over the tumult, "We're in a firefight. The fire is unbelievably heavy. I've never seen anything like this."

"What are you gonna do?"

"We're gonna have to get the hell out of here. There is no way we can advance into this shit. No way in hell. And if we stay here, they're gonna chop us up."

"Come back then."

Boccia set up a machine gun at the base of the incline and started laying down a covering fire. He yelled at the squad on the right side of the trail, and they slowly worked their way down, dragging the wounded with them. Once the squad was down, he put them on-line also, and they likewise started laying down covering fire. Everyone in the squad on the left managed to make it down except for Snyder, who was still pinned down behind the large log, where he found himself in his own little war. Rifle fire was pouring down on him from enemy positions all around the two knolls. Rounds thudded into the front of the log without stopping. From the same position, enemy soldiers were rolling grenades down at him. Most were exploding in the front of the log, showering him with rocks and tree bark. One grenade, though, actually hit his helmet, bounced high in the air, and exploded behind him.

Snyder found his mind focused on one thought: I've got to get out of here or these bastards are gonna kill me. As he was thinking this, a grenade went off nearby and stunned him. He passed out for a fleeting second, and when he came to, he heard someone pop the cork of a champagne bottle. What? Am I dreaming? He looked over the top of the log just an inch or two, and, there, standing in full view only fifteen feet away, half out of a spider hole, was an NVA soldier. The man had a stick-handled grenade in his hand, and Snyder realized suddenly that the sound he had heard was that of the man pulling the string fuse. Snyder watched as the man's arm went back, then knelt there transfixed at the sight of the grenade coming right at him. The grenade hit a vine halfway across and exploded, but it woke up Snyder to the fact that he was finished if he did not get out of there immediately.

He jumped up and made a dash backwards, but tripped and fell. He tried getting up, but discovered that the strap on his gas mask had gotten tangled in some vines and pinned him to the ground. He squirmed to get free, and some enemy riflemen saw him move and poured fire in his direction. Below, his own men fired up the trail to suppress the enemy fire, and Snyder found himself right in the middle of a crossfire, with waves of red and green tracers flowing over him from both directions. Snyder pulled on the strap, but still could not get free. Finally, in desperation, with bullets kicking up dirt all around him, he pulled out his bayonet and cut it free. Then with a wild lunge, he leaped free of the vines and ran like a madman down the trail, bullets kicking up dirt behind him all the way.

Below the incline, Lieutenant Boccia turned his platoon around and, while three men laid down covering fire, started them back down the trail. At the edge of their previous NDP, they hunkered down and waited. Fighter-bombers arrived minutes later and once again started pounding the clearing with 500-pound bombs and napalm. While the planes worked,

Boccia put his wounded on makeshift stretchers, and they were carried back to the battalion CP.

Back at the battalion CP, Colonel Honeycutt had followed Bravo's difficulties on the trail with an ever-rising feeling of frustration. But they were not his only problem. Capt. Dean Johnson was reporting that Charlie Company's advance straight east up their ridge was meeting small but tenacious enemy resistance. Snipers in the trees in their front and in the draws on both sides of the ridge were methodically tracking the company's advance, taking potshots, then quickly disappearing into the jungle.

Delta Company was experiencing even worse problems. Not only were snipers tormenting the column, but the company was finding its move down the side of the ravine an experience similar to mountain climbing. The sides of the ravine varied in slope from twenty-five to thirty degrees, with some areas nearly vertical. In places, the men had to back their way down, holding onto vines and trees to keep from falling.

To compound things for Honeycutt, he had the problem of putting his staff back together. He did so with a steady stream of replacements cannibalized from a number of rear-area detachments and staff, with a final result that was far from satisfactory. In the midst of all this, he held a tense meeting with Gen. Lloyd Picou, the division artillery officer, to discuss the gunship accident. During the meeting Picou agreed to Honeycutt's request that any gunships coming into the 3/187th's AO would first have to check in with the battalion CP before they were given clearance to fire.

When Picou left, Honeycutt ordered his detachment of engineers to begin construction of an LZ for Bravo Company on the southeast side of the saddle near its present NDP. Nearly seven hundred meters of rough trail now separated the battalion CP and Bravo's rear, and as they pushed up the mountain, that distance was going to get bigger and bigger. If that push turned into a prolonged fight, Bravo was going to need a closer point from which to be resupplied and to evacuate their wounded.

Getting the LZ constructed, however, turned into a major problem. At 1030 the engineers arrived over Bravo's position in a Huey helicopter. The ship went into a hover just above the tops of the trees, and the engineers, burdened with chain saws and rucksacks loaded with plastic explosives, started rappelling through a hole in the canopy.

Above on the mountain, the NVA watched the action and waited patiently. They let one engineer get on the ground, but when the second was halfway down the rope, dangling helplessly below the canopy, they opened up on the ship with a number of light and heavy machine guns. The first burst shattered the ship's windshield and ripped up the tail section. The pilot screamed back to the engineers that he was going to pull away, and one of them cut the rope. The engineer dangling from it plummeted down through the trees and hit the ground, breaking both legs.

The ship pulled off, with enemy tracer rounds tracking it all the way, and flew east away from the mountain. When Honeycutt heard the news, he was furious. He honked up a FAC plane circling nearby. "Dump the world on their asses. Do you hear me? Let the bastards have it."

The FAC plane did just that. In the next thirty minutes, he brought in four fighter-bombers with a total of thirty bombs against the enemy positions.

Thinking the enemy fire was suppressed, the ship carrying the rest of the engineers returned at 1205 and again went into a hover over Bravo's NDP. There was no enemy machine-gun fire this time, just a single RPG. It sailed down off the mountain and hit the ship's rotor with a blinding flash. The ship shuddered under the impact, and the pilot tried desperately to bring it under control. He could not. It dropped like dead weight through the trees, and with its giant blades slashing away through tree branches and vines, crashed into the side of the mountain, bounced, then rolled over on its top.

The men toward the rear of Bravo's column rushed back down the trail and pulled the four crewmen and six engineers from the wreckage, then backed away as the ship exploded and the ammunition inside started cooking off.

While men from Bravo Company organized stretcher parties to haul out the ten wounded, fighter-bombers returned to bomb the enemy machine-gun positions. This time they went in with the max—1,000-pound bombs with delayed-action fuses. When the fighter-bombers finished, all five supporting firebases likewise brought their fire to bear on the enemy positions, and for the next thirty minutes ten howitzer batteries sent barrage after barrage into the west face of Dong Ap Bia. When they stopped, two pairs of Cobra gunships took over, and for the next twenty minutes rocketed and strafed. Finally, at 1400, the fighter-bombers returned with yet more 1,000-pounders and cannon fire.

While the bombers worked, Honeycutt ordered another group of engineers to move cross-country from the battalion CP to Bravo's NDP and to continue work on the LZ, then honked up Captain Littnan and told him to try to push another platoon through the clearing.

Lieutenant Eward's 2d Platoon took the point this time, and took it with confidence. After all the prep fire, most men in the platoon were convinced that the enemy positions around the two knolls had been knocked out and that they would be able to just sweep through them. They were badly mistaken. While Eward's men did manage to advance a few feet farther, they were eventually sent reeling back down the mountain by a blizzard of automatic-weapons fire.

Honeycutt's two other maneuvering companies were having equally bad experiences. Still moving down the treacherously steep sides of the ravine, the men in Delta Company were now being harassed by so many snipers that they were forced to recon the trail ahead of their march with flechette rounds fired from their recoilless rifle. In five hours they had managed to cover only five hundred meters, and their pace, rather than quickening, was slowing.

Charlie Company, moving straight east up the ridge, now had a plethora of enemy groups shadowing it. Snipers pecked away at the column from all sides. Although most of the fire was inaccurate, the constant shooting unnerved the men and caused some to panic at the slightest noise or movement.

At 1820 the company was ambushed. From the high ground above the trail, the NVA hit the front of the column with six or seven RPGs. They all exploded in the trees, and the rain of shrapnel wounded eight men. The company responded by calling in mortars on the enemy positions, then gunships and artillery. The artillery fire must have hit an enemy ammo cache, for a secondary explosion ripped through the enemy positions. When Charlie started a second push, the enemy soldiers fled the area. After moving only seventy-five meters farther, however, the front of the column was once again pummelled with rocket grenades, and the company ground to a halt.

No one was wounded in this second ambush, but back at his CP Honeycutt had to admit reluctantly to himself that neither Delta nor Charlie Company was going to be in position by morning to take part in his multicompany push against the mountain. Neither, in fact, was even close to being in position.

CHAPTER 11

SIDESHOW AT FIREBASE AIRBORNE

While Honeycutt's men settled down for an uneasy night, North Vietnamese troops in the northern A Shau were preparing to go on the attack. Their target, however, was not the NDPs spread out below Dong Ap Bia, but Firebase Airborne, one of the five artillery positions supporting the 3/187th. Only a few hours away was one of the bloodiest, and what for the Americans would be the most disastrous, sapper attacks in the history of the Vietnam War. The attack would confirm the suspicions that many high-ranking officers in the division were already entertaining, namely that the North Vietnamese intended to fight, and fight savagely, to hold the northern A Shau.

To understand the forthcoming events at Airborne, however, we need to backtrack twenty days. During the early morning hours on April 22, a FAC plane, while on a routine reconnaissance mission over the northern A Shau, spotted some huts on a ridge 2,000 meters below the peak of Dong Ngai. It was not an exceptional discovery, coming as it did in an area that the troops in the 101st Airborne Division already referred to as the "warehouse area," a 10-square-kilometer patch of jungle on the eastern side of the A Shau, out of which flowed a good portion of the enemy supplies and munitions for Thua Thien Province.

A thorough search of the area would have likely turned up dozens of similar bamboo-and-thatch huts, any of which could have been part of an active enemy base camp or one long abandoned.

Either way, the huts were legitimate targets, and a few minutes after the discovery, fighter-bombers began inundating the area around the huts with 250- and 500-pound bombs. The first couple of passes did little but blow gaping holes in the jungle, but the second or third bomb runs set off a series of secondary explosions that rocked the area with the ferocity of an erupting volcano. Balls of fire gushed up over the tops of the trees, and the red flashes of exploding ordnance rippled in waves across the jungle terrain.

There were North Vietnamese dug in all around the ridge above the huts, and though they could have easily fired on the fighter-bombers, they chose not to. Instead, they decided to wait out the situation and let the Americans make the next move.

The next day B52s hit the area even harder, with hundreds of tons of 1,000-pound bombs. Again, there were huge secondary explosions, conclusive evidence for the intel people that the enemy was using much of the southwest side of Dong Ngai as an ammo cache.

To exploit this cache and find out just how extensive it was, an aerial rifle platoon from the 2/17th Cav was ordered in. The entire platoon arrived in a CH47 Chinook helicopter. As the giant twin-rotored ship was hovering over a bomb crater, letting troops down by a rope ladder through a small hole in the canopy, it was hit by furious bursts of ground fire and sent crashing down through the tops of 100-foot-high trees. Seven men were killed in the crash and two badly wounded. The survivors, badly shaken, barely had time to form a perimeter before a platoon-size enemy force attacked down the mountain and tried to overrun them. The GIs managed to kill or wound about half of the attacking force, but lost five more of their own men and had to put in a distress call for immediate reinforcements.

Two fresh platoons from the 2/17th Cav were dispatched to the mountain, but as they CA'd in, they likewise ran into a fire storm. They managed to get on the ground, but lost two ships in the process and suffered ten wounded. The reinforcements were able to expand the perimeter, but soon found themselves defending against a number of small but intense ground attacks.

Fearful that the 2/17th Cav was in imminent danger of being overrun, Gen. Melvin Zais, the commander of the 101st, called Colonel Honeycutt to Camp Eagle. In a hurried meeting, Zais told Honeycutt that the situation on Dong Ngai was critical and the 2/17th so badly battered that they needed to be immediately relieved. After relieving them, Honeycutt was ordered further to take up the attack on Dong Ngai and clean out the numerous bunkers and trenches on the mountain.

Even though they lost two observation helicopters and a Cobra gunship to ground fire, the 2/17th managed to hold on the rest of the night. Early in the morning of April 25, Honeycutt moved his Bravo Company to Firebase Blaze, where they quickly staged for a combat assault on the mountain.

At Firebase Blaze, Capt. Barry Robinson, Bravo's CO, due to be replaced in a few days by Captain Littnan, gathered his platoon leaders together and briefed them about the situation on Dong Ngai. Lts. Frank Boccia, Marshall Eward, James Dickey, and Charles Denholm stood silently as the captain talked. "The 2/17th Cav is getting their asses kicked," he said bluntly. "Since yesterday morning they've lost over forty men, and if we don't get up there and help them soon, they're going to be wiped out. It is bad up there, and I mean really bad!"

The casualty figure stunned the assembled officers, though worse news was already on the way. As the four lieutenants prepared their men for the CA, Captain Robinson got another call from Honeycutt, with a change of plans. In just the last hour, Honeycutt told Robinson, the 2/17th had lost another forty men repulsing a savage enemy ground attack. Their perimeter was now so beleaguered that the colonel did not think it would even be safe to CA troops into it. He had decided instead that it would be better to put Bravo and Delta in on top of Dong Ngai and then have them attack down toward the 2/17th, putting the enemy, he hoped, in a slowly closing vice. The Air Force had already cleared an LZ about two hundred meters from the peak of the mountain, and he told Robinson to use it for his initial assault. Once all of Bravo was down and the top of the mountain secure, Delta was then to CA in.

The plan looked good on paper, but when Boccia heard that his platoon would be going in first, he had to fight off a feeling of panic. If the NVA had antiaircraft positions on the lower slopes of Dong Ngai, it seemed logical they would have them near the top also, and Boccia seemed certain that Bravo was heading right for a hot LZ.

Premonition aside, Boccia quickly got his men aboard their six lift-ships, and at 1530 they all took off for the northern A Shau, followed closely by the ships carrying the rest of Bravo Company. Boccia rode in the lead ship, along with Sp.4's Dennis Helms, Tim Logan, Nate Hyde, Doug Walton, and Terry St. Onge. It took the ships about ten minutes to cover the thirteen kilometers from Blaze to Dong Ngai. When they arrived, the whole formation went into a hover over the valley floor while two fighter-bombers worked the area around the LZ with 500-pound bombs and napalm.

At 1600, preceded by a final prep by gunships, the lead ship started its run toward the LZ. Boccia's premonition proved true. When the ship was about 1,000 meters away, the door gunner on the left side, Pfc. Jon Fleagane, spotted muzzle flashes coming from the trees to the right of the LZ. He counted five or six of them, but as the ship closed the gap to 500 meters, their number doubled. When the ship was only 250 meters out and closing, the copilot of the ship screamed into his intercom, "Get that fucking machine gun working!"

Fleagane did not need to be told. Before the captain finished his sentence, the young Pfc. had his finger on the butterfly trigger of his M60 and was raking the trees below. On the left side of the ship, the crew chief also opened up with his M60.

Fleagane went after the muzzle flashes with a fury, holding the trigger down for a solid thirty seconds before he let up, then holding it down for another twenty. But he did not seem to be doing any good. Everywhere he looked now about the LZ he could see more and more flashes. He kept firing, nonetheless, just raking the side of the mountain with wild bursts.

When the ship was about one hundred meters away, he started spotting bunkers and spider holes all over the side of the ridge and even a few makeshift bamboo ladders that he knew snipers used to climb into the tops of trees. He fired a few bursts into the tops of trees where he thought snipers were, but there was just too much down there for his one gun.

At sixty meters and closing the enemy found the range, and the ship was hit by a torrent of enemy fire. Fleagane and the crew chief, however, kept firing, raking the area around the LZ as the pilot, Major Daugherty, started the ship in.

The LZ was narrow and choked with splintered trees and debris, and Daugherty had only a few feet to spare on either side of his blades. With bullets still hitting the ship, the major eased it into a hover about ten feet off the ground. In quick succession, Logan, St. Onge, Helms,

Hyde, and Walton leaped from the ship and scrambled into the surrounding jungle. But when it was Boccia's turn, his gas mask container got hooked on an eyebolt on the floor and he could not move. With the ship taking fire and Boccia pulling madly at his gas mask, Captain Watson turned around and screamed at Fleagane, "Push him out."

Just as Fleagane started to push Boccia, the ship suddenly drifted back a few feet off the center of the ridge, and the push sent Boccia off into space. The lieutenant landed roughly on a pile of logs, then tumbled fifteen feet down the steep side of the ridge before he caught himself.

Above, Daugherty started the ship up again, and Fleagane rushed back to his machine gun. Off to his left, not more than twenty meters away, he saw two NVA soldiers behind a log. He turned the gun toward them and was just starting to depress the trigger when an RPG hit the ship right under the pilot's seat. To Fleagane it sounded as if a giant had hit the bottom of the ship with a sledgehammer. He looked into the cockpit and saw that the explosion had blown off Captain Watson's left arm, splattering the cockpit with blood.

The ship dropped like a rock, its blades slashing wildly through the trees before snapping off and careening through the jungle like huge knives. The ship hit the ground with such force that its skids buckled and the transmission broke through the back wall and shattered Fleagane's left arm.

The door gunner, stunned, sat there on the floor of the ship for a long moment, and then he saw something that would haunt him for the rest of his life. Though bleeding profusely, Captain Watson pulled a machete out from under his seat, wiggled out of his seat, and charged up the ridge toward the enemy position. He had not covered fifteen meters and was only a foot or two away from St. Onge, who was standing behind a tree, when an RPG struck the captain right in the chest. The explosion blew him and St. Onge into pieces all over the area.

Fleagane scooted across the floor to the other side of the ship and started pulling Daugherty out of his seat. As he did, a sniper opened up on them and shot the major through the knee. Fleagane managed to get him out of the ship and behind a log, but a second later the same sniper shot the major in the back.

Fortunately for both Fleagane and the major, Boccia moved his men up and formed a perimeter around the downed ship, then helped to get the two men back into the safety of a bomb crater. With his men laying down covering fire on the enemy positions above, Boccia called in Cobra gunships. While they raked the area, the lieutenant was then able to get a medevac in to take out Fleagane and Daugherty.

A few minutes later, Honeycutt arrived overhead and took control of the seven lift-ships still hovering west of the mountain. He was faced with a difficult decision. If he did not reinforce Boccia's position, they would likely be overrun. To send further lift-ships into a hot LZ, however, would only risk losing some of them to ground fire. He decided to reinforce the position.

Although it took heavy fire, the first ship managed to squeeze into the LZ, drop off six men, and get away. The pilot of the second ship, however, panicked when he started receiving fire and crashed into a tree. The ship tipped over on its side and dropped into the jungle to the left of the LZ. The third ship in managed to get six more men down, but the pilot of the fourth, likewise unnerved by the heavy enemy fire ripping into his ship, backed into a tree with his tail rotor and crashed into the jungle on the right of the LZ. The fifth ship, although it was not hit by ground fire, lost its torque as it was hovering to drop off its men and crashed right on the LZ, blocking it for any further use.

Boccia was forced to call off any further lifts. With night approaching, he had the machine guns stripped off the four downed ships and formed a perimeter around the seven men injured in the crashes. Boccia had no sooner set up than a platoon-size enemy force started probing the perimeter. His men drove them back with machine-gun fire, but they continued probing the perimeter the rest of the night.

In the morning, Honeycutt moved to reverse the deteriorating situation on Dong Ngai. In quick succession he CA'd the rest of Bravo Company and two platoons of Alpha into the lower LZ. After securing the perimeter and helping the 2/17th Cav haul out their dead and wounded, both companies began sending squad-size RIFs up the mountain, probing the enemy positions.

With the lower LZ secure, the colonel had fighter-bombers and gunships pound the enemy positions above Boccia's perimeter. Then, after waiting for the pilots of the downed ship to repair it and clear the LZ, he ordered Captain Sanders to CA in Delta Company and reinforce Boccia. The first five of Delta's ships managed to get their troops down, but the next two ships were shot down, and the LZ was once again blocked.

At 1540, Honeycutt himself landed on the lower LZ and took personal command of the troops there. He was just setting up his CP when the enemy bombarded the entire position with heavy mortar fire. The mortar attack lasted for more than an hour. On its heels, a company-size enemy force launched a ground attack, hitting the perimeter from two different directions. Enemy soldiers charged through the jungle firing their AK47s from the hip. Grenadiers and recoilless-rifle gunners ripped the enemy with flechette rounds and broke the momentum of the attack. Thirty minutes later, they regrouped and attacked again. At one point, they breached the north end of the perimeter and seemed about to overrun it, but Honeycutt had napalm dropped less than fifty meters from the U.S. position. One bomb inundated an entire enemy squad as they were preparing to attack. Toward evening the enemy broke off the attack and retreated back up the mountain, leaving ten of their dead behind.

On the morning of April 26, Honeycutt put the 3/187th on the attack. Capt. Gerald Harkins, the CO of Alpha Company, choppered into the upper LZ at first light and took charge of the hodgepodge of units stranded there. As soon as he arrived he held a meeting of all his officers. "I cannot remember seeing a mess like this," Harkins said, pointing to the LZ still littered with lift-ships. "This looks like a damn Keystone Kops movie."

Harkins wasted no time in organizing the different groups into platoons and immediately went on the offensive. After securing the high ground around the LZ, he expanded his perimeter, then ordered Lieutenant Boccia and his own 3d Platoon leader, Lt. Daniel Bresnahan, to start attacking straight down the mountain.

With the upper LZ finally secure, Honeycutt ordered a platoon each from Bravo, Alpha, and Delta companies to push out from the lower LZ and start attacking up the mountain. Honeycutt preceded their advance with a massive airstrike, which resulted in a number of huge secondary explosions. Shortly after the airstrike, Delta's platoon overran a huge enemy arms cache less than two hundred meters from the lower LZ. Included in the cache were more than ten thousand Chicom rifle grenades and twenty thousand rounds of small-arms ammo.

Nearby, Bravo's 4th Platoon, led by Lieutenant Denholm, overran an equally large cache. Their advance up the mountain, however, was stopped a short time later by a reinforced platoon of NVA occupying about fifteen bunkers. Denholm called in airstrikes on the bunkers, but the bombs had little effect. After a long artillery prep, Denholm and his men assaulted the bunkers on-line. Using the 90mm recoilless rifle,

Denholm's men knocked out most of the bunkers in less than an hour and killed fifteen enemy soldiers.

To the east, also advancing on-line, Alpha Company's 2d Platoon, led by Lt. George Bennitt, also overran about ten enemy bunkers, killed seven NVA, and uncovered another large cache of weapons and ammo.

The three platoons stopped for the night about two hundred meters from the upper LZ. With first light on the twenty-eighth, after an hour of airstrikes, they once again started attacking up the mountain. At the same time, a platoon from both Alpha and Bravo companies started an attack down the mountain. About thirty to forty NVA soldiers were caught between the two forces and killed. The linkup of the two forces was effected later in the afternoon, and the area for two hundred to three hundred meters on all sides of the upper LZ was secured.

With this accomplished, Honeycutt ordered a detachment of engineers to begin the construction of Firebase Airborne near the site of the upper LZ. The firebase was needed to support the final mop-up of Dong Ngai. The engineers worked all through the night of the twenty-eighth clearing the jungle from the ridge and by late afternoon on the twenty-ninth— although the position was far from finished—had three howitzer batteries in place.

With Alpha securing the Firebase, Bravo and Delta companies started the slow torturous process of rooting out the last enemy soldiers on the mountain. Neither company had any significant contact on the twenty-ninth. But in the late afternoon on the thirtieth, after a sharp firefight with an entrenched enemy platoon, which they routed, Delta discovered a cache containing more than twenty tons of rice and hundreds of 122mm rockets and RPG rounds.

For the next four days, Delta continued uncovering smaller caches while fighting a running battle with small groups of NVA snipers and trail watchers. On the morning of May 4, however, while the company was riffing northeast toward the peak of Dong Ngai, they ran head-on into an NVA bunker complex defended by a company of infantry with heavy weapons.

Sanders's men managed to take out a number of the bunkers with recoilless-rifle fire, but had three ground assaults thrown back. After the third assault failed, Sanders called in mortars, gunships, and, finally, airstrikes on the bunkers. The mortars and gunships had little effect on the deep bunkers, but the airstrikes did the job. Using pinpoint bombing, the fighter plane hit the bunker complex with nearly thirty napalm bombs and turned it into a huge bonfire.

As soon as the airstrikes ended, Delta's men charged up the mountain and swept into the NVA positions. They were not met by rifle fire, but by the nauseous smell of burning flesh. In the bunkers and trenches, they discovered the bodies of fifteen enemy soldiers, many of them still burning. Delta moved through the position quickly in pursuit of the rest of the NVA company, but most of the enemy escaped, carrying with them many of their dead tied to bamboo poles. This fight was the last attempt by the NVA to hold Dong Ngai. After it, the rest of the units in the area abandoned their positions and moved farther northwest into new bivouacs.

The 3/187th suffered five killed and fifty-four wounded in the 13-day fight for the mountain; but the North Vietnamese losses were far worse. Not only did they lose more than one hundred killed and hundreds of tons of supplies, but they also had one of their major logistical bases in the A Shau wiped out. Yet, even as their forces were retreating from the mountain, the cadre of the 6th NVA Regiment were already planning their revenge.

The Rakkasans would later be awarded a Valorous Unit Citation for their actions on Dong Ngai, but for the time being they had little time to gloat over their victory. On May 8, with hardly a moment's rest, the entire battalion was lifted to Camp Evans, the 3d Brigade base camp, so they could get ready for Operation Apache Snow two days later. They were replaced on Firebase Airborne by a 2d Brigade company, Alpha 2/501st, under the command of Capt. Gordon Johnson. The other three companies in the battalion, earmarked, like the 3/187th, to take part in Operation Apache Snow, were likewise choppered into Camp Evans and from there to Firebase Blaze.

Honeycutt was there when Alpha 2/501st arrived to take over the firebase, and he did not like what he saw. The troops seemed too overly confident to suit him, and after talking with a few of them, he discovered why. He felt they were under the impression that the fight for Dong Ngai was over, the mountain secure, and that they were in for some easy duty guarding a firebase.

Before he left Firebase Airborne, the colonel cornered two young lieutenants and tried to give them some parting advice, "You better get dug in deep here," he told them. "You better get some more wire up, and you better get some patrols out, and you had better start actively defending this place. We just finished kicking the fucking shit out of the NVA up here, and they're gonna be back looking to put some smoke on your ass."

Honeycutt did not know if the officers would heed his advice or not, but he did not have time to concern himself with it. At the moment he had the start of Apache Snow to worry about.

The position Alpha 2/501st inherited from the Rakkasans was far from ideal. The engineers had built the firebase on the north end of a long ridge running parallel to the valley floor. The main position was about two hundred meters long and twenty-five wide, with a howitzer battery in the center and one on each end. On a nearby small knoll, about fifty meters higher than the ridge, they had cleared an area for two guns of the 81mm mortar platoon. Both the main position and the knoll were surrounded by fighting holes and a single strand of concertina wire.

On the coastal plains such a position would have easily been defended, but in the center of a jungle-covered mountain like Dong Ngai, it was fraught with hazards. While the west and northwest sides of the position overlooked steep ground and could easily be defended, the northeast and south sides had gradual slopes and offered an attacking force an easy approach to the heart of the firebase. Compounding the problems the defenders faced was a thick, double-canopy jungle that stopped only a few feet from the wire. While the engineers had been able to clear the jungle from around the immediate vicinity of the firebase, they had had the time to chop back only a few feet of it outside the wire.

As soon as Alpha took over the position, they immediately set out trying to improve it. In order to strengthen the perimeter, a number of fighting holes were added, and both the original and new ones provided with overhead cover. To provide better fields of fire, the jungle was chopped back about five meters, and then two rows of concertina wire, seeded with many trip flares, were added.

To defend the nearly 450 meters of perimeter, Captain Johnson assigned each of his platoons a section of it. On the north and northeast sides, he placed Lt. Howard Pitt's 2d Platoon; on the west and northwest sides, Lt. Patrick Cushing's 1st Platoon; and on the south side, Lt. Bruce Saunders and his 3d Platoon. Saunders was also given responsibility for protecting a mortar position on the small knoll.

If the Americans knew the shortcomings of Firebase Airborne's defensive system, so likewise did the cadre of the 6th NVA Regiment, an elite infantry unit bivouacked in deep caves on Doi Thong Mountain, only twenty-five hundred meters away. A year before, during the Tet Offensive, the 6th was one of the units that seized the Citadel in Hue, then for over a month put up a savage defense against the U.S. Marine and ARVN forces trying to retake it. During this fight, they suffered nearly 50 percent casualties and were finally forced to retreat back into the mountains. In the past year, though, they had rebuilt their depleted ranks from a steady stream of replacements coming down the nearby Ho Chi Minh Trail and were now ready to go back on the offensive.

As would be learned later from a captured NVA soldier, around May 8 or 9 the cadre of the 6th drew up an operations order calling for the complete overrunning of Firebase Airborne and the destruction of everyone and everything in it. The plan was detailed and listed the specific mission of every unit taking part. Spearheading the attack would be forty-six men from the K12 Sapper Battalion, another unit that had fought at Hue, and infantry from Companies 3 and 4 of the 806th Battalion. Supporting the attack would be an 82mm mortar battery.

Led by a recon unit, the attacking force left their bivouac on Doi Thong Mountain around 1700 on May 12 and by nightfall were in their attack positions less than thirty meters from Airborne's wire. The assault was scheduled for 0100, but due to logistical problems was postponed two and a half hours.

At 0200 the sappers moved out from their assault positions and began slowly crawling toward the wire. Most of them wore nothing but loincloths or shorts, but a number were completely naked. All possessed that steely-eyed, cold, methodical professionalism which was their trademark. They approached the main position from the north and northeast and the knoll from the north, east, and northwest.

The sappers who moved up first were tasked with the job of breaching the wire, but they were followed by others carrying satchel charges and AK47s who were to exploit the breach once it was made. Behind them would follow the infantry.

These first sappers were well-built, husky men, picked specifically for their job because of their agility and their catlike moves. Each carried nothing but a small pair of wire cutters and a few thin strands of bamboo. Each sapper approached the concertina wire on his stomach, slithering forward as noiselessly as a snake, his eyes and ears attuned to the slightest movement or sound. His body undulating, he moved over certain strands of wire and under others, always feeling ahead gently for trip flares. When he found one, he took a thin strand of bamboo from his mouth and tied down the striker. When each man had neutralized all the flares in his section, he started back, cutting each strand of wire until a gap had been opened through all three rows. By 0300—without alerting a single man guarding the perimeter—the sappers had opened gaps in six different sections of the wire.

Around 0310, Pfc. Mark Weston, an 81mm mortar gunner taking his turn on bunker guard on the west side of the knoll, thought he heard movement below him in the wire. Although he was manning an M60, he had specific orders not to use it unless under direct attack. Instead, he threw a grenade out at the noise. The grenade exploded a few feet beyond the wire, and in the millisecond following the explosion, Weston thought he heard an agonizing groan. Hearing the explosion, the mortar platoon sergeant, S.Sgt. George Parker, rushed over to the bunker. For the next five minutes he and Weston kept their eyes peeled on the wire, but could not see a thing.

Nor could Sp.4 Greg Bucknor, a grunt from 3d Platoon detailed to help guard the knoll. Bucknor had been standing in his fighting hole on the east side of the knoll for the last two hours with his eyes glued to the wire, and though sappers had been moving around in it most of that time, he had not seen or heard them. But he could see other things. The night was clear and full of stars, and he watched as green and red tracers filled the sky around Dong Ap Bia, less than seven kilometers away, in beautiful parabolas. And below in the center of the valley, he could see the headlights of a large North Vietnamese convoy slowly threading its way south down either Highway 548 or one of its branch roads.

Bucknor's watch was up around 0315, and he awakened his replacement, Sp.4 Ernest Williams, who was sleeping behind the hole. When Williams was behind the gun, Bucknor wrapped himself in his poncho liner against the cool mountain air and fell instantly into a deep sleep.

A few minutes later, however, he found himself being violently shaken awake. He looked up to see Williams kneeling over him, screaming, "Get up! Get up! We're being hit!"

Bucknor jumped into the fighting hole beside Williams, who had a pile of grenades in front of him and was throwing them out into the wire as fast as he could pull the pins. Bucknor looked down on the main position and saw mortar rounds exploding everywhere. One of them hit an ammo dump in the center of the position, and he watched in horror as two men were blown into the air, their arms and legs flying in all directions. After the initial two-to-three-minute bombardment, the NVA gunners started marching their rounds across the main position.

In the flashes of the explosions, Weston could see that the men trying to man the howitzers were getting knocked over like bowling pins.

A few seconds later, the enemy gunners also opened up on the knoll. Within thirty seconds, twenty to thirty rounds came crashing down on the small position. And with the mortar rounds came a flurry of rocket grenades fired by NVA soldiers in positions all around the firebase.

The GIs on both the main position and the knoll dived into their bunkers and fighting holes to avoid the shrapnel. And while the mortars fired and the GIs huddled under cover, the enemy sappers soundlessly slipped through the holes in the wire and scattered into all parts of the firebase.

After moving through the wire at the north end of the main position, sappers threw satchel charges into five or six bunkers, then coldly shot the soldiers inside crying out in pain. Another group charged into the two howitzer batteries near the north end, destroying five of the guns with satchel charges and shooting down fifteen men in the gun crews. One sapper fired an RPG into an exposed metal conex container that was being used as a fire-directional control center by one of the batteries. When the two men inside started screaming and moaning with pain, two other sappers stood outside and riddled the container with bullets. The commander of the battery, Capt. Moulton Freeman, tried to organize a defense around one of the gun pits, but was gunned down.

Other sappers, specifically trained for deep penetration, charged forward toward the center of the main position. Some carried nothing but satchel charges, and they threw them at any target they encountered on the way. Other sappers followed behind with AK47s, firing away at the GIs milling about in confusion. They moved quickly, darting in and out of the shadows like phantoms. In the confusion they created, GIs shot at shadows and sometimes at each other.

Sappers had also penetrated the wire in a number of places on the northeast side of the knoll and in the gap between the knoll and the main position. Once through, they scattered around the circular position and started flinging satchel charges up into the perimeter.

Pfc. Mark Weston, the man who had thrown the grenade earlier, was crawling low, trying to get back to his mortar position, when a satchel charge landed right next to him, ripping open his right leg and butt. He yelled for a medic, but Doc Kreiger was at that very moment hit himself by an explosion that peppered his head and arm with shrapnel and split open his left leg.

S.Sgt. Parker, who had been sitting at his CP near two logs in the center of the position, rushed toward his mortars at the start of the attack. On the way there he was knocked down three times by explosions. When he finally arrived at the position, he worked with Sgt. Anthony Branco and three or four other men and quickly got the two mortars cranked up and ready to fire illumination. Before they could drop the first round down the tube, however, two satchel charges landed right in front of the guns. The explosion wounded three men and knocked Parker senseless. He did not know how long he was unconscious, but when he came to he could barely stand up. His head felt spongy, and his legs were weak and rubbery. He had the urge to lie down and rest for a minute, but in the back of his mind, a voice kept prodding him. You've got to get back on that gun, it said. You've got to get some illumination. If you cannot see the bastards, they're gonna completely overrun this place and kill everybody on it.

The thought drove Parker back to the gun position. With Branco they tried to stand the two guns back up, but discovered that the steel legs had been blown off both of them and bent like pretzels. Improvising, Parker held one of the tubes against his shoulder while Branco dropped in the first illumination round. It burst brilliantly overhead, then, dangling from its parachute, drifted down slowly, lighting up the entire firebase. Branco was getting ready to drop in another round when two or three more satchel charges went off in front of the gun. The explosion sent both men sprawling and burned the powder bags off every round in the ready rack.

"I need some help here," Parker screamed.

Bucknor jumped out of the fighting hole he was sharing with Williams and rushed over to Parker. "What do you want me to do?"

"Keep those sonofabitches off me," Parker said, pointing down at an area below where the satchel charges were coming from.

In the meantime, Branco ran down to a bomb crater where the mortar rounds were stored, stripped the powder bags off them, and recharged the burnt rounds. Seconds later they got up their second illumination round. When some sappers tried to move forward and throw more satchel charges, Bucknor raked them with rifle fire and sent them reeling backwards.

The attack on the knoll seemed to go into a lull, a short hiatus, for a few minutes, but then it suddenly exploded with fury again. Already through the wire on the northeast side of the knoll, a group of five or six sappers, followed by infantry, charged up the gradual slope of the knoll, throwing grenades and satchel charges before them.

Sp.4 Richard Powell, a mortarman fighting from the top of a bunker on the northeast side of the knoll, pointed his M16 right at the charging figures and emptied a full magazine. On both sides of him other GIs were firing like madmen, firing and screaming and throwing grenades. Two or three of the sappers went down, but two or three others got close enough to lob satchel charges right into the perimeter. In the space of a few seconds, a dozen of them went off with an ear-splitting roar. Powell was knocked unconscious, and when he came to a moment later saw that except for Pfc. Vick Burnette manning an M60 to the right, everyone on this section of the perimeter was either dead or wounded. He got back up and started firing again, but seconds later was blown into the air and off the top of the knoll. He landed near the bottom of the saddle between the knoll and the main position. He knew he was hurt badly, but the fear and adrenaline kept the pain from registering. He looked around in confusion. On the knoll, Burnette was the only one still firing. With his M60 he was firing long bursts at the enemy sappers and infantry coming up the slope. He was hitting some of them, but others were flitting by and disappearing into the heart of the position.

While watching Burnette fire, Powell sensed something behind him. He turned his head slightly and saw a flash of bare skin, and then a naked sapper rushed by him through the saddle and up the west side of the knoll. Behind the sapper came three NVA soldiers wearing Russian steel helmets, AK47s at their hips. Powell tensed his body and played dead, and a few seconds later another small group of helmeted soldiers rushed by.

On the knoll, Burnette spotted the men and turned his machine gun on them. He knocked down two in the group, but one of the sappers let fly with a satchel charge before he fell. The explosion blew off Burnette's left leg above the knee and knocked him unconscious. Instead of finishing him off, the NVA charged right past him, spraying bullets in all directions. They killed two GIs and wounded a number of others, then stopped in the center of the knoll for a moment. Spotting the mortar position, they started across after it. Four or five GIs, however, had formed a perimeter on the back side of the position to protect the guns. They cut loose at once with their M16s and killed or wounded every one of the NVA.

On the northwest side of the knoll, a medic had found Burnette and tied a tourniquet around his upper thigh, stopping the bleeding. He tried to pull Burnette away from the perimeter, but he refused to leave. On one leg, he hopped and crawled back to the bunker and started firing the machine gun again. A group of three or four NVA infantrymen tried to rush the position, but he cut them all down. In the confusion of the shooting, another enemy soldier managed to crawl up unseen below Burnette's bunker. With a sudden movement, he leaped up and pulled the gun from Burnette's hands, then rushed down the slope with it. Undaunted, Burnette grabbed an M16 lying nearby and a bandoleer of magazines and started firing again.

Still lying at the bottom of the saddle, Powell had watched the NVA soldier pull the machine gun from Burnette's hands. With a rifle he had found lying nearby, he raised up slightly and shot the man. Then, seeing a group of four NVA soldiers coming his way, he dropped the rifle and played dead again.

Two of the soldiers rushed up the side of the knoll firing, but two others stopped to check out Powell. For Powell it was an agonizing, heart-pounding moment. For what seemed like an eternity, the two soldiers stood over him talking excitedly. At any second, he expected to be either bayoneted or shot in the back, and he tensed his body to receive it, but then inexplicably they rushed up the hill. For long seconds afterwards, all Powell could do was lie there and gasp for breath, his heart fluttering wildly.

The main position was still a scene of chaos, with sappers running around all over the firebase. Some of the NVA infantry had occupied the overrun bunkers on the north side of the perimeter and had set up machine guns. With those, they kept a steady fire on the center of the firebase. While they fired, other enemy infantrymen trickled in through the wire in preparation for a final push. Although GIs had shot a number of sappers, five or six others, loaded down with satchel charges, were still lurking around the position causing chaos and death.

The Americans, however, were slowly recovering from the terrible shock of the attack and starting to fight back. When Lieutenant Cushing, the CO of 1st Platoon, was seriously wounded by an RPG, Sgts. Ken Counts and Roger Barski, the 1st and 2d squad leaders, organized a hurried defense line on the northwest side of the perimeter and began firing back at the enemy infantry trying to get through the wire to reinforce their comrades. There were numbers of stragglers milling around the overrun howitzer batteries, and Barski and Counts gathered them up and put them under their command.

While they were working on repulsing the attack on the north end of the position, the enemy launched another attack against 2d Platoon's section of wire on the northeast. From twenty to thirty meters away, enemy soldiers pummelled 2d Platoon's bunkers with about thirty RPGs. Three of them made direct hits on bunkers. With screams of wounded and dying GIs filling the air, sappers and infantry charged through four gaps cut in the wire. There was no surprise to this attack, however. The more than thirty GIs manning the perimeter met the enemy troops with a blizzard of rifle and machine-gun fire. Under the light of mortar illumination rounds, the GIs cut down the NVA two and three at a time as they tried to weave their way through the three rows of wire. The wire was soon filled with dead sappers, and the NVA infantry waiting just outside the jungle retreated.

With the threat to 2d Platoon's section of the perimeter gone, Lt. Howard Pitts took seven of his men and linked up with the ragtag group under Counts and Barski. Together they started a counterattack, pushing the enemy soldiers out of their foothold in the northern perimeter.

At 0400, a C47 Spooky gunship arrived over the firebase. On both the main position and the knoll, strobe lights were put out to mark the firebase's perimeter. Directed by Capt. Pierce Graney, the battalion airmobility officer, the gunship began slowly circling just outside the perimeter, its six miniguns crackling out a rain of fire.

The gunship fire stopped cold an enemy attempt to feed fresh troops into the north side of the perimeter, and those already inside began deserting their positions and running back through the wire. They were followed closely by GIs intent on revenge. It was the same situation on the knoll, where the sight of the gunship, coupled with strong counterattacks, put the enemy in retreat. The fight went on sporadically for the next hour, but by first light, except for some scattered fighting on the south side of the main position, where GIs were routing a few NVA diehards from bunkers, it was over. At 0600 Phantom jets arrived over the mountain and went at the trails down which the NVA were withdrawing with 500-pound bombs, napalm, and cannon fire.

The morning light revealed a horrific scene. The firebase was covered from end to end with dead NVA and GIs. Twelve sappers, their faces burned and blackened, their bodies shredded, hung in the wire on the northeast side of the main position. One man still clutched a pair of wire cutters, another a pistol. Seven GIs lay sprawled around the gun pits of the howitzer batteries. Two more were found huddled in the conex container, their bodies riddled with bullets. A number of other

Americans were found dead still in their bunkers. Many had died unaware that they were even under attack. And everywhere there was debris, the junk of war—rifles, satchel charges, and grenades; unexploded RPGs and mortar rounds; powder bags; belts of machine-gun ammo, M16 magazines and piles of bloody bandages.

In the cleanup of Firebase Airborne, thirty-nine enemy bodies were discovered. Two badly wounded sappers were found huddling outside the wire. One died later of his wounds, but the other lived to tell brigade interrogators the story of the attack from his point of view. There were undoubtedly more enemy dead and wounded, as indicated by the many blood trails found in the area around the firebase, but even an approximate figure of their number is impossible.

The Americans suffered twenty-six killed and sixty-two wounded in the 1½-hour battle. On the basis of body count alone, this constituted an American victory, and that is exactly how the spokesman at division level portrayed it to the press.

In reality, most high-ranking officers in the division were shocked by the outcome of the battle. While none expressed this opinion publicly, in private most admitted to each other that the battle had been a debacle. "We held the firebase," Col. Joe Conmy, the 3d Brigade commander, would say in an interview after the war, "but it was the worst result from a sapper attack that I have ever seen."

SFC Louis Garza, B/3/187th, near Bravo's NDP (Courtesy of Louis Garza.)

PFC John Snyder, B/3/187th, with captured SKS rifle and pith helmet. (Courtesy of John Snyder.)

CPT Luther (Lee) Sanders, CO of D/3/187th, in a river valley or ravine some-
where in the northern A Shau. Delta had great difficulty in similar country on
13 May when their medevac was shot down. (Courtesy of Lee Sanders.)

SP4 Johnny Jackson, A/3/187th, was awarded a Silver Star on the 20th for
leading Alpha's successful assault. (Courtesy of Johnny Jackson.)

SP4 Michael Vallone, SP4 William Jennings, and SP4 Robert Spear after the battle. (Courtesy of Michael Vallone.)

Pickup Zone for Operation Apache Snow; near FB Blaze. (Courtesy of John Comerford.)

SP4 Ron Storm (with canteen), B/3/187th, and friend waiting for chopper after battle. (Courtesy of Ron Storm.)

SP4 Emil Hoffman and SP4 Michael Rocklen, D/3/187th, at Camp Eagle. (Courtesy of Michael Rocklen.)

1LT Robert Schmitz, A/1/506th, at Camp Evans. (Courtesy of Robert Schmitz.)

1LT Frank McGreery, A/3/187th, on P2 at Camp Eagle. (Courtesy of Frank McGreery.)

1LT Charles Denholm, B/3/ 187th, on the radio. (Courtesy of Charles Denholm.)

CPT Gerald Harkins, CO of A/3/187th, in his hammock. (Courtesy of LCL Gerald Harkins.)

PVT Seth Randolph, A/3/187th, inspecting tunnel on Dong Ap Bia. (Courtesy of Michael Vallone.)

A-Frame tunnel on Dong Ap Bia. (Courtesy of Michael Vallone.)

SP4 John Comerford, C/3/187th. His fire helped cover Charlie Company's withdrawal on the 14th. (Courtesy of John Comerford.)

SP4 Leonel Mata and SP4 John Comerford (front) and SP4 Bill Batten and unknown soldier (rear), C/3/187th, on PZ Camp Eagle before start of Apache Snow. (Courtesy of John Comerford.)

General Melvin Zais, Commander of the 101st Airborne Division. (Courtesy of Defense Audio Visual Agency.)

Soldiers from the 3/187th cleaning up after the battle. (U.S. Army photo, Courtesy of Pratt Museum.)

SP4 Don (Doc) Krieger, E/2/501st, medic on FB Airborne. (Courtesy of Don Krieger.)

Doc Stinger and SGT Matthew Randolph, B/3/187th, resting at NDP on ridge below Dong Ap Bia. (Courtesy of Ron Storm.)

CHAPTER 12

THIRD RIF

With morning, the news of the enemy ground attack against Firebase Airborne spread like a prairie fire through the four companies of the 3/187th. Although few men knew specific details about the casualty figures, it was common knowledge that Alpha 2/501st had suffered a disaster of major proportions.

As the nearly 350 men of the battalion prepared to move out that morning, many wondered if as bad a fate was awaiting them. If the NVA were willing to fight so fanatically and suicidally to overrun Airborne, what might they do if they decided to fight for this mountain? It was a question few men wanted to think about.

At 0656, a FAC plane appeared and began circling the mountain, waiting for a target. Convinced that all the bombing was having little effect on the NVA positions around the clearing, Captain Littnan had Lieutenant Eward personally crawl up to the edge of the clearing and mark it with smoke so the fighter-bombers could better pinpoint their bombing. Once Eward marked it, the FAC plane marked it again with a phosphorous rocket. Minutes later, two Phantom jets started their runs, this time using 1,000-pound bombs with delayed-action fuses.

Two hundred meters below the clearing, Captain Littnan held a quick conference with Lieutenant Boccia, whom he had picked to lead yet another probe on the clearing. "After these jets get done prepping the clearing, I want you to move your men up until you are about seventy-five meters from the bunkers," Littnan said. "I've got three more sets of fighters on the way. The first two sets are going to hit the bunkers one more time. Then I'm going to have the third set make a pass at the clearing, but not drop their bombs. This should make the gooks keep their heads down. When the third set starts in, I want you to rush up there and try to get in that bunker line before the gooks can react. And for Christ's sake, don't get caught in that clearing the way Denholm did."

Boccia nodded and rushed forward to join his platoon, which he quickly moved into assault positions about seventy-five meters below the clearing. They were hardly in position, though, before circumstances destroyed Littnan's plan.

Two hundred meters across the large draw on the other ridge, Charlie Company, which had been moving rapidly since early morning, suddenly had the front of its column ambushed by enemy soldiers firing from bunkers between the two ridges. Pinned down, they called for an airstrike on the bunkers.

Littnan radioed Boccia with new instructions. "Tell all your men to get on the left side of the ridge and stay low. They're going to put the airstrike right between you and Charlie."

At 0805 the first fighter-bomber went in and dropped a 1,000-pound bomb about two hundred meters northeast of the front of Charlie Company's column. A second after the explosion Boccia was on the horn to Littnan, "Charlie, that HE is landing too close to us."

"Hold on, I'll check it," Littnan said, then radioed the FAC pilot, who was flying to the west of the mountain, observing the airstrikes. The pilot, however, assured him that the bomb had hit right on target.

Littnan passed the news on to Boccia, but when the next 1,000-pounder hit, Boccia was again on the horn. "That shit is landing too close, Charlie, I know it is. We've got shrapnel falling all around us."

Littnan considered Boccia a fine officer, but felt that at times he was too emotional. He knew also that the sight of a 1,000-pound bomb heading for the ground tended to get people excited, tended to make them think it was landing closer than it actually was, which is what he imagined was causing Boccia's reaction. Still, once again he checked with the FAC, and once again he was told that the last bomb had likewise hit in the target area.

Boccia took the news silently. On the left side of the ridge, his platoon hunkered down, awaiting the next bomb. It hit a few seconds later, and the lieutenant looked up to see a giant white flash. And then it seemed as if someone had taken a giant machete and chopped off the tops of every tree on the right side of the trail. A second before the explosion, Boccia had been looking up at triple-canopy jungle, and now he could see clear sky. Fist-size chunks of dirt, rocks, tree branches, and bark showered 1st Platoon. Nearby, Sp.4 Phillip Nelson, hit in the side by shrapnel, gasped and doubled up.

Boccia keyed the handset of his radio trying to get through to Littnan, but discovered that Sargeant Garza was on the frequency giving routine instructions to some listening posts guarding the platoon's left flank. In the distance he could see the next fighter-bomber getting ready to make his bomb run. The plane was over Laos, but turning east toward the mountain.

Thirty seconds later, Boccia managed to get Garza off the line and in to Littnan. "Stop that fucking plane," he screamed. "Stop him, for Christ's sake. You're hitting us."

The fighter-bomber, however, was already in his dive. Boccia watched mutely as the bomb separated from the plane's wing. It was another 1,000-pounder, and it was so close he could actually see its fins open; then the jet kicked in his afterburner, and Boccia went to the ground.

This bomb went off just like the last one, with a huge white flash. Boccia looked up to see another large hole blown in the canopy, a hole large enough for a helicopter to drop through.

"Those are too close," he screamed again, furious.

"What's your problem?" Littnan asked, also getting angry.

"I said they're too close."

"Goddamnit, I'm telling you they're not too close."

At that moment, Boccia heard a commotion behind him and crawled over to see a group of men gathered around a fallen man. He pushed his way in and found Doc Schoch, the platoon medic, frantically working on Sp.4 Myles Westman. It was a wasted effort. A piece of shrapnel had taken off the entire back of his head, and he died within seconds.

Westman was a big, blond Swedish kid from Minnesota, a Billy Budd–like innocent, beloved by everyone in Bravo Company, and his death devastated the platoon. Sp.4 Tim Logan, who had been a particularly close friend of Westman, leaned over the body and started crying. A number of other men stood up and started raging against the jets.

Boccia himself lost control, screaming into the handset, "You're killing my fucking people! You're killing them! Those fucking bombs that aren't supposed to be landing too close just killed one of my men! Do you hear me?''

Littnan listened to Boccia raging, then yelled back, ''Shut the fuck up, Frank, and get off the horn. That's an order.''

Littnan had no idea what had happened up ahead, but he knew the FAC monitored the company command net, and he did not want him thinking he had done something wrong if, in fact, he had not. He turned to his first sergeant, William Murtiff, and told him to rush up the trail and check out the situation. Five minutes later, Murtiff brought back his report.

Overhead, the FAC pilot, his voice breaking with grief, asked, ''Did we do anything wrong? Is someone KIA?''

''Yes, we have a KIA, but it isn't your fault. It was the kid's own fault. He was sitting above the military crest of the ridge, and he didn't have his helmet on.''

Littnan did not discuss the incident any further with Boccia, but he vowed to himself that if the lieutenant ever threw a similar fit, he was going to relieve him of his command on the spot. The incident, however, negated the possibility of 1st Platoon's mounting an attack, and so he pulled them back and moved Lieutenant Eward's platoon forward.

At 1030, two more airstrikes were brought in against the clearing, and at 1100 Lieutenant Eward started the 2d Platoon up the trail. As they moved forward, First Sergeant Murtiff joked with the men around him. ''Can you smell that rice?'' he said, lifting his nose toward Dong Ap Bia. ''That's what we're havin' for supper tonight. Hmmmm! Can you smell it?'' Men smiled weakly at the sergeant. They were in no mood for humor.

Pfc. Octavian Espinoza took the point for the platoon, and Pfc. Phil Trollinger slack. They moved out at a slow walk, neither man aware that right after 1st Platoon had pulled back snipers had climbed into a number of trees in the draws on both sides of the ridge. They found out when they were about seventy-five meters from the clearing. At that moment a number of single shots slashed through the treetops just feet above the column.

''Snipers!'' someone screamed. ''In the trees!''

Both Espinoza and Trollinger dropped flat to the ground. To the left, in a tree on the side of the ridge, Trollinger spotted a muzzle flash. He flipped his M16 on automatic and sprayed the tree, then watched as a sniper tumbled out head first and crashed to the ground. Behind

Trollinger two or three men spotted another muzzle flash in a tree and massed their fire against it. Another sniper fell to his death.

The platoon kept advancing forward, foot by foot. As they did, the sniper fire got heavier, until the ten or fifteen men in the front of the column were all steadily putting out rounds.

"Over there," a man fourth or fifth toward the back of the column screamed, pointing to a large tree. "There's one! Get the sonofabitch!" Five or six men opened up automatic at once. A rifle dropped through the tree branches, and a few seconds later the sniper fell forward, dangling by a rope around his waist just below his perch.

When rifle fire failed to bring down another sniper, the 90mm recoilless rifle was brought forward and the whole top of the tree shredded with a flechette round. Slowly the column advanced up the trail, with the men now dodging from tree to tree, leaping over fallen trees, or crawling under them, and all the time spraying fire into the trees on both sides.

When Espinoza reached the steep incline before the clearing, they started taking fire from the knolls again. Espinoza started up the incline, crawling forward on his hands and knees, his eyes riveted on the trail ahead. Behind him followed Trollinger and then the platoon sergeant. As they crawled, rifle and machine-gun fire careened through the trees overhead, thumped hollowly into logs and trees, and kicked up dirt on both sides of the trail. Soon both knolls were visible ahead. Bombs and shell craters covered the area around them.

Espinoza was just moving into the clearing when an NVA soldier popped out of a bunker between the knolls and threw a stick-handled grenade at him. The blast wounded Espinoza, Trollinger, and three other men, including the platoon sergeant, who was blown into the air and sent rolling down the trail. The four other wounded men limped and crawled back down the trail, and not a second too soon. In an instant, ten grenades sailed out of the enemy bunker line and went off all over the trail like a string of firecrackers.

Lieutenant Eward rushed two squads forward. They formed a short skirmish line across the top of the ridge and started maneuvering forward, firing as they advanced. The clearing was a roar of noise. When a machine-gun position in a bunker on the left side of the trail held up the advance, the recoilless rifle was again brought forward. The gunner again fired a flechette round into the bunker aperture and shredded the two NVA inside.

But the NVA were once again showing incredible fire discipline, refusing to commit all their firepower until they absolutely had to. They let the skirmish line advance another ten meters and then gave Eward's men exactly what they had given Denholm's.

As if on signal, twenty to thirty NVA came out of their bunkers and spider holes, out of trenches, and from behind logs and cut loose with everything they had. RPGs splattered into treetops, raining shrapnel down on the line, and grenades exploded all over the trail. Three men in the line were hit instantly, and the rest broke and started backing up, dragging their wounded with them. The attack was over within seconds.

When Captain Littnan heard of the failure of the attack, he fell into a momentary fit of depression. Jesus Christ! he thought to himself. What in the hell is it going to take to get those bastards out of there? For three straight days we've hit them with 500-pound and 1,000-pound bombs. We've hit them with napalm and tons of artillery rounds, and none of it seems to be doing any good. What more can we possibly do? The captain did not have an answer to his own question, but in the back of his mind the conviction was slowly growing that there were a lot of NVA on Dong Ap Bia and that they were dug in and had no intention of leaving.

Captain Littnan was hardly alone in his perception of the seriousness of the situation around Dong Ap Bia. At 1220 that afternoon, Colonel Bowers, whose 1/506th was still running RIFs near the A Sap River, got orders from 3d Brigade telling him to halt his present operation, then turn his Currahees north and start a cross-country march toward Dong Ap Bia. His new mission: Launch another attack against the mountain from the south.

As the 3/187th and 1/506th maneuvered to attack Dong Ap Bia, NVA units were also on the move all around the mountain. Their tactics, as at Firebase Airborne, were simple: To make the Americans aware that they were not safe anywhere in the northern A Shau and that they were vulnerable to attack from any direction at any time.

It was a lesson Charlie 3/187th learned the hard way. When the main body of the company moved up the ridge on the twelfth, the 1st Platoon, under Lt. Joel Trautman, was left behind to construct and secure a small LZ, from which wounded could be evacuated and ammunition and supplies brought in. It took Trautman's men less than a few hours to chop the LZ out of the jungle, after which they dug fighting holes on both sides of the ridge and settled in to await any calls from the rest of the company. The platoon spent the twelfth quietly, but early that morning Trautman had to detail one of his squads to carry ammunition across the draw and up the large ridge to Bravo Company.

This weakening of 1st Platoon was something NVA scouts likely spotted. In the early afternoon, a large squad of enemy soldiers slipped down from Dong Ap Bia, moved quietly through the triple-canopy jungle in the large draw, then began slowly crawling through the elephant grass up the side of the ridge toward 1st Platoon's perimeter. Their intention was to get close to the perimeter, and then, firing wildly, to rush forward and overrun the LZ. Like the sappers at Airborne, they counted on the shock value of such a sudden attack to throw the Americans off guard, making any kind of organized defense impossible.

Fortunately for the platoon, Pfc. David McCarty, a soldier guarding the north side of the perimeter, spotted movement in the grass below him. When he was sure it was enemy soldiers, he loaded a flechette round in his 90mm recoilless rifle, took careful aim, and fired. All he got, however, was a click. The round was a dud.

At that same moment, probably realizing that they had been spotted, the enemy soldiers leaped to their feet and sprayed rifle fire across the entire south side of the perimeter. They killed two men instantly and wounded McCarty and four others.

Lieutenant Trautman heard the firing and rushed over to see his perimeter in chaos. The wounded and dead were sprawled out around their fighting holes, and, everyone else, shocked by the suddenness of the attack, was either hugging the ground or cowering in the bottom of his fighting hole. No one was firing back, and the NVA, steadily firing, were advancing rapidly. Trautman tried to get some men in the center of the LZ to help him fire back, but they likewise would not respond.

Finally, Pfc. Otis Smith, a black kid whom Trautman had always considered both unmotivated and a troublemaker, jumped up, chambered a round in his rifle, and said, "Come on, I'll help you get the sonofabitches."

Together they started down the side of the ridge, firing as they moved. Still advancing, the NVA stopped, and their fire slackened. Smith's move had motivated the entire platoon, and men opened up all along the perimeter, pouring fire down on the enemy skirmishers. The NVA went for cover and began retreating.

Trautman let off a few parting shots at them, then noticed that Smith had taken an AK round in the arm. He was holding a handkerchief over the wound and walking back up toward the top of the ridge. A medic was trying to tend the wound, but Smith kept pulling back. "Get away from me," Smith said. "I'm okay."

Trautman was amazed. He realized he had been wrong about Smith. He wondered how many other men he would find himself wrong about before this fight ended.

Almost fifteen hundred meters straight north of Charlie Company's LZ and five hundred meters east of the battalion CP, Delta Company was finally reaching the bottom of the deep ravine they had started down the afternoon of the 12th. In that time, they had managed to cover only eight hundred meters, but it had been eight hundred meters down 30-degree slopes and through the heart of deep primeval jungle choked with vines and overgrown with thick stands of bamboo and thorny bushes. The march had been an agonizing ordeal, and it had left every man in Captain Sanders's company near exhaustion.

The pointman stopped the company at the edge of the ravine and Captain Sanders moved up to the front. Sanders stood at the edge of the treeline and looked out. Below him was a steep bank about ten feet high and a rocky river bottom. The river bottom was strewn with large boulders, driftwood, and fallen trees. Sanders could not see the river, but he could hear the roar of water over rocks.

Since Lieutenant Mattioli's 3d Platoon was already at the front of the column, Sanders had them move to the right and set up a position to cover the crossing. He then ordered Lt. Jerry Walden to move 1st Platoon into the river bottom and across the river. There he was to secure the other side with one squad and start moving the rest of the platoon up the large ridge on the north side of Dong Ap Bia.

First Platoon started out about 1210. The men had to hold on to vines and small trees and slither backwards down the steep bank, an ordeal that took nearly fifteen minutes. Once the entire platoon was down, they started off in a column, crossed the chilly waist-deep mountain river, and began moving up the ridge on the other side toward the mountain. About 50 meters up the ridge, Walden stopped the column and set up a perimeter facing the mountain.

With the east side of the river bottom secure, Lt. Thomas Lipscomb started his 2d Platoon down. When they reached the edge of the river, Sanders radioed the platoon to halt for lunch.

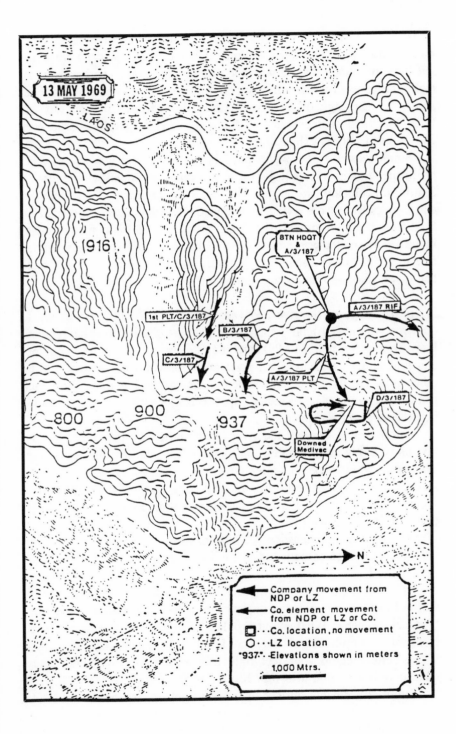

13 MAY 1969

LAOS

1916

BTN HDQT
&
A/3/187

A/3/187 RIF

1st PLT/C/3/187

B/3/187

C/3/187

A/3/187 PLT

D/3/187

800   900   937

Downed
Medivac

N

Company movement from
NDP or LZ
Co. element movement
from NDP or LZ or Co.
▣ ···Co. location, no movement
○ ···LZ location
"937." ·Elevations shown in meters
1,000 Mtrs.

For Pfc. Mike Smith, 3d Platoon rifleman, the break came not a minute too soon. The terrible climb down the side of the ravine had left him so drained that he was not sure he could take another step. To make things even worse, the temperature was hovering around 100 degrees. At the edge of the river, Smith did what most men did: He filled his three canteens, then collapsed wearily against a large rock and groaned out his exhaustion.

Smith was just starting to open a can of C-rations when an RPG hit in the streambed to his right and showered his squad with shrapnel. Smith miraculously was not hit, but Pfc.'s George Pickel, Jerry Spence, and George Blair were seriously wounded. A second later, another RPG, fired from the high ground south of the river, hit 3d Platoon's perimeter in the treeline on the west side of the river bottom. The explosion wounded five men, including Lieutenant Mattioli, who was blown off the bank and down into the rocky river bottom.

At the edge of the river, Private First Class Smith was moving to help his wounded friends when a sergeant stopped him. The sergeant threw four or five belts of M60 machine-gun ammo over Smith's shoulder and told him to get across the river and join Walden's platoon on the other side. He gave the same order to the machine gunner, Sp.4 Jack Little, and the assistant gunner, Sp.4 Bill Cochran. "Let's go, move it," the sergeant screamed.

Smith rushed through the river, then started up the ridge. Behind him came Little and Cochran, and behind them the rest of their squad. The ridge was steep, and after covering less than ten meters, Smith staggered, felt himself getting faint, and collapsed to the ground.

A sergeant from Walden's platoon was over him in a flash. "Get up! What's wrong with you?"

"I've got heat exhaustion," Smith gasped.

"Bullshit! Get up now and move up there."

"I can't . . ."

"Do you hear me troop? I said get on your feet." When Smith still did not move, the sergeant flew into a rage and started screaming, "You chickenshit! What's your problem? You scared of being out here? Is that it?" Smith did not answer, and finally the sergeant exploded, "You better get on your feet right this second, or I'm gonna court-martial your ass. You hear me? Right now!"

Smith still did not answer or move to get up, but he did crook his head and, looking back down the ridge a few feet, saw that both Cochran and Little had also collapsed from the heat and were lying prostrate in the center of the ridge. When the sergeant threatened Smith with court-martial yet again, Smith looked up weakly and thought to himself: What are you gonna do, send me to Vietnam? A minute later the sergeant moved up the ridge, still cussing and fuming.

Farther up the ridge, Captain Sanders had joined Lieutenant Walden and the rest of 1st Platoon, and together they were pushing toward the high ground. Sanders had called a medevac for the wounded, but wanted to set up a position higher on the ridge in order to better suppress any enemy fire when the ship arrived. Sanders had moved about one hundred meters up the ridge when the medevac arrived. The ship had a large red cross painted on each side, clearly marking it as a noncombatant. It went into a hover about one hundred meters above the canopy and just north of the spot where the wounded lay. On the radio, Sanders told the pilot not to come in until 1st Platoon had better secured their ridge.

The pilot, however, concerned because some of the seriously wounded needed immediate help, disregarded Sanders's request and started his ship in. Since the gap in the jungle canopy over the river was too small for the ship to drop through, the pilot went into a hover about one hundred feet above the ground and had his medics lower a large metal basket down through a gap in the canopy.

On the ground, medics loaded Private First Class Pickel into the basket, then stood back to watch as the medics in the medevac began winching him up slowly. When the basket was about fifty feet in the air, an NVA soldier on the high ground to the south fired an RPG right at the hovering ship. Around the clearing and on the opposite ridge, twenty to thirty men watched in horror as the rocket grenade sailed down off the mountain and struck the ship's rotor. There was a giant flash above the trees, and the ship, wobbling and shaking like a huge washing machine out of balance, dropped straight down through the canopy. Sp.4 Willie Springfield, an RTO who had guided the ship in, and Sp.4 Miguel Moreno, one of the wounded, were both struck by the huge blades. Pickel, trapped in the basket, was crushed by the ship.

Blood and pieces of flesh flew in all directions, but when the ship's blades stopped, men rushed at the ship from all directions, pulling away the wounded still on the ground, then going after the four crewmen inside the ship. They were able to get only the pilot out, however, before the ship exploded and burst into flames. Around the ship twenty-five men stood and watched helplessly, knowing that the copilot and two medics were still inside.

Twenty-four-year-old Pfc. Michael Rocklen was one of the watchers. He finally turned away and, feeling a rising nausea in the pit of his stomach, ran about twenty meters north of the streambed and ducked behind a rock. He could not believe what was happening to him. A year before he had been in graduate school in Connecticut, leading a soft, decadent life; and, now, here he was in this streambed in Vietnam with dead men all around him. It seemed too bizarre to be true, too unreal.

It was then he started gagging. Well, Rock, he thought, just before he vomited, this is what your college degree did for you.

Up above, on the ridge, Captain Sanders watched the explosion with a sinking feeling in his stomach. This has got to be the worst day of my life, he thought. Absolutely the worst. He radioed the men standing around the crash site, trying to get more specifics on the accident, but, instead of an answer, got the hysterical voice of one of his platoon sergeants. "You gotta get us out of here," the sergeant screamed. "We're all gonna be killed if you don't."

The sergeant was a lifer, and Sanders could not believe the man was acting so hysterically over the incident. He angrily squelched the sergeant's voice, feeling that the NCO's fear might contaminate the entire company. He turned to his first sergeant, Thomas Stearns, who was standing nearby and who had also heard the sergeant's voice, and said, "Go down there and get that bastard out of here. Relieve him or knock him out—do anything you want. But just get his cowardly ass out of here."

"Roger that, sir," Stearns said. "No problem. I'll take care of him."

At the battalion CP, when Captain Addison brought Honeycutt the news that the medevac had gotten shot down, the colonel was incredulous.

"What are you talking about? Medevac helicopter? There ain't no medevacs out here! What in the hell is going on here?"

"I don't know," Addison said, "but I just got a message from Delta saying a medevac had been shot down."

A moment later Honeycutt got through to Sanders himself. They spoke over the scrambler so the NVA could not listen in. As if unwilling to believe what he was hearing, Honeycutt shook his head as he listened to Sanders tell about the crash.

"How many wounded and dead do you have?"

"I've got seven wounded and seven dead."

"Jesus!"

"Can you send us another medevac?"

"No way, Sandy. They'll shoot that sonofabitch down; you'll never get out of there."

"What do you want us to do?"

"You'll have to carry them out. Can you make it out with everybody?"

"There's no way. We can carry the wounded, but we'll have to leave the dead behind and come back and get 'em later. Can you send us a platoon to help?"

"Yeah, I'll have Alpha send one down right away."

Sanders was still holding the handset in his hand when a soldier came up and said, "Sir, come here quick!"

He followed the soldier up the ridge until they were behind 1st Platoon's perimeter, spread out across the ridge. Lieutenant Walden stepped over and said, "They're comin' down, Captain. You can hear 'em."

Sanders looked up toward the top of Dong Ap Bia and listened carefully. The sound of men moving through bamboo was as clear as the sound of the mountain river below. "They're maneuvering to attack us," he told Walden. "Put two M60s on-line. We're gonna start withdrawing."

Although Lieutenant Mattioli was among the wounded, his platoon still held the west bank above the river bottom. Sanders told them to remain in position and lay down covering fire if necessary. Next he ordered Lieutenant Lipscomb to move his platoon back down into the river bottom, improvise stretchers for the seven wounded, and start carrying them up the other side.

The most seriously injured was the pilot. He had second- and third-degree burns over much of his body, and his left foot was badly crushed.

The basket was salvaged from the crash site, and he was loaded in it and shot up with morphine.

In the delirium of the drug, he looked up at the men hovering over him and said, "I'm sorry for what I did. I really fucked up, didn't I? I really let you guys down."

Private First Class Rocklen took the pilot's hand and tried to comfort him. "You didn't let anybody down. Don't talk that way."

When Lieutenant Lipscomb and his men had the wounded out of the river bottom, Captain Sanders and Lieutenant Walden started leapfrogging 1st Platoon down the ridge, a squad at a time. Seventy-five meters up the ridge, Sanders could see enemy soldiers. There were a lot of them, and they were darting from tree to tree. They really want to put the hurt on Delta Company, Sanders thought. It was a fight, though, that the captain simply could not risk. Unable as he was to get resupplied by air or to take out his wounded, he knew that this river bottom could quickly become Delta's last stand.

It took 1st Platoon about fifteen minutes to move down the ridge. The first part of the platoon was just moving back across the river when the NVA hit them. RPG rained down from the mountain as thick as a flock of birds and began impacting all over the river bottom. Machine-gun fire raked the same ground, with green tracer rounds ricocheting off rocks and careening in all directions. The men in the river bottom fired back up at the mountain, but it was impossible for them to see targets. Worse, the NVA infantry were now running down the ridge in an attempt to pounce on 1st Platoon while they were still in the river bottom.

Fortunately for Delta Company, Sanders was able to honk up a circling FAC plane. Two fighter-bombers arrived soon after and without a marking round started sweeping the ridge the NVA infantry were moving down with long bursts of cannon fire. The fire rained havoc on the exposed infantry. Those not killed by the first runs of cannon fire scattered into the draws and ravines.

The fighter-bombers gave 1st Platoon time to climb back up the steep 10-foot bank and into the thick jungle. It was now 1650, and under the thick canopy it was already growing dark.

If Delta's movement down the side of the ravine had been difficult, their climb back up, burdened now with the wounded, was a nightmare. While the pilot was in the basket, the other wounded had to be carried on improvised stretchers made from rubber ponchos and bamboo poles. It took four men to carry each stretcher, and they moved the wounded forward a foot at a time, with each of the bearers grabbing a tree or vine for support, then heaving the stretcher forward a foot or two, then repeating the same motion again. In the 100-degree heat men became exhausted quickly, and the bearers had to be changed every fifteen minutes or so.

In the first thirty minutes the column covered thirty meters, and in the next about forty. At 1850, Alpha Company's 3d Platoon linked up with Delta on the side of the ravine. They had left their rucksacks behind and double-timed their way down, but it had still taken them nearly three hours. They reported that there were small groups of enemy soldiers roaming about everywhere on the west side of the ravine and that they had been sniped at a number of times. Third Platoon took over from the exhausted men of Delta, and the column started moving again.

Around 1900 Honeycutt and one of his RTOs walked out to the edge of the ridge where his CP was. From there he could see down into the ravine. It was an eerie sight. The bottom of it was now as dark as a cave, and the fog was just starting to roll down off the top of Dong Ap Bia and sift down into it. And with the fog came a wet chill and sharp gusts of mountain air. The temperature dropped twenty degrees in a few minutes.

Honeycutt radioed the column and asked one of the medics about the condition of the wounded. From the medic, he learned that six of the wounded were going to survive, but that the pilot was going to die if he was not given immediate medical attention.

"Can you make it out of there tonight?"

"We think so."

"Good."

One of the men from Alpha Company's 3d Platoon who was carrying the basket was not worried just about the pilot's safety, but also about that of everyone in the column. Sgt. Tim Ard knew the surrounding jungle was filled with NVA patrols, and yet the pilot was moaning with the pain and thrashing about in the basket. At one point Ard asked the man to please keep quiet, but the pilot did not seem to understand him. During a rest break, he discussed with the three other soldiers carrying the basket the possibility of gagging the pilot, but they all finally decided against it. The man had suffered enough without having to accept the further indignity of being gagged.

About 1940 the column reached the steepest part of the ravine. For the next twenty to thirty meters the land lay at a 45-degree slope, and not even four men could handle a single stretcher. Instead, the men formed two lines and passed the wounded up between them. For over thirty minutes, they grunted and groaned and wrestled the stretchers forward. In the dark, men were continually losing their footing and falling backwards, their rifles and helmets clattering against rocks. Under the jungle canopy it was now a dark tunnel, and as the men struggled forward, they were tormented further by hordes of mosquitoes and by thumb-size leeches that either dropped from tree branches onto their necks or slithered up their pants legs.

Still they struggled forward, silently, cursing under their breath, and at 2000 reached the edge of their NDP of the night before. In two hours they had covered maybe two hundred meters. Before them lay another six hundred.

At the battalion CP, Colonel Honeycutt knelt before his radios with Captain Addison and Major Collier and continued monitoring the minute-by-minute progress of the men below. Around twenty men from the other three platoons of Alpha had gathered around the CP, holding a kind of silent vigil for the pilot. Similar groups had gathered around radios on every NDP around the mountain.

"How are you doing?" Honeycutt asked the medic again.

"We think we can make it."

A few minutes later, however, just as the column was pushing out from the NDP, it started raining. It began as a light drizzle, but quickly became a downpour, a wild jungle storm with lightning that lit up the mountain like giant illumination rounds. The column lurched to a halt. The men covered the wounded with rubber ponchos and huddled next to them, thinking to wait out the rain. But the rain fell only harder.

When they realized it was not going to stop soon, the stretcher bearers tried moving in the rain, but it was impossible. The soil had turned quickly into a deep, sticky mud, and in places the water was rushing down the sides of the ravine in sheets.

"Can you make it?" Honeycutt asked.

"No, we can't," the medic said. "It's impossible."

"Keep trying."

"It's impossible."

"How far have you moved in the last thirty minutes."

"Maybe twenty feet. People keep falling backwards and sliding back down. We're doing the wounded more harm than good."

Around the radios, Honeycutt, some of his staff, and a number of men from Alpha Company maintained their vigil. After about an hour, the rain stopped, but the ground was now a quagmire. Two hours later, Honeycutt received the message that the pilot had died. Around the battalion CP and at the different company NDPs, men took the news silently and grimly.

In the bowels of the ravine, the men protecting the remaining wounded still had more of an ordeal to face. Although most were now so exhausted they barely had the strength to move, they were to get little sleep that night. At 2100 lights were spotted approaching the NDP from the north. Thinking they were either an enemy patrol searching for the NDP or scouts for a large enemy force getting ready to attack, Delta's forward observer called for artillery fire. Thirty to fifty rounds slammed into the ridge above Delta's position, and the lights went out. Half an hour later, however, more lights were spotted approaching the NDP from the river bottom. Another heavy dose of artillery fire put them out. Small groups of enemy soldiers, however, continued probing for Delta's position the rest of the night.

One thousand meters to the south of Delta's NDP, Charlie Company's 2d and 3d platoons were also settling down for an uneasy night. Like Lieutenant Trautman's 1st Platoon, they had had a rough day. Since morning they had been able to cover only 175 meters up their ridge, and it had been through a gauntlet of sniper fire. They had luckily suffered only five wounded to the fire, but the constant harassment had left the men in the platoon as nervous and skittish as wild horses. To compound things their NDP—strung out on both sides of the ridge—lay just 150 meters below Dong Ap Bia.

At 1940, right after the two platoons finished digging in, enemy mortarmen from positions just across the border in Laos opened up on the NDP with their giant Russian 120s. Although they fired for only a few minutes, the enemy gunners, supplied with exact coordinates, walked the rounds perfectly from one end of the position to the other, seriously wounding five men and destroying the equipment of an Army camera crew preparing to film the morning assault.

Thinking that the mortar fire was a softening up for a ground attack, the men waited in their fighting holes, their rifles and machine guns pointing down into the draws. After a tense 10- to 15-minute wait, one soldier, thinking he saw sappers moving up out of the draw to the north, cut loose at them with his M16. It was just a single burst, but it set off a panic up and down the perimeter. An instant later, nearly every man in the two platoons was firing like crazy into the draws.

"I'm the LP, don't shoot," a man's voice cried out above the firing. "Stop shooting, for Christ's sake!"

The fire slackened, sputtered up for a moment, and then stopped. A GI, who had been on listening post in the big draw on the north side of the perimeter, stumbled up the hill, a radio on his back and a poncho liner draped over his head like a shawl. "What the fuck are you doing?" he screamed at the men on the perimeter. "Don't you know there's LPs out? For Christ's sake!"

When they were certain they were finally safe, the three other LPs also made their way back up to the NDP. "Don't shoot," they all yelled over and over again. "Hold your fire!"

Unbelievably none of the four LPs was hit, but the sight of them seemed to make little impression on the men. A few minutes later, another soldier, spooked by what he thought was movement in the draw, cut loose at it with his M60. Panic once again rippled down the perimeter, and soon nearly sixty men were firing like crazy.

Sp.4 John Comerford, whose fighting hole was on the northern end of the perimeter, looked down into the draw below and, try as he might, could not see a thing.

"Stop firing," he screamed repeatedly down the line, but no one paid him the slightest attention.

Finally he got out of his fighting hole and ran up and down behind the perimeter, yelling at the men over and over again, "Hold your fire! What in the hell is going on down there? There's nothing down there."

Again no one paid him any attention. In fact, a few minutes later he saw that someone had even called in a Spooky gunship. Soon it was circling the position, adding the fire of his six miniguns to the panic on the ground.

To Comerford it was all pure lunacy. It seemed to him as if Charlie Company had been struck by some kind of collective madness. In his six months in Vietnam, Comerford had never seen soldiers so "completely freaked out."

The gunship quit firing around 2000, and over the mountain a deep, eerie quiet settled. At the battalion CP Honeycutt was getting a situation report from one of his company commanders when a Vietnamese voice broke into the company net. "Blackjack!" the voice said, using Honeycutt's call sign.

"Who is this?" Honeycutt said.

But instead of an answer, the voice continued, "Blackjack! Calling Blackjack!"

Honeycutt was about to say something, but stopped himself, realizing that the man, obviously an enemy soldier sitting in a command bunker up on Dong Ap Bia, did not want to talk, but only to taunt him.

"Blackjack!" the voice came back a few seconds later, in an arrogant, sneering, contemptuous tone. "Blackjack! Can you hear me? Calling Blackjack!"

CHAPTER 13

FIRST ASSAULT—HARD TIMES FOR CHARLIE COMPANY

With morning, Honeycutt started his companies in motion for what he wanted to be the first concentrated attack on Dong Ap Bia. He gave Bravo the mission of continuing the attack up the main ridge. In close support, Charlie Company was detailed to launch another attack up a small finger 150 meters to the south of Bravo. Delta, in turn, once it had evacuated its wounded and dead from the ravine, was to move back down the ravine, back across the river bottom, and attempt to once again launch an attack up the north side of the mountain. Honeycutt hoped that with three companies going up the mountain simultaneously, the NVA would not be able to concentrate their fire against any one of them. Although the colonel was not positive Captain Sanders could get Delta in position fast enough to have an impact on the fight, he simply could not risk postponing the attack for fear the NVA might use the respite to further strengthen their position on the mountain.

Honeycutt knew for a fact that the NVA were using the large draw on the southwest side of Hill 900 to shuttle fresh troops and supplies up to the mountain at night. He had requested that the 1/506th attempt to cut this draw, but so far the Currahees had not advanced close enough to the mountain to do so. For now the 3/187th was going to have to go at the mountain alone. It was not a situation the colonel relished, but he had no other choice.

The artillery, which had been firing sporadically at Dong Ap Bia all night long, picked up the pace at first light. Every battery on each of the five supporting firebases began hurling volley after volley into the top and west face of the mountain.

A FAC was already overhead as the artillery worked over the mountain. When the guns stopped firing at 0646, he marked a number of targets on the mountain he wanted hit, then pulled aside for the first of a number of pairs of fighter-bombers. They arrived with Snake and Nape, a deadly combination of high-drag bombs and napalm. For the next hour the mountain shuddered under the impact of 500- and 1,000-pound bombs and was scorched by lethal doses of napalm.

In their NDPs, the men of Bravo and Charlie companies stood silently, mutely, and watched the destruction above them. Large trees were tossed into the air like matchsticks by the explosions; smaller ones were shredded and pulverized. Small rocks and dirt rose in geysers and showered down over the mountain as thick as snowflakes.

In Charlie Company's NDP some of the men saw the body of a North Vietnamese soldier tossed into the air like a rag doll. Everywhere on the mountain the napalm set fire to dry patches of bamboo and fallen trees, and from a dozen spots on the west face of the mountain, bonfires raged, belching out thick clouds of black smoke.

At 0800 both Bravo and Charlie pushed out from their NDPs and started a deliberate move toward the mountain. Again, the men had left their cumbersome rucksacks behind and carried only their weapons, bandoleers of ammo, grenades, and three or four canteens of water.

In Bravo's sector, Lieutenant Eward's 2d Platoon led the assault, with Lieutenant Boccia's 1st Platoon right behind; in Charlie's sector, Lt. James Goff's 3d Platoon led off, followed by Lieutenant Sullivan's 2d Platoon. One hundred meters to the rear, Lieutenant Trautman and his men still had their job of guarding the LZ.

At 0810, Bravo's 1st Platoon came up over the incline and started toward the clearing. When they reached the edge of it, Eward sent one squad up the left side of the ridge, one up the right, and the third up the center of the trail. The squad in the center had two machine guns. They moved up about ten meters and took up position behind some logs and then, with the riflemen in the squad, started pouring fire onto the two knolls. At this signal the other two squads started advancing

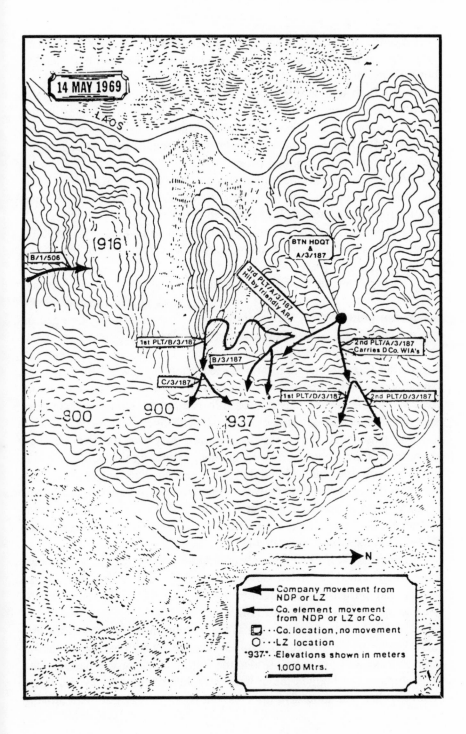

up the sides of the ridge, firing as they moved. Their intention was to get close to the knolls and then rush the enemy bunkers from the flanks, but they did not get close enough.

When both squads were about ten meters into the clearing, the NVA set off two or three giant claymore mines which they had hung in the trees facing the trail. The steel pellets ripped into the front of both squads, wounding four men and causing an instant panic. Dragging the wounded, both squads pulled back.

While the squad on the trail kept fire on the knolls, Eward regrouped his other two squads and sent them forward yet again, only to have them run into even more claymores and suffer three more wounded.

"I can't advance," Eward finally reported to Littnan. "Every time I try to maneuver a squad up there, they blow claymores on them."

Charlie Company's 3d Platoon went on the attack at about the same time as Bravo. Lieutenant Goff moved his men up the ridge with two squads on point. When they were about 150 meters from the edge of the mountain, the front of the column began receiving heavy fire from three bunkers about 20 meters up the ridge. The two squads spread out across the face of the ridge and started crawling toward the bunkers. The bunkers had A-frame log roofs covered by as many as five feet of dirt. While the two squads poured rifle fire on the bunkers, recoilless-rifle teams knocked all three of them out with flechette rounds.

The platoon advanced rapidly forward. Just past the bunkers they came to a saddle about twenty meters deep. Running through the saddle was a narrow trail, and about sixty to seventy meters above it was the western edge of Hill 900. In between were two rows of bunkers, positioned so they could support each other with fire. Many of the bunkers were A-frames, but many others were just large spider holes, carefully camouflaged with logs and tree branches.

Lieutenant Goff moved his platoon down into the saddle at a double-time, then turned them left down the narrow trail. When the platoon was spread out across the length of the trail, he started the men forward on-line up the western face of Hill 900.

The NVA opened up as soon as the platoon made its move forward. Like Bravo on the thirteenth, Goff's men ran into withering fire and a rain of RPG and grenades. Under the initial shock of the barrage, the men stopped and hugged the ground or huddled behind rocks and trees. They lay there for about five minutes, but NCOs finally got them moving again. "Keep moving," they shouted over and over again. "Move up there, you men. Let's go, move up."

The men did, crawling forward on their stomachs, dodging from tree to tree, and all the time firing like crazy up at the enemy bunkers. Grenades boomed all up and down the line, and RPGs went off continuously in the trees overhead. The 3d Platoon had six wounded before they closed on the second bunker line. There again the recoilless-rifle teams moved up and went at the bunkers with HE and flechette rounds. "Backblast!" the gunners shouted before firing. "Look out behind! Backblast!" Up and down the line, the crackboom sound of the 90mm mingled with the sound of exploding grenades and RPGs. And over it all was the continuous crack and clatter of small-arms fire, a roar of noise that never stopped.

It took 3d Platoon about thirty minutes to overrun the second bunker line. As they were preparing to push out from it, however, their line was lashed with sniper fire coming from a dozen spots in the trees ahead.

Sp.4 Tyrone Campbell was advancing with his squad on the far right of 3d Platoon's line when a sniper cut loose at him. Five or six shots kicked up dirt in front of him, and he ran forward and dived behind a large log. There were two men already huddling there. Campbell was turning to see if he knew the men and saw them both wince as bullets hit them. The shot meant for him ricocheted off the top of the log. Out of the corner of his eye, he had spotted the rifle flash at the top of a tall tree about thirty meters to the left. Campbell flipped his rifle on automatic and emptied an entire 20-round magazine into the tree, then quickly changed magazines and fired again. Leaves fell from the tree like snowflakes, and a second later, the sniper tumbled forward, dangling grotesquely five feet below his perch by a rope he had tied around his waist.

Campbell checked the men near him, but they both seemed dead.

"Help me, somebody," a voice called out ahead. "Help me, please!"

Campbell crawled forward through splintered tree trunks toward the voice. At the bottom of a bomb crater, he found a man from his platoon. He had been shot in both his right arm and leg and was thrashing around in terrible pain. "Give me some morphine, man. I'm shot bad. Oh, fuck, this hurts. Hurry, man, give me something." Campbell jammed a morphine Syrette in the man's butt, then, while the morphine calmed him, bandaged the man's wounds.

After he finished bandaging the man, Campbell just lay there and observed the scene around him. It did not seem like he was watching a battle, but a wild melee, a giant street fight. To his right a man aimed a 90mm recoilless rifle and blasted a bunker twenty meters up the mountain. Another man, with an M60, jumped up, fired off a long burst, then dropped under cover again. Wounded men were staggering back down the mountain, holding bandages over their wounds. Behind him, men carrying boxes of ammo and sacks of grenades were running up and down the hill. Up above he caught quick glimpses of pith-helmeted NVA soldiers as they popped quickly out of trenches and spider holes, let off with a quick burst of AK fire, then ducked under cover again. Other NVA, without exposing themselves, were rolling grenades down the steep sides of the mountain. While Campbell watched, a Phantom jet came down and went at the west face of the mountain twenty meters below the top. Two canisters of napalm separated from the plane's wings, and the jellied fire burst for thirty meters across the top of Hill 900.

At 0903 Honeycutt got a call from Captain Johnson with the news that Charlie's 3d Platoon had moved through the second bunker line and was pushing toward the top of Hill 900 forty meters away. It was the best news the colonel had had in five days, but it was soon to prove illusory.

A few minutes later, the NVA launched a counterattack against 3d Platoon's line. Enemy infantry swarmed down from the top of the mountain and began maneuvering against the front of the platoon. Another group of enemy soldiers slipped down from Hill 937 and began pouring enfilading fire into the platoon's left flank. And still another group, which had hidden in the large draw during the attack, moved out of it and began shooting into the platoon's rear. At 0903, 3d Platoon had seemed on the verge of topping the mountain. At 0931, it had two dead, fifteen wounded, and was slowly disintegrating as a fighting unit.

Honeycutt was unaware of 3d Platoon's sudden reversal. He was certain that at any minute he would get a message saying they had topped the mountain. He got just the opposite, a frantic call from Captain Johnson.

"I'm gonna have to pull back," Johnson screamed over the clatter of gunfire.

"What?" Honeycutt said.

"Third Platoon has taken a lot of casualties. They've been hit real hard. We've got to pull back."

"You're shit gonna pull back," Honeycutt snapped. "You pull back now and you'll expose Bravo's right flank. Where are they taking fire from?"

"From their left flank and from their rear—from the draw."

"Then start maneuvering some people around and do something. You've got two other platoons that aren't doing anything. Get 'em movin'. Are you listening to me?"

"Yes, sir."

"You pull off that mountain now and they're gonna shoot your fuckin' ass off. You hear me?"

"Yes, sir."

Captain Johnson was holding Lt. Donald Sullivan and his 2d Platoon in reserve at his company CP about thirty meters below the low saddle. He held a quick conference with Sullivan, apprised him of 3d Platoon's situation, and ordered him to move quickly forward to start another attack on Goff's left.

Sullivan double-timed his men forward up the ridge, then down the low saddle. From the saddle they followed the trail around the mountain, passed behind 3d Platoon, then formed a skirmish line and started up the mountain.

While Sullivan and his men advanced, Captain Littnan moved up the trail on the main ridge until he found Lieutenant Boccia.

"Frank, I want you to move your men back up and start another attack," Littnan said.

Boccia was incredulous. "You're shitting me."

"No, I'm not shitting you."

"Jesus."

"You got any ideas about what you wanna do?"

"The way I figure it, the only chance we've got is to try what we planned yesterday, which is to have the jets make a fake run on the mountain and then get in there before the NVA can respond."

"Okay, let's try it then."

Boccia knew his plan had only a slim chance of success, but it was all he could think of. He hoped desperately it would succeed, though in his mind's eye he could already picture his men rushing wildly forward into a murderous wall of rifle- and machine-gun fire. Already he could see the wounded and dead sprawled all over the clearing, could hear their screams of hurt and confusion. The thought threw him into a deep depression, but try as he might he could not shake it from his mind.

Boccia gathered his platoon around him and solemnly announced, "We're going back up!"

"What?" five or six men said almost at once.

"You heard it. Get your shit together."

"Jesus Christ!" a man yelled. "That fucking Honeycutt wants to get us all killed!"

"If that sonofabitch wants to take this fucking mountain so bad," another shouted, "why don't he do it himself?"

Boccia let the men bitch. It did not bother him in the least. It was healthy for soldiers to bitch and complain. It was natural. Only a raving lunatic would have been eager to go back up that mountain. The time to worry about soldiers, Boccia knew, was not when they bitched and complained, but when they became silent and moody and refused to express their feelings. That's when you had real trouble on your hands.

Boccia moved his men forward. They passed Eward's men on the trail, then moved up the incline before the clearing. They were just moving into their attack positions when Boccia got a call from Littnan. "Stop the attack, Frank," Littnan said. "I've got to call it off."

"What happened?"

"I just got a call from Blackjack. Charlie Company is in some real bad shit, and he wants you to go over and help them."

Boccia breathed a sigh of relief. He felt suddenly like someone who had had a death sentence commuted at the last minute.

Sp.4 John Comerford was not feeling anything but absolute and total terror at the moment. With the rest of Lieutenant Sullivan's 2d Platoon, he had advanced up the side of the mountain rapidly for about thirty meters, but then the NVA had suddenly dumped the world on their heads.

Like everyone in the platoon, Comerford was hugging the ground. The mountain had about a 30-degree slope, and he just pointed his M60 uphill and sprayed bullets wildly. He did not aim at targets because he could not see any. Occasionally he caught a quick glimpse of NVA soldiers raising up quickly to fire their rifles or an RPG, but before he could bring the M60 around they were back under cover again.

The enemy, though, could see him. Machine-gun rounds were zipping just inches over his head, showering him with leaves, pieces of bark, and tree branches. As he lay there firing, he saw a pineapple-shaped grenade bouncing down the hill toward him. About ten feet away it hit a rock, leaped into the air, and struck his helmet, finally exploding about fifteen feet behind him. Comerford was not hit by any shrapnel, but the experience left his heart in his throat. Still, Comerford could count himself lucky. In the last thirty minutes over half the men in his platoon had been either wounded or killed, and it was obvious enough from the intensity of the enemy fire that the situation was only going to get worse.

One of Comerford's friends, Pfc. Leonel Mata, was finding a similarly hopeless situation with Charlie's 3d Platoon. Although from the 2d Platoon himself, Mata had been detailed by Captain Johnson early in the attack to carry ammo for Lieutenant Goff's men. For the last hour, burdened with boxes and cans of ammo, he had been sprinting back and forth from Captain Johnson's CP up the mountain to the rear of 3d Platoon.

On his last trip up, he carried two sandbags filled with M79 grenades. He was able to run up the mountain for about thirty meters, but after that the fire was so intense that he had to crawl on his hands and knees. Mata crawled through a surreal landscape of shattered tree stumps and shell and bomb craters. There was battle junk everywhere—discarded helmets, M16 rifles, bandoleers of ammo, canteens, and pieces of clothing. As he climbed higher and higher up the mountain, the noise got louder, and so did the number of wounded. Medics were attending to some wounded behind logs and trees. Others were limping or crawling down the hill on their own, hurrying to get away from the maelstrom of fire up ahead.

When Mata finally reached 3d Platoon, he moved in behind Lieutenant Goff. Fearlessly, Goff was standing behind a small tree and, with an M79 grenade launcher, steadily shooting grenades up at the enemy bunkers. The lieutenant was like a machine, firing, reloading, then firing again, over and over again. When he saw Mata, he grabbed one of the sandbags, filled a pouch around his neck with grenades, then went back to firing. Goff was like a man possessed. Unfortunately his personal bravery was not going to be enough to save Charlie Company.

Lieutenant Boccia and his platoon arrived at Bravo's CP a little after 0930. Boccia stepped aside to talk with Littnan.

"So what exactly happened to Charlie Company?" Boccia asked.

"Frank, from what I've been able to figure out, they got hit pretty bad."

"What do you mean by *bad*?"

"I mean *bad*!"

Boccia put Sp.4 Johnny Hernandez on point and Sp.4 Anthony Bresina on slack. The lieutenant took the fourth position back. On cat's feet Hernandez led the platoon down the south side of the ridge and into the draw. At the bottom of the draw, he found the trail and started the column moving toward the southwest. He followed it one hundred meters to the center of the draw and then stopped the column. There the trail branched off east toward Dong Ap Bia and farther southwest toward Charlie Company's LZ.

Thinking to take a shortcut in order to get to Charlie Company's aid quicker, Boccia instructed his pointman to take the trail east. The trail ran up a small finger and right through double-canopy jungle. There was not much lower growth, and Hernandez was able to make good time for about seventy-five meters. After that, however, the trail entered a huge sea of bamboo. Most of the bamboo was taller than a man and intertwined with elephant grass and thorny vines. The trail began narrowing as it entered the bamboo, until it finally became nearly impassable. In order to move through it, each man had to separate the bamboo with his hands, then force himself through the small gap.

Hernandez moved the column about forty meters into the bamboo, then suddenly stopped cold in the trail. He motioned Boccia forward, and together they moved up a few more meters. Hernandez pointed uphill, and Boccia listened to the unmistakable sound of North Vietnamese soldiers talking. It was difficult to tell how many there were, but they were all talking so loud that it was obvious they were not concerned about being heard. So these are the men shooting into Charlie Company's rear, he thought.

Boccia considered for a moment the idea of launching a grenade attack against the enemy soldiers, but quickly rejected it. Not only did he not know how many men were in there, but he didn't know what kind of defensive positions they were in. And if they, in turn, counterattacked, his only retreat would be back down the trail, with no room to maneuver because of the walls of bamboo. It would be like trying to fight in a tunnel, and he feared his platoon could very quickly get wiped out.

Instead, he had the platoon turn around and move back down the finger. At the branch in the trail, he had the pointman turn the platoon east and start up the other side of the draw toward Charlie Company's LZ. As they moved up the side of the ridge, Boccia radioed the LZ. "We got a bunch of bad guys down in this draw. Hold your fire until we clear the area, and then let them have it.'' Five minutes later, the four 81mm mortars on the battalion CP and a howitzer battery from one of the supporting firebases were slamming volleys of rounds into the enemy position in the draw.

While Boccia was moving out of the draw, Captain Littnan tagged the 4th Platoon for a final go against the clearing. After two airstrikes with 1,000-pound bombs and a hard 15-minute artillery prep, Sfc. Louis Garza, who had taken over 4th Platoon after Lieutenant Denholm was wounded, led his men forward for yet another assault. Garza was an experienced soldier, noted for his absolute fearlessness under fire, and considered by most enlisted men in the 3/187th as the best NCO in the battalion, but all that was not going to be enough. In the next thirty minutes, he led three separate assaults on the clearing and had nothing to show for it except seven more wounded.

After the third failure, Captain Littnan came forward to discuss the situation.

"What do you think I should do?" Garza asked.

"Give it another shot."

"I think I'll just go up with six men this time."

"Do you think that'll be enough?"

"I don't know. We might be able to maneuver better with a smaller group."

"Give it a try then. We gotta do something."

Once again they went forward, moving this time along the left side of the ridge. Garza himself took point, and the other five men followed at two- to three-meter intervals. When they were about thirty meters from the clearing, a sniper opened up on the men from some trees to the left of the knoll. Garza tried to locate the sniper, but could not. In frustration he called the other five men up and had them move in beside him. "Fire into those trees over there. Put your rifles on automatic and just spray the tops."

The shooting was wild and indiscriminate, and at once three snipers crashed down from the cluster of trees and thudded onto the ground. Three! Garza could hardly believe his eyes. Everyone quickly put in a new magazine, and Garza directed their massed fire to some trees just behind the knoll. Again the firing was wild, and this time a single sniper crashed down.

To both Garza and Littnan the results were like a sudden revelation.

Both now realized that the majority of the fire they had been taking all this time had been coming from the trees, not from the bunkers. Sitting in perches at the top of 100-foot-high trees, the snipers had easily survived the hundreds of bombs, rockets, and artillery rounds directed against the bunkers.

Garza put his platoon in a skirmish line this time. Rather than reconning by fire into the jungle directly ahead, Garza now had his men mass their fire into the treetops. As they fired and walked forward, sniper after sniper crashed to the ground.

Moving rapidly now, the platoon pushed forward through the clearing and into the bunker line. There they discovered that all the bombing and shelling had indeed been effective. Everywhere they looked there were collapsed bunkers and trenches dotting a Verdun-like landscape of shattered tree trunks and swimming-pool-size bomb craters.

Honeycutt called for a body count, but the platoon had difficulty furnishing one. There were no bodies, only parts of them. The bunker line was a grim sight. Torsos without heads jutted out of spider holes and collapsed bunkers. Arms and legs were scattered all over the area, and the leaves and trunks of trees were covered with clots of black blood and pieces of flesh.

The NVA, however, were far from finished. Even as the 4th Platoon consolidated its position, it started receiving heavy fire from the second row of bunkers only thirty meters farther up the ridge.

Bravo's small victory was easily diminished by the grim, desperate situation Charlie Company was in. Both 2d and 3d platoons were still pinned to the side of the mountain. Together they now had around thirty-five men wounded and two killed, and their casualties were mounting by the minute.

They were also discovering that there was no safety anywhere around Dong Ap Bia. A little after one in the afternoon, a group of enemy soldiers slipped up out of the draw and at point-blank range shot up a large party of stretcher bearers carrying wounded through the saddle behind 2d and 3d platoons. Another seven or eight men were wounded in the incident, and when a relief party set out from the company CP to help these new wounded, they too were ambushed.

Charlie Company was, in fact, slowly coming apart at the seams, unraveling like a ball of thread. It was not a company any longer, but a mob of men pinned down on the face of the mountain. When Captain

Johnson asked for permission to withdraw this time, Honeycutt had no choice but to grant it. Honeycutt, in turn, not wanting to expose Bravo's right flank, radioed Littnan and told him likewise to start withdrawal. It was a bitter pill for Bravo to swallow. What they had spent five days and more than thirty casualties to take, they now had to give up without a fight.

Sensing the withdrawal, the NVA went on the attack. Enemy skirmishers in twos and threes came out of the bunkers above and started maneuvering down the mountain. Firing and throwing grenades, they pushed toward both the front and flanks of both of Charlie's platoons and took up positions ten to twenty meters away.

Ten minutes after the start of the withdrawal, disaster struck Lieutenant Sullivan's 2d Platoon. While Sullivan and his RTO, Sp.4 Ron Swanson, stood by watching helplessly, an enemy soldier slipped down the mountain and fired an RPG at a line of wounded passing through a clearing below 2d Platoon's position. The rocket impacted against a man being carried in a rubber poncho by four other men and went off with a blinding flash.

Swanson himself was blown off the ridge and thirty feet down into the draw. When he scrambled back up onto the top of the ridge, he came across a scene of slaughter. The man on the stretcher had been blown into pieces all over the trail, and three stretcher bearers were dead. One of them, Swanson discovered, was his friend Willie Chapman. Nearby two other men lay dying. One of the dying men, his left leg blown off, was trying futilely to crawl out of the clearing; the other, his entire body peppered with shrapnel, had one hand over his face and was crawling around in circles. Although not wounded, one of 2d Platoon's squad leaders, a very young sergeant, was kneeling at the edge of the clearing, covered with blood and pieces of flesh, staring ahead in wild-eyed shock.

While the medic gave morphine to the kid who had lost his leg, Swanson held him in his arms and tried to comfort him. The kid opened his eyes for a second, then closed them and began slowly reciting the Lord's Prayer.

To the right of the clearing, Sp.4 John Comerford had watched the scene in disbelief for a couple of minutes, too stunned even to react. Finally, he realized that he had better do something to suppress the enemy fire on the mountain as the rest of 2d Platoon's wounded were being moved through the clearing. If not, this entire section of trail was going to turn into a big slaughterhouse.

With his M60 machine gun in one hand and two metal ammo cans in the other, Comerford started back through the jungle and up the side of the saddle. On his way up, he came across three men who had retreated from the fight earlier and were hiding behind a cluster of large trees. Like a lot of men in 2d Platoon at the moment, they were terror-stricken and wanted no more to do with the fight. Comerford asked one of the soldiers to help carry the ammo containers and to be his assistant gunner, but the kid—huddling against a large teak tree and shaking like a frightened rabbit every time a volley of machine-gun fire ripped through the trees overhead—did not respond.

Comerford moved on. Ten meters farther up, at the edge of a small bamboo stand, he came across another soldier kneeling behind a tree. The kid had an M60 and three or four belts of ammo. Comerford asked him to help, and the kid jumped up without a word and followed him up the mountain. Together they pushed their way through the thick bamboo at the top of the saddle and onto the base of the mountain. There Comerford set up his M60 and began firing up at the mountain, raking the area just below the skyline. While he fired, the kid belted ammo and fed the gun. Every time he saw an enemy soldier come out of a spider hole or trench and try to take a shot at the clearing, Comerford brought his 60 around and drove the man back down.

The NVA, however, quickly got a fix on his position and were soon popping away at him with RPGs. When one hit a bit to his right, he jumped up and moved to another position. When one hit close again, he again moved. After the third near miss, however, he decided it was time to pull back.

While he and his assistant gunner moved back through the stand of bamboo on the side of the saddle, Comerford saw movement in some bushes on his left and wheeled the 60 around. "Who is it?" he screamed, his finger pushing ever so slightly against the trigger.

"Don't shoot," a voice said. A sergeant, one of 2d Platoon's squad leaders, stood up, an embarrassed, sheepish look on his face. The man was a lifer, and Comerford bristled at the thought of a career man showing such abject cowardice.

"What in the hell are you doing hiding in there?" Comerford snapped.

The sergeant lowered his eyes, but did not speak.

"You better get your ass down there and help some of those people. Get going!"

Comerford gave him a hard look and thought: At the drop of a hat, I'd blow your shit away.

The sergeant turned and ran down the saddle and disappeared.

Around this same time, at Charlie Company's LZ, two hundred meters to the rear of the fight, Lieutenant Trautman received a frantic call from Captain Johnson, who was near the saddle behind his 2d and 3d platoons trying to organize the withdrawal. "We've got 50 percent dead and wounded," Johnson yelled. "You've got to get up here and help us out."

For a moment after Johnson rang off, Trautman stood there dumbfounded. He already had one squad on the other side carrying ammo for Bravo Company and did not see how he could be expected to help two platoons withdraw with only two squads.

Still, realizing he had no choice in the matter, he quickly rounded up his platoon and had everyone shuck his rucksack and then led them forward at a run up the ridge. He came across Johnson about one hundred meters up the trail. He was kneeling on one knee near a clump of trees fifty meters or so behind the saddle, his head hanging like that of a penitent in church, oblivious to the furious sounds of battle just a short distance away. A piece of shrapnel slashed through the trees overhead, but Johnson did not respond, did not so much as turn his head or lift an eyelash.

"What's going on, Captain?" Trautman asked. "What do you want me to do?"

Johnson did not move or respond in any way.

"Captain!"

Again nothing.

"Captain, give me an order."

When he still got no response, Trautman walked up the trail toward the fight. A short distance away, he ran into a young soldier he knew and from him got some details on the situation of 2d and 3d platoons.

When he finished talking with the soldier, Trautman started back down the trail to get the rest of his platoon and discovered that Johnson had disappeared. My God! he thought. The man has two platoons pinned down on the face of that mountain. He's already taken 50 percent casualties. He gives me a distress call and then just leaves. This is incredible!

Trautman realized he was going to have to organize and lead the withdrawal himself. With his RTO he started up the trail, his two squads trailing behind him. The jungle was thick on the ridge, but started thinning out as they neared the saddle. As they started down the saddle, enemy soldiers spotted the platoon and turned their fire on them. Trautman led the platoon quickly down into the saddle, then in behind 2d and 3d platoons. With bullets thudding into logs and trees and tearing up the dirt around him, Trautman started crawling up the side of the saddle toward the mountain. He moved about ten meters, then looked back to discover that his RTO had not followed him. The kid was lying on his side behind a large tree, cowering from the incessant fire.

"Get up here," Trautman yelled.

The RTO looked up at Trautman, but did not move.

Trautman crawled back down to the kid. "What's the problem here? Come on, let's go!" He pulled the kid's arm, but he would not budge. At that same moment an RPG hit a tree nearby. The kid shrieked in pain, clutched his left arm, and started screaming, "I'm hit! I'm hit!"

"Let me see," Trautman said. The lieutenant pulled the kid's hand away, but could find nothing but a small red dot, no bigger than a pinprick.

"Is that all you got?"

The kid moaned, "It hurts."

"Yeah, I'll bet it does."

Trautman was both furious and disappointed. He had relieved his old RTO only a few days before because the kid had been too slovenly in his dress and unmilitary in his attitude, and had given the job, in turn, to this new kid because he was so neat, clean, and professional.

The kid groaned again, squeezing the wound so that some blood trickled out. "I'm hurt! I gotta get out of here."

Trautman angrily pulled the radio off the kid's back, then shoved him down the hill. "Get your ass out of here! Do you hear me? Get the hell away from me, you chickenshit!"

The kid leaped to his feet and, no longer holding his wound, rushed hell-bent down into the saddle. Trautman looked back down the column until he spotted his old RTO, then shouted, "Hey, you wanna be my RTO again?"

"Sure, why not?"

Trautman could not believe it. The kid bolted up the slope and slipped on the radio, not the slightest bit scared.

It was around one in the afternoon when Lieutenant Boccia and his platoon climbed out of the draw and arrived at Charlie Company's LZ. Boccia was shocked to discover that there was no security at all around the position. No listening posts in the surrounding jungle. No guards around the perimeter. Nothing.

Boccia led the platoon forward up the trail, and they soon came across a row of bodies. Some of the bodies were badly torn up, and a soldier behind him named Brown started vomiting at the sight.

Boccia grabbed Brown by the shoulder and pushed him forward. "Keep movin', man. Don't get yourself wrapped up in this shit."

Boccia stepped over to have a closer look at some of the bodies and was shocked to discover that two or three of the men were not even dead. Why wasn't someone caring for them? He called Doc Schoch, and the medic quickly went to work trying to save the men.

A little farther on, the lieutenant came across a very young soldier lying up against a tree. "Where's your CO?"

The kid looked up blankly, but did not speak.

"Did you hear me? Where's your CO?"

When the kid again did not answer, Boccia moved on. He finally got an answer from a wounded soldier lying on a stretcher in the center of the trail. "I think he's up there," he mumbled, pointing east.

Boccia found Captain Johnson just a short distance farther up the trail. He was just sitting on the ground, staring off into space.

"Captain Johnson, I'm from Bravo Company."

Johnson looked up and mumbled, "Glad you're here."

"What would you like me to do, sir? I'm one-six from Bravo Company."

"Do?"

"Yes, sir. What would you like me to do?"

When Johnson did not answer, Boccia had to do everything in his power to keep from flying into a rage. He wanted to scream, "Look, man, you're a captain in the fucking United States Army? Get off your fucking ass and do something," but he did not. Instead, he ordered his men to set up security around the LZ, then, recognizing an officer he knew, went over to him. The officer had been shot in the leg and was sitting against a tree, holding a bandage against the wound. From him, Boccia learned the grim details of Charlie Company's disaster. In two hours, they had lost their first sergeant, two of three platoon leaders, the company executive officer, two platoon sergeants, six squad leaders, and forty enlisted men. Boccia could not imagine anything worse happening to a company and found himself becoming more sympathetic with Captain Johnson.

Boccia walked back down the trail and stood beside Johnson. "Could you send a squad up and bring back our stuff?'' Johnson asked after a while.

"Yeah, sure." Boccia knelt down next to the captain.

"You know, I lost my entire company up there," Johnson said. "Goddamn! I lost my entire company, and I don't even know what I did wrong."

At the moment Charlie Company's failure was being mirrored on a much smaller scale by Delta Company. Tabbed by Honeycutt to launch a critical flanking attack against Dong Ap Bia from the north, they had instead spent most of the morning and early afternoon struggling back down the west side of the deep ravine in an attempt to recover the seven bodies left near the river on the thirteenth.

For Delta it was another descent into hell. Anticipating the move, small enemy patrols were roaming the jungle and harassing their every step. After fighting their way through a number of small ambushes, Delta reached the river at 1354. As they were recovering the bodies, however, a platoon of NVA—hidden on the ridge opposite the river bottom—pounded the company with RPGs and machine-gun fire. Captain Sanders had to call for gunships and a massive dose of artillery to suppress the enemy fire. When the fight ended twenty minutes later, Delta was burdened with ten more wounded, over half of whom needed to be carried on stretchers. With this added burden, Sanders knew that he would be lucky to make it out of the ravine by nightfall, let alone return and launch another attack against Dong Ap Bia.

At 1400 Lieutenant Trautman was finally in position to start directing the withdrawal of 2d and 3d platoons. From a position between both platoons, he established a CP and began the slow, agonizing process of bringing back down the fifty to sixty men still scattered across the face of the mountain. First he had one of his squads set up a continuous supply line to the rear of both platoons, then had another start laying down suppressing fire on the enemy bunkers. While they fired, he had the third squad break into two- and three-man teams and rush up the side of the mountain to start pulling out the dead and wounded. When the dead and wounded were all down, he began bringing down the rest of the men.

The next three hours were a grueling, frightening experience for Trautman. He was nearly blown apart numerous times by RPGs and once had a grenade explode only three feet away from his position, though miraculously he was not hit. By 1600, though, he had everyone down off the mountain and heading back to the LZ. They made it down just in time, for a few minutes later the heavens exploded, and a monsoon rain crashed down across the entire northern A Shau.

At Charlie Company's LZ the wounded were stretched out in two rows down the center of the trail. Nearby, in another row, lay the dead. Most of the wounded lay there silently, stoically, oblivious to the pelting rain, to the mud, to the icy chill floating down with the fog off the mountain. A few of them smoked cigarettes, cupping their hands over them to keep them lit or holding them under helmets and ponchos. Occasionally a man moaned or cried out sharply against some terrible pain, but most endured it with gritted teeth.

Crazy Rairdon arrived in a small, bubble-shaped LOH to take out the dead and wounded. The 20-year-old Rairdon was already somewhat of a legend in the division because of his willingness to fly in and out of tight spots with a total disregard for his own safety, and he proved that it was a reputation well earned. With fierce gusts of wind buffeting the ship and rain blowing through his open window, he made the trip back and forth from Charlie's LZ across the draw to the battalion LZ, where the wounded were backloaded on Hueys for the long trip to hospitals on the coast. Each time he landed on Charlie's LZ, enemy riflemen raked the surrounding area with long bursts of fire or pummelled it with RPGs. Every time he took off and started back across the draw, enemy machine gunners tracked him, filling the air around the tiny ship with hundreds of green tracer rounds. It took him twenty, possibly twenty-five, trips, but eventually he had all the dead and wounded out.

While Crazy Rairdon was making his last trip across the draw, Lieutenant Boccia got a call from Colonel Honeycutt.

"How are things going over there?" Honeycutt asked.

"We've got all the casualties out."

"Is everything else cleared up?"

"Yes, sir."

"I want you to get everything added up and moved back here. You do what it takes to get yours and Charlie's people back. Understand what I mean?"

"Yes, sir. I understand."

Boccia was struck by the oddity of the conversation. This is not the way a battalion commander should be talking to a mere platoon leader, he thought. It seemed obvious to Boccia that Honeycutt knew that Captain Johnson was not in control of the situation and that he wanted Boccia himself to take command of the withdrawal. He did not know how else he could interpret the conversation. Without giving it another thought, he gave the order for the platoon leaders to start organizing their men for the move back across the draw.

As soon as Lieutenant Trautman got the order, he lined up his men and did a quick head count, only to discover to his shock that the RTO who had shown such cowardice earlier was missing. He figured the kid had gone out with the wounded, but discovered instead that he was dead. Ironically, the kid had been running to the rear down the saddle, thinking he was headed for safety, when a North Vietnamese soldier had popped out of the jungle and shot him.

In order to protect Charlie Company's left flank, Bravo Company had kept a platoon in position around the two knolls until all of Charlie was down. Then they started their own withdrawal.

To help them carry some of their wounded, Honeycutt dispatched a platoon from Alpha Company. Here again, fate turned against the 3/187th. When the platoon was about halfway between the battalion CP and Bravo's NDP, two Cobra gunships inexplicably appeared out of nowhere and raked the rear of the column with minigun fire. Before the gunship pilots realized their mistake, four men lay seriously wounded on the trail.

Sp.4 Johnny Jackson, who had been walking near the front of the column, rushed to the rear to find his best friend, Sp.4 Edward Brooks, lying in the center of the trail, his stomach and chest ripped open.

Jackson was a 20-year-old black man from Little Rock, Arkansas, and Brooks a 21-year-old white from Boston. Out of these different backgrounds, however, they had developed an incredible friendship. It was ending quickly, however, for Brooks was dying. While a medic bandaged his wounds, Jackson held Brooks in his arms.

"What happened?" Brooks mumbled.

At that moment someone nearby screamed, "It was our own shit! Goddamn cocksuckers!"

Brooks perked up at the words and looked Jackson in the eye. "Tell me it wasn't our own shit, man. Tell me it wasn't."

"No, it wasn't ours, man," Jackson said.

Brooks died a few seconds later.

When Honeycutt heard about the gunship incident, he immediately got on the horn to the brigade S-3, Major Montgomery. "Where in the fuck did those gunships come from?"

"We don't know."

"Did you authorize them?"

"No."

"Did any of my people request ARA?"

"Not that I know of."

"Where in the fuck did they come from then?"

"We don't know."

"Jesus Christ! What in the fuck is going on around here? This is turning into a goddamn three-ring circus."

It would not be until the next morning that Honeycutt would discover what had happened, that the gunships had been firing in support of the 1/506th and had somehow got their coordinates confused.

It was around 1700 when Lieutenant Boccia finally had his own platoon and the thirty-one survivors of Charlie Company ready to start the 600-meter trip back across the draw to Bravo's NDP. The column of men looked exactly like what it was—a group of soldiers, defeated and exhausted, withdrawing from a battlefield. Some of the soldiers carried four or five M16s, some two M60 machine guns. One man had an armful of M79 grenade launchers, another a stack of helmets. At least half the men were carrying two rucksacks, and nearly everyone was draped with extra bandoleers of M16 magazines or belts of machine-gun rounds. The equipment they could not carry—rucksacks, ponchos, canteens, boots, and bloody clothing and bandages—was stacked in a pile twenty feet wide and ten feet high and set on fire.

By the light of this huge bonfire, the column started out, Boccia's platoon on the point and Johnson's thirty-one men bringing up the rear. It was pitch-dark under the jungle canopy in the draw, and the column moved at a snail's pace. In order to keep from losing anyone, Boccia had each man hold onto the rucksack of the man in front of him. Like blind men groping for objects in a dark room, the men stumbled forward.

After the column had moved about one hundred meters, Boccia got a call from Captain Johnson. "I think we ought to stop and set up an NDP," Johnson said. "It's too dark to be moving around like this."

Boccia tried to ignore the request. He did not want to set up anywhere with Charlie Company. They were shell-shocked, exhausted, and incapable of functioning any longer as a cohesive fighting unit.

Boccia kept moving, but five minutes later he got another call. "Look," Johnson said, "I think we ought to stop. I don't want to be wandering around in the dark out here."

"We don't have far to go," Boccia said. "Just hang on."

When they were two hundred meters deep in the draw, Johnson called for a third time, snapping, "Look, I'm ordering you to stop."

Boccia ignored the call, and instead honked up Captain Littnan. "Sir, we're about four hundred meters from your position. Charlie wants to stop, but I think we're close enough to make it. What do you think?"

"Of course, you're close enough."

Boccia radioed Johnson and relayed the message, but Johnson only got angrier. "No, damnit, we're gonna stop right here. Are you listening to me? I gave you a direct order."

"This is Bravo one-six. No, I think we're goin' in."

As Boccia spoke, Sp.4 Tim Logan, one of his machine gunners, stumbled and fell face first on the trail. A chain reaction followed, with men crashing into each other. Logan was carrying two 50-pound rucksacks, his machine gun, and ten belts of ammo and was near the point of complete physical collapse. Boccia helped him to his feet, then felt around in the dark trying to locate all the gear.

"What's wrong?"

"I can't go on," Logan said, his breath coming in spasms. "I can't take another step."

"You've got to," Boccia said and gave Logan a hard shove. Logan staggered under the shove and seemed about to fall again, then reached down for the last of his reserve and started forward.

It took the men another hour and a half to cover the last four hundred meters to Bravo's NDP. There the men stumbled to their places around the perimeter and collapsed wearily to the ground.

Captain Littnan walked up the trail from his CP and handed Boccia a hot cup of coffee. "You really didn't want to spend the night out there, did you?"

"Are you shitting?"

After all his companies had settled into their NDPs and put out their listening posts and ambush patrols, Honeycutt called each of his company commanders for a final casualty figure. When he got them, they only confirmed what he already knew, which was that the situation was becoming critical. During the hard day's fighting, his companies had had twelve men killed and over eighty wounded and had gained not a foot of ground. While he was sure the enemy had paid an even more grievous price, their forces on the mountain, instead of weakening, only seemed to be getting stronger each day.

When Col. Joe Conmy, the 3d Brigade commander, choppered in the LZ right before dark, Honeycutt brought him to the CP, where they immediately went into a huddle. In the dark and under a drizzling cold rain, with artillery pounding the top of Dong Ap Bia one thousand meters away, Conmy listened calmly to Honeycutt's appraisal of the situation.

"Joe, this fight is getting awful rough," Honeycutt said. "I don't know how many of the bastards are up there, but I know there's a helluva lot of them. The bastards have got heavy weapons. They've got communications. They're dug in. They've got a defense in depth, and they're movin' fresh troops up those draws from Laos every night. Every night, and I don't have the manpower to stop them. We're in a goddamn fight here, Joe—and I mean a fight!"

Conmy, who had himself commanded infantry units in both World War II and Korea, had been carefully watching the fight and had come to similar conclusions. "I agree," he said. "This is the toughest fight I've seen in three years over here. If there's been a tougher one, I don't know what it is."

"Joe, we've got to have some help out here," Honeycutt continued. "The 506th has got to get their asses in gear and get involved in this fight. This is a goddamn Dak To battle, and we're fighting it with a fucking battalion."

"The 506th is moving, and we're getting the ARVN prepared to move also."

Honeycutt knew the 1/506th was moving, but as far as he was concerned, they were not moving fast enough. His feeling about the battalion's progress would remain unchanged throughout the battle.

The situation on Dong Ap Bia was also becoming a primary concern for Maj. Gen. Melvin Zais, the commander of the 101st Airborne Division. Like Conmy, he had been keeping a close watch on the fight developing around the mountain. What he had seen so far ran contrary to all his experiences with the North Vietnamese. In past battles, the general had always known the North Vietnamese to fight hard for a time, but then quickly withdraw from the battlefield as the preponderance of American firepower turned against them. Except for a few prolonged fights, like Ia Drang and Dak To, it was a pattern they had almost always adhered to. Now, suddenly and inexplicably, at an insignificant mountain called Dong Ap Bia, they had decided to stand and fight.

About the same time Honeycutt and Conmy were meeting, General Zais called Gen. Jim Smith, the assistant division commander, to his headquarters at Camp Eagle to seek his advice on whether to continue attacking Dong Ap Bia.

General Smith, who had already spent two-and-a-half years in Vietnam and was likewise very familiar with NVA tactics, was also troubled by the battle raging on Dong Ap Bia. He took the enemy's sudden decision to tenaciously defend such an insignificant mountain as an indication that the North Vietnamese might be embarking on a new strategy to fight the war. He was not quite sure what the new strategy might be at this point, but he was certain that if anything could be surmised from the fighting so far, it was that the North Vietnamese were in the Vietnam War "to stay." Regardless of this belief, he recommended that General Zais not only continue the fight, but also that he pursue it "to a successful conclusion."

Although Zais was at this point under pressure from several people outside the division to pull out of the battle, he took Smith's advice. It was a decision which would soon be the focal point for a fiery debate in the U.S. Senate and which some would consider, like the Tet Offensive of 1968, one of the major turning points in the entire Vietnam War.

After Colonel Conmy departed, Honeycutt radioed Captain Johnson and told him to report to the battalion CP. When Johnson arrived, Honeycutt took him off to the side so they could talk privately. Johnson was still nervous, and the colonel knew he had to settle him down.

"You were getting a little too excited out there today," Honeycutt said as they stood facing each other in the darkness. "You're not looking at the big picture. You're screaming, and you're hollering, and you're exciting people for no goddamn reason. You weren't in that bad a fix. You had two fuckin' platoons that weren't doing anything, and you were almost ready to break and expose Bravo's right flank, and I don't wanna hear any more of that shit. If you can't run that company, then let me know, and I'll get someone else. But I don't want you carrying on like you were up there today. Do you understand what I'm saying, Captain?''

"Yes, sir, I understand."

"Do you have any questions?"

"No, sir."

"Is there anything your men need?"

"No, sir. We've got everything we need."

"Good. Then you might as well go back to your men."

Honeycutt really had no intention of relieving Johnson. In reality, he thought he was a good officer. He had been in some heavy action and had gotten excited, but in two wars the colonel had seen a number of officers react similarly, men who eventually settled down and became fine officers.

Nevertheless, he decided to keep Charlie Company at the battalion CP for a couple of days so Johnson could reestablish rapport with his officers and get control of his company again.

Night fell over the mountain like a shroud, a deep night without stars. In an instant the jungle turned from green to black. Just above the peak of Dong Ap Bia black clouds swirled in the cool night air. The drizzling rain continued, dripping down through the jungle canopy as if through a leaking roof. On the NDPs, most men were already sound asleep, lying beside their fighting holes, wrapped in their cloth poncho liners and covered with their rubber ponchos. But others, as if wanting to sort out the day in their minds, sat in small groups around the NDPs, smoking and talking.

On the northern edge of Bravo's NDP, Lieutenant Boccia was sitting with just such a group, although at the moment there was not much talking going on. There were six men besides himself in the group, and he had never seen any of them so quiet and introspective, so moody and depressed.

What had happened to the usual bitching and complaining, he wondered. Where were the horseplay and practical jokes? The lieutenant was beginning to get worried, when one of the soldiers suddenly leaped to his feet, ran to the edge of the perimeter, and looked up toward Dong Ap Bia. "Hey, Ho Chi Minh," he yelled. "We're gonna kick your ass off that mountain tomorrow. Do you hear me, Ho? Tomorrow we're comin up there, and we're gonna kick your fuckin' ass."

Two men near Boccia laughed at the kid's proclamation, and soon everyone in the group was grinning. Boccia felt very relieved.

On the other end of the perimeter, Sp.4 Andrew Hannah was sitting on the edge of his fighting hole, softly singing, when a friend, Pfc. Joseph Price, crawled over and nudged him.

"I need to talk with you," Price said.

"What is it, man?"

Price sat down across from Hannah and put his feet in the fighting hole. "I'm not gonna make it out of this sonofabitch, man. If we go up that mountain again tomorrow, I'm gonna be killed. I know I am."

"Bullshit!" Hannah said. "What are you talking about?"

"I know I am, man. I just know it. I ain't gonna make it out of this. I can feel it."

"Man, don't be talkin' that shit. That's crazy talk." Price was oblivious to Hannah's words.

"Listen to me now because I wanna tell you something. Are you listening?"

"Yeah, I'm listening. But I don't wanna hear you talkin' that bullshit."

"Look, since we're both from the same area in Florida, I want you to escort my body back."

Hannah was stunned. The request was like a hard punch to the stomach. It was unreal. Both of them were indeed from the area around Panama City, Florida. They had, in fact, grown up only a few miles apart, though, in the completely segregated, early 1960s, Hannah had attended an all-black school and Price an all-white one. It was not their different backgrounds, however, that bothered Hannah, but the fact that his friend was so certain of his death that he was even planning the details of his funeral. Hannah had heard a lot of men in Vietnam talk fatalistically, but he had never heard anything like this.

"What do you say, man?" Price asked after a while. "Will you do it?"

"Man, you're crazy," Hannah said. "Didn't I just tell you I didn't wanna hear that kind of talk?"

Another man not sleeping at the moment was Captain Sanders, Delta's CO, only for a much different reason. A moment before, while walking around his NDP checking his men, Sanders had chanced to look through an opening in the jungle up at Dong Ap Bia and had seen something that set his heart fluttering.

For a second he thought he might be hallucinating, that after the exhausting two days his mind was finally starting to play tricks on him, but the longer he looked up at the mountain the more he realized that what he saw was real, that there were indeed fires burning all over the sides of Dong Ap Bia. Although it was difficult to tell because of drifting fog, he estimated that there had to be at least a hundred of them. Like Christmas-tree lights, they ran in three irregular rows all the way around the mountain, from the edge of the ridges all the way to the military crest.

After two tours in Vietnam, Sanders knew enough about the NVA to know what the fires were being used for. They were cooking fires, and their sudden appearance on a night like this meant that the hundreds of enemy soldiers up there had come out of their tunnels and bunkers and were cooking up a three- or four-day supply of rice, preparing, Sanders knew, for a long fight. They are up there, he thought, and they don't give a damn if we know it.

CHAPTER 14

SECOND ASSAULT

Catching catnaps, Honeycutt slept near his radios all through the night and monitored his company net. Most of the reports he received during the night were routine stuff—small probes and minor enemy harassments—and he paid them little concern. About two in the morning, however, one of Bravo Company's ambush patrols, set up on the side of the large ridge, reported that a large group of enemy soldiers was slipping down from Dong Ap Bia and into the draw. Honeycutt did not put a lot of credence in this first report. He assumed the enemy soldiers were either a small reconnaissance patrol or possibly some sappers moving down to probe Bravo's NDP. But when Bravo's second ambush patrol, set up farther northwest along the ridge, turned in a similar report, Honeycutt realized the enemy was planning something, and he was sure he knew what it was.

"Those bastards are gonna try and get down in that draw," he told Captain Addison. "They figure we won't be able to spot them in the morning fog, and when the companies move up to their assault positions, they'll move in right behind them. Then when the fog burns off, they're gonna climb out of that draw, get on the ridges, and hit the companies in the rear." Honeycutt had to admit that it was a gutsy and ingenious idea, but he intended on spoiling it—and in a big way!

Rather than having his companies go into the attack at first light

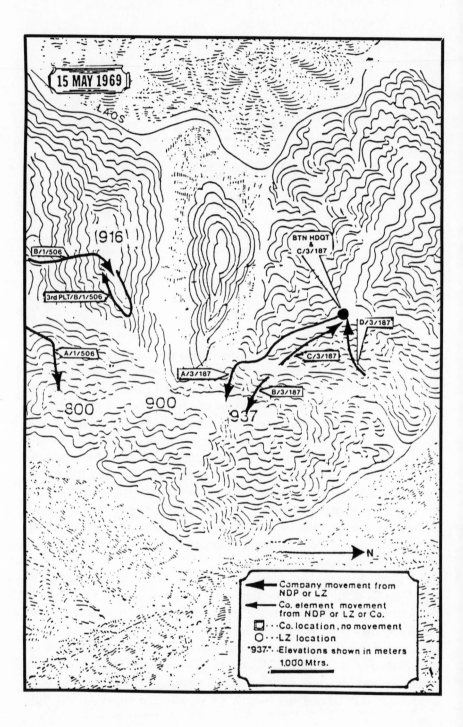

15 MAY 1969

LAOS

916

B/1/506

3rd PLT/B/1/506

A/1/506

800   900   937

BTN HDQT
&
C/3/187

D/3/187

C/3/187

A/3/187

B/3/187

N

Company movement from
NDP or LZ
Co. element movement
from NDP or LZ or Co.
▢···Co. location, no movement
○···LZ location
·937·Elevations shown in meters
1,000 Mtrs.

on the fifteenth, he instead had Alpha and Charlie companies exchange positions, with Alpha taking up responsibility for the assault in the southern ridge, while Charlie moved back and took up security for the battalion CP. Bravo, of course, would continue the attack up the main ridge. The colonel had hoped to have Delta finally start the flanking attack from the north, but by midmorning, he got word from Captain Sanders that Delta was still struggling to get the dead out of the ravine and could not be counted on to take part in the assault. The colonel also got unpleasant news concerning the 1/506th. Because the Currahees had been on the move since the thirteenth, Honeycutt had expected them to be in position by late morning to cut the NVA supply routes from Laos and to launch another attack on the mountain from the south. He discovered, though, that in the forty hours since they had started their push north, they had managed to advance only fifteen hundred meters. At the moment they were still twenty-five hundred meters from the top of Dong Ap Bia.

Just as on the fourteenth, Honeycutt realized he was going to have to go at the mountain with only two companies. Around noon, after a solid four-hour prep of the mountain with artillery and airstrikes, Honeycutt ordered Alpha and Bravo to start their move toward the mountain, telling them that he wanted their advance to be slow, deliberate, and coordinated. When both companies were about half the distance to their assault positions, he ordered them to stop and take up positions along the ridge facing the draw.

A few minutes later the NVA infantry in the draw, thinking that Alpha and Bravo were in their assault positions, started moving up toward the ridges. They thought they were moving into the rear of the companies, but instead walked right into a wall of rifle and machine-gun fire. Stunned by this unexpected fire, the NVA infantry retreated back into the draw. Honeycutt already had a pair of fighter-bombers circling, and while the grunts kept the NVA pinned in the draw, he gave them the go-ahead. They came in from the northwest, one right on the tail of the other, and, with their 20mm cannons growling hoarsely, swept the draw from end to end. When they made a second run, it was with napalm and 500-pound bombs. The third run was with cannon fire again.

When the fighter-bombers had expended their ordnance, Honeycutt's artillery liaison officer adjusted artillery fire on the draw and bracketed it with hundreds of 105, 155, and 8-inch howitzer rounds. He finished with a pair of Cobra gunships, and for the next fifteen to twenty minutes, they swept the draw from end to end. When they finished, an entire company of North Vietnamese infantry lay dead.

It had been a slaughter, and for most men in the battalion a sweet revenge for all the friends they had lost during the previous five days to NVA bullets, grenades, and RPGs. Still, it was a revenge they had little time to savor, for the battalion was still a long way from the top of Dong Ap Bia.

At 1320, with fires still burning in the draw and black smoke curling up through the jungle canopy from a dozen spots, both Alpha and Bravo started forward again.

When the companies reached their assault positions, the artillery began working over the mountain one final time. Every gun available joined in so that as many as fifty to sixty rounds were impacting on the mountain at the same time.

As Lieutenant Boccia listened to the artillery crashing into the mountain, he found himself wondering about the North Vietnamese soldiers up there huddling in their bunkers and spider holes. What were they thinking? What were they feeling? After five days of enduring round-the-clock shelling and bombing, they must have realized that we were more than determined to take that mountain. And with that realization must have also come an acceptance of the fact that before this fight was over they were almost certainly going to die.

While Boccia mulled over these thoughts, he was stunned by what sounded like a speeding train passing overhead, followed by an ear-splitting boom and an even louder explosion. Boccia was familiar with the sounds of all the howitzer rounds, but had never heard anything that went off with such force. Boccia turned to the company FO, Lt. Russ Crenshaw, who was standing nearby. "What in the hell was that, Russ?"

"You mean you don't know?"

"No."

"That was a 16-inch shell from the battleship *New Jersey*."

"You're shitting?"

"Nope. They're goin' all out today."

At his company CP, Captain Littnan was talking with one of his platoon leaders and preparing to give the order for Bravo Company to move out when he felt a burning sensation on the inside of his right leg a few inches above the top of his jungle boot. He winced at the sharp, hot pain. It felt as if someone had held a burning cigarette to his leg. He looked around in confusion, wondering what had burned him, until he noticed a soldier about ten meters behind him. The soldier was standing stock still in the center of the trail, his mouth hanging open in shock, his M16 at his hip, the barrel still pointed at Littnan's legs.

Littnan stepped out of the line of fire and walked up to the soldier. He was tempted to punch him, but stopped himself at the last minute when he realized the kid was so scared that he was only vaguely aware he had fired the rifle. Instead, he pushed the barrel of the M16 down and smiled. "Son, the next time you fire that rifle at anybody, make sure it's at someone in a different uniform. Okay?"

"Yes, sir."

"Good."

Both companies moved out from their assault positions around one o'clock in the afternoon. For Bravo, Sfc. Garza and 4th Platoon took the point, and for Alpha Lt. Frank McGreevy and his 1st Platoon.

Garza immediately discovered that the ground around the knolls that they had overrun on the fourteenth was going to have to be retaken. The NVA had moved back into the area, reoccupied many of the old bunkers, and dug new spider holes. They had also reseeded the area with claymore mines. In order to test the defenses, Garza had two squads maneuver forward on opposite sides of the ridge. They both managed to cover less than fifteen meters before a roar of exploding claymore peppered the two pointmen with steel pellets and sent the rest of the men in retreat back down the ridge.

Garza was immediately on the horn with Littnan. "We can't move against those claymores. If we try to form an assault line, they'll wipe us out."

"What do you wanna do?"

"I need something to remove those claymores. Some bombs or something."

"Hold on, I'll call headquarters and see what's available." Littnan was back on the horn five minutes later. "I've got a FAC plane and two fighter-bombers on the way. Go up there and mark the area you want hit."

Garza gathered together three riflemen and his RTO and led them crawling up the ridge. While the riflemen covered him, he rushed forward and threw three smoke grenades in front of the knolls, then joined his men in a bomb crater, where they huddled together, holding their rucksacks over their heads.

Once the FAC had also marked the knolls, the two fighter-bombers struck the area with twelve 250-pound bombs and cut a swathe through the center of it with cannon fire. The fire set off a number of claymores, and before the NVA could set out more, Garza led a second assault. The men moved forward in a line, reconning by fire, the recoilless-rifle teams firing flechette rounds ahead of the advance. Although they suffered another three or four wounded, they quickly overran the enemy positions around the knolls and killed seven or eight enemy soldiers. Many more, however, escaped and headed higher up the mountain.

Around the knolls, Garza reorganized his line and started advancing again. When they took heavy fire to their front, Garza, as he had on the fourteenth, screamed above the shooting, "Fire into the trees. Snipers! Shoot into the trees!"

The cry went down the line, and more than twenty men flipped their rifles on automatic at once and let loose with a wild volley. A sniper fell immediately, and a few seconds later another, and then a third.

On the right side of the line, a recoilless rifle boomed, and a bunker ahead disintegrated in a blinding flash. Up the trail a light machine gun barked, and two GIs dropped.

The men inserted new magazines in their M16s, and Garza screamed, "Shoot into the trees! Keep moving! Don't stop firing!" The men raked the trees ahead with a long volley, and within seconds of each other, three more snipers crashed to the ground.

The line advanced, but in the next few minutes, four or five more GIs were wounded. Garza radioed Littnan for reinforcements, and the captain rushed forward a squad from 1st Platoon. The new men quickly moved up and joined the skirmish line.

Two of the replacements were Sp.4 Anthony Bresina and Pfc. Wayne Olson. The two men took up positions in the line near Garza, who had a prominent position in the center of the ridge. Bresina was not sure what was happening or what exactly he was supposed to do, so he did like everyone else, just sprayed the trees ahead, going after the snipers.

Most of the snipers were well hidden by the leaves, but after advancing about twenty meters, Bresina actually saw one. The man was crouched in the V of two large branches near the top of a very tall tree about thirty meters away. Olson also saw him, but before he could shoot, Bresina moved forward and said, "I'll get him." Bresina aimed carefully and emptied a 20-round magazine into the man, only to find the sniper still in his perch. He quickly put in another magazine, squeezing it off this time in three or four short bursts. He was positive this time he had hit the man, but still nothing happened. Beside him, Olson joined in and let fly with a full magazine, but the sniper still did not move.

It was not until the skirmish line advanced a little farther that Bresina saw that the sniper had tied himself into the tree with a piece of rope. What fascinated Bresina, however, was that the man had used smaller pieces of rope to tie tourniquets around both his arms and legs. What dedication, Bresina thought. The sniper must have gone up that tree knowing positively that he was going to die.

The 4th Platoon quickly killed the last of the snipers and advanced through the treeline, where they were confronted with a view of the top of Dong Ap Bia less than 150 meters away. From the treeline to the top, the ground was now almost bare of jungle. Only about fifty limbless, leafless trees dotted the landscape. The rest had been knocked down by bombs and artillery, then further shredded and pulverized. Many of the bunkers in the second line of defense, however, were still intact, and during the night NVA soldiers had dug new positions in place of those destroyed and then carefully camouflaged them to blend in with all the debris scattered all over the face of the mountain.

As Sfc. Garza and his men broke from the treeline, they were met with a torrent of fire and were driven flat to the ground. The fire was so heavy, in fact, that Bresina was sure the advance had been permanently halted. Every man around had quit firing and had sought shelter under a log or in a shell crater.

Bresina had difficulty believing what he saw next. With bullets hitting all around him, Garza stood up and started screaming up and down the skirmish line. "Come on, everybody, get up! Move it! Let's go!" Garza had his pockets filled with grenades and was throwing them at the enemy positions up ahead as fast as he could bring back his arm. "Let's go," he screamed again. "Come on, let's go get those bastards!"

Bresina, who thought a number of NCOs in the company were chickenshit, had never seen anyone braver than Garza. Like most men in the company, he had always thought highly of Garza, but never more so than now.

Garza got the response he wanted. Up and down the line men got up and started moving forward again, firing and crawling and firing again. Slowly the line inched its way up the mountain, until after a 10-meter advance it was stopped by an enemy heavy machine gun positioned under a large log 20 meters away. The machine gun raked the entire line, its bullets splintering logs and causing the men in the platoon to take cover in terror. Two or three men let loose with a grenade shower on the position, but all their throws landed short. Bresina, who was carrying an M72 LAW, finally slid forward behind a large log, cocked the weapon, then popped up quickly and fired. Up ahead the machine gun and the two soldiers manning it disappeared in a white flash.

The skirmish line jerked forward again and moved another twenty meters closer to the top of the mountain. At this point, the slope of the mountain got even steeper, and the men had difficulty standing up. As the Americans drew ever closer, the NVA started rolling grenades down on them.

One of the grenades exploded only a few feet away from Pfc. Jordy Pitre, a man in Bresina's squad, and sent him flying down the side of the mountain. Sp.4 Andrew Hannah rushed over to help Pitre, but before he had taken more than a few steps, he was knocked flat by another exploding grenade. With a head feeling like mush, Hannah struggled to his feet and stumbled forward into the bomb crater where Pitre lay. He held his friend in his arms and discovered that he had been hit in the head and mouth with shrapnel and was slowly strangling. Since the position was too exposed, Hannah grabbed Pitre by the shirt collar and dragged him down the mountain. When he was far enough behind the skirmish line, he dropped his friend in a bomb crater and started screaming furiously for a medic.

When none arrived, he yelled up for Bresina to come back and help him. With bullets hitting all around him, Bresina scrambled back down the mountain and leaped into the bomb crater next to Hannah. Hannah was holding Pitre in one arm, and the wounded man, his lips turning blue and his throat gurgling as he struggled to breathe, was flailing his arms about wildly.

Bresina knew what he had to do, but did not know if he could. Already he felt overcome with nausea just at the thought, already both his hands were shaking, already he felt slightly faint. You've got to do it, he told himself. You've got to force yourself. If you don't, he's going to choke to death. If you don't, he'll be dead in another minute or two. With a trembling hand, Bresina reached down and pulled the bowie knife from the scabbard on his right hip, then slowly brought the knife up to Pitre's throat. As the point of the knife touched the skin, he hesitated. His hand was still shaking while his mind prodded him, Do it! Do it! With a force of will, he drove the knife into Pitre's throat and pushed it through the cartilage. A rush of air swirled around the tip of the knife. With his hand still trembling and while Hannah held down Pitre's hands, he rotated the knife and enlarged the hole.

"Here," Hannah said, holding up the end of a ballpoint pen.

Bresina took the piece of plastic and stuck it in the hole, then watched Pitre's chest heave as air rushed back into his lungs.

When Bresina turned back to the fight, he discovered that the attack had permanently stalled. In fact, 4th Platoon was starting to pull back a short distance so the second bunker line could be softened up by artillery and airstrikes. Bresina helped Hannah carry Pitre down to the edge of the trees, where they huddled together to wait out the airstrike. The first fighter-bomber hit the side of the mountain with a 1,000-pound high-drag bomb. Bresina was bounced off the ground by the explosion, and looked around to see bloody parts of bodies and chunks of debris raining down all around him. After performing the emergency tracheotomy on Pitre, the sight of body parts raining down from the sky was almost more than he could take.

The airstrike knocked out a number of the large A-frame bunkers facing 4th Platoon, but not all of them. When Garza started the skirmish line forward again, they were quickly pinned down by two large bunkers on the right side of the ridge. When neither the recoilless rifles nor M79 grenadiers could manage to put rounds into the bunker apertures, Garza called Littnan and requested gunships.

The request was passed up through channels, and a few minutes later an LOH scout ship arrived over the mountain. Littnan honked him up and read him his instructions, "We're gonna pop green smoke out in front of 4th Platoon's position. I want you to start out and give me one rocket one hundred meters southwest of the smoke. After that we'll adjust." Littnan then read the exact azimuth he wanted, and the scout pilot passed it on to his two Cobra gunships overhead.

On the skirmish line, Garza pitched a green smoke grenade as far as he could out in front of him, then everyone in 4th Platoon took cover. The first gunship went into his run from the wrong direction, coming in along the ridge from the top of Dong Ap Bia, rather than toward it. Worse, rather that firing just one round, as requested, he salvoed every rocket on the ship.

About fifty to seventy-five meters behind 4th Platoon, Captain Littnan was sitting on a tree stump checking some coordinates on a map when one of the rockets exploded in the trees right above him. He jumped up at the impact, then took two steps forward before he realized that the entire left side of his body was shredded. He stumbled forward another step or two, then pitched forward on his face. He pulled himself up on one knee and found his RTO kneeling over him, holding out the handset. Littnan took the handset and heard Honeycutt screaming, "We're being hit with fucking ARA again. We're gonna get the bastards out of the area." Littnan dropped the handset and passed out.

Not more than twenty meters away, Pfc. Joseph Price—who only fourteen hours earlier had asked Andrew Hannah to escort his body back to Florida—was likewise sitting on a log when a piece of shrapnel hit him in the back of the head. He instantly leaped to his feet, looked around in confusion, and screamed, "Mother, Mother!" then fell over.

Pfc. Paul Samuel, one of Price's best friends, rushed over and held the bleeding man in his arms and started calling for a medic. But before one could get there, Price died.

When Sp.4 John Snyder arrived on the scene a few minutes later, he found Samuel standing near Price's body, sobbing like a baby. "I held him in my arms, and he died," Samuel cried. "He just died!"

Snyder left Samuel to his private grief and ran forward to the company CP. He was shocked to see the surrounding area littered with wounded. When he discovered that one of Littnan's RTOs was one of them, he took over the man's radio.

He was soon talking with Honeycutt. "What's the situation up there?" Honeycutt asked.

"We got a lot of wounded here, sir—about fifteen I'd say—and two dead. The CP's wiped out."

"Who's in command?"

"I don't know. There's no one left here. I'll call Lieutenant Boccia."

Snyder yelled down the trail for Boccia, who came at a run, and grabbed the handset.

"Whatever you do, Boccia, continue the assault. Do you hear me? Don't back off! Keep pushin' to the crest."

"Sir, we don't have enough men to get our wounded out. We need some immediate medevacs."

"I'm sending someone up to replace Captain Littnan, and I want you to continue the assault. Do you hear me?"

"Yes, sir."

"Good. Now get movin'."

On the mountain, obviously aware of the disaster which had struck Bravo, the NVA launched a counterattack against 4th Platoon. While a squad of NVA bombarded the front with RPGs, enemy riflemen began maneuvering against the flanks of the platoon. To compound matters, a squad of enemy soldiers had somehow gotten into the draw and was pouring fire into the platoon's rear.

Sensing an envelopment, Garza decided to pull the platoon back into the treeline. At the knolls, they formed a hurried defensive perimeter. The NVA moved a platoon quickly into the draw in an attempt to cut off the platoon.

Sp.4 Hannah, who with four other men was carrying Pitre on a rubber poncho, heard someone scream, "Look out! Get down!"

The four men set the poncho down, and Hannah huddled over Pitre, who was screaming, "Oh, my God, I'm gonna die! I'm gonna die! Oh, God! Oh, God!" Pitre flailed wildly with his hands, grabbing at Hannah's face and pulling at his shirt.

Hannah was pushing Pitre's hands down with one hand and straightening the pen in his throat with the other when an RPG exploded in the trees overhead, almost knocking him unconscious.

Nearby someone screamed, "Here they come! They're in the draw! Get 'em!"

Another man screamed, "Put out some fire. The fuckers are comin' up."

Hannah lay across Pitre's body, and then he saw them: ten to fifteen enemy soldiers moving on-line out of the draw, their AKs barking. He leaned forward slightly and fired a short four-round burst and saw one of the NVA soldiers knocked backwards into the jungle. He turned his rifle to the left and dropped another man. He looked to his right to see an enemy soldier preparing to fire an RPG, but an M79 grenadier shredded the man with the full force of a flechette round. The grenadier reloaded and turned to the right just as two enemy soldiers broke from the thick jungle and side by side charged him. The grenadier ducked behind a tree to avoid the fire, then at a range of twenty meters shot both NVA point-blank with another flechette round. One enemy soldier took the full force of the round and was killed instantly, but another, slightly wounded, kept charging. He was just about on top of the ridge when two or three GIs hit him with rifle fire and sent him rolling back down the side of the ridge.

The attack against 4th Platoon's right flank was not an isolated incident. Squad-size groups of enemy soldiers were coming out of the draw all along the length of Bravo's column. Toward the rear of the column, two squads of NVA tried to mount a rush on Bravo's LZ, which was then crammed with wounded, but were stopped by Sp.4 Logan and Pfc.'s Snyder and Maryniewski, who drove them back with a blizzard of machine-gun fire.

With Bravo's right flank under attack and 4th Platoon withdrawing, Boccia knew that it was impossible to follow Honeycutt's order to continue the attack. He was, in fact, more concerned about Bravo's being overrun than in mounting another assault on Dong Ap Bia.

A few minutes after the start of the enemy counterattack, he radioed Lieutenant Eward, whose platoon was right behind Garza's; and during a hurried discussion, they agreed to split command of the company, with Eward taking charge of the front of the column and Boccia the rear. Fearful that the enemy might charge down the ridge and roll the company up like a carpet, Eward rushed one of his own squads up to strengthen Garza's position. At the same time, Boccia started running up and down the ridge, directing the defense against the enemy soldiers who were still trying to come out of the draw.

While Bravo was being counterattacked, Alpha Company's 1st Platoon was still fighting its way up the ridge against intense sniper fire. Unlike Charlie Company before them, they did not make it to the saddle, but were stopped thirty meters short by fire from three or four bunkers spread out across the ridge.

Although Lieutenant McGreevy believed any attack he launched was doomed to failure, he moved quickly to try to take out the bunker. He put his 1st Squad, an extra machine-gun team on loan, under the control of the platoon sergeant, Michael Lyden, then took personal control of the 2d Squad and started maneuvering them to the right along the edge of the ridge. While Lyden's men lay down fire, the 2d Squad inched its way upward.

The NVA kept up a steady harassing fire on both squads as McGreevy and his men advanced up the ridge, but as they continued closing the gap to the bunkers, enemy gunners cut loose with everything they had. A dozen rocket grenades rained down on the 1st Squad's position. As always, they fired into the trees just above the heads of the men, and within thirty seconds five men were hit by the rain of shrapnel. They also turned their fire on 2d Squad, volleying them with RPG and furious bursts of heavy machine-gun fire. McGreevy quickly had two wounded of his own, but kept his men advancing, advancing, and firing.

When McGreevy was only twenty to thirty meters from the bunkers, he decided to look back and signal Lyden. For some reason the platoon sergeant was standing up at that moment; a second later he was struck in the chest by an RPG. The explosion killed Lyden instantly and wounded two or three men nearby.

McGreevy watched it all as if it were happening in slow motion. Lyden, like Westman in Bravo Company, was one of those men beloved by everyone in the platoon, but especially so by the lieutenant. A coal miner from northern Illinois, Lyden was a natural storyteller, with an incredible sense of humor. McGreevy was so stricken with grief by his death that for a long moment he did not know if he could continue the attack.

He finally did, however, though it was a futile gesture. He had not advanced his men more than a few more meters before the NVA pounded both squads with more RPGs, wounding another four or five men.

With more than half his platoon wounded, McGreevy ordered a withdrawal and started the 2d Platoon back down the ridge. Once back with the other two squads, McGreevy organized parties of stretcher bearers and started the entire column in reverse.

On the mountain the NVA troops spotted the withdrawal and started climbing out of their bunkers. Some enemy soldiers rushed down into the draw in order to attack McGreevy's left flank while others charged straight down the ridge. The enemy move coincided with a wild thunderstorm which burst over the mountain with the ferocity of a bomb strike. Lightning flashed angrily through the sky, and the rain came down in sheets.

McGreevy remained in the rear with two other men to cover the withdrawal. Although it was difficult to see distinct shapes in the jungle, he could make out the flitting movement of NVA soldiers rushing through the semidarkness under the canopy and could catch glimpses of pith helmets and AKs.

The lieutenant flipped his M16 on automatic and sprayed the jungle.

He emptied his magazine with three quick bursts, then slammed in another, backpedaled a few steps, and fired again. Every time he fired, he thought, I can't let what happened to Charlie Company happen here.

In the column, Pfc. David Dean, one of the stretcher bearers for Lyden, felt as if he were in a bad dream, a terrible nightmare that try as he might, he could not awaken from. Dean had likewise been good friends with Lyden, and having to carry his friend now—a man he had partied with on many weekends at Lake Charles just outside of Fort Polk—was almost more than he could bear. And now the rain on top of it all, and all the wild shooting and screaming . . . it had to be a dream.

A moment later, he found out for sure that it was not a dream. It was real, as real as the NVA maneuvering at the column from the draw. He and the three other bearers dropped Lyden, fell into the oozing mud, and cut loose at pith helmets emerging from the jungle below. Half a dozen M16s ripped away at the enemy soldiers on both sides of him.

Dean picked up his corner of the poncho a moment later and started struggling forward again. But a little farther down the trail he again had to stop, this time to shoot at snipers who were in trees in the draw. He fired and he fired, but in the rain, he could not tell if he was hitting anything or not.

At 1520 Capt. Butch Chappel, Captain Littnan's replacement, choppered in to the battalion LZ, where Honeycutt stood waiting for him. On the edge of the LZ, in a drizzling rain, Honeycutt gave Chappel a hurried briefing, then had Crazy Rairdon shuttle the captain the seven hundred meters up to Bravo's LZ.

Lieutenant Boccia was there to greet Chappel when he landed. "What's up, Captain?"

"I just talked with Blackjack," Chappel said. "We're gonna continue the attack."

"You gotta be kidding?"

"No. Those are my orders. Let's go. We've got to get moving."

"Captain, this company has had 50 percent casualties in the last five days. My own platoon is down to fifteen men, and the other two platoons are in even worse shape. There's just no way in hell we can mount another attack."

"Those are my orders, Lieutenant."

Boccia started to protest again, but Chappel cut him off. "Let's hop to it, Lieutenant."

"Yes, sir."

The attack started at four in the afternoon and was over in minutes. During the fighting along the draw, the NVA had for the second time in two days reoccupied the area around the knolls and rigged the surrounding trees with claymores. As the two platoons crawled up toward the clearing, the enemy started blowing the directional mines down on them. Three men were wounded by the first blasts, and both columns stopped. Already exhausted by a day of hard fighting and demoralized by the gunship accident, the men of the platoons simply did not have the heart for yet another fight through the knolls. Instead, each man found whatever cover he could and refused to budge. Boccia had been right. Bravo Company was indeed finished.

When Captain Chappel heard the news from Eward and Boccia, he radioed Honeycutt, who now had no choice but to call off the attack. Then, fearful that a weakened, exhausted Bravo Company strung out for a hundred meters along the ridge might be an easy mark for an enemy ground attack during the night, Honeycutt instructed Chappel to pull back down the ridge four hundred meters and form a combined NDP with Alpha Company once it had moved back across the draw.

On Bravo's LZ, Boccia supervised the abandonment of the position when the last of the wounded were loaded aboard Crazy Rairdon's LOH and the rest of the company trudged off down the ridge with all the ammunition and as much of the discarded equipment as they could carry. Boccia and five of his men gathered up the remaining rucksacks, ponchos, and clothing and built another huge bonfire. Then, with the fire shooting flames fifteen feet into the air and each of them draped with belts of M60 ammo and lugging five or six M16s or M79s, the six men started the ignominious walk back down the mountain. For Boccia, this was becoming an all-too-familiar scene.

The day's defeat had left a bitter taste in the mouth of a lot of men, but not more so than in that of Colonel Honeycutt. As far as he was concerned, the gunship rocketing of Captain Littnan's CP had been singly responsible for stopping Garza's attack. Like a domino, it had set off a chain reaction of disasters, all of which he had been helpless to stop.

When Bravo and Alpha were safely in their NDP, he called the new artillery liaison officer to the CP and gave him a message to carry back to division. "I want you to make sure everybody gets this. And I mean the artillery people and the gunship pilots and the liaison officers . . . everybody. I don't want any more ARA out here if they can't shoot the enemy instead of us. I'm tired of taking more casualties from friendlies than from the enemy. The next goddamn sonofabitch who comes out here and shoots us up, we're gonna shoot his fuckin' ass down. And that's final. Now you go back and tell 'em that."

At their new NDP, the troops of Alpha and Bravo companies dug fighting holes around their perimeter, then sent out listening posts and ambush patrols in the surrounding area. Once the perimeter was secure, they began processing in replacements being shuttled in from Camp Evans. They were badly needed. Alpha had lost seventeen men during the day, and Bravo nineteen; and both showed sixty-seven men on their rosters, which was about half the ideal strength of a rifle company.

Unfortunately, most of the replacements were not infantrymen, but cooks, truck drivers, and other rear-area men. The replacement sent to Sp.4 Anthony Bresina's squad was a short, chubby cook from Camp Evans. He arrived just as fighter-bombers were dropping 500-pound bombs on Dong Ap Bia. He stood there in wild-eyed terror as the bombs went off, his hands shaking, his mouth hanging open like a trap door.

"What the fuck are you doin' out here?" someone asked.

"I'm a replacement," the cook mumbled.

"You?"

"Yeah."

"You've gotta be shitting me?" someone else said.

"No, I don't think so."

Like sharks moving in for the kill, the squad moved in around the cook. They all knew him. Earlier in the year, after more than two months in the bush, Bravo Company had returned to Camp Evans for a two-day stand-down, every hour of which they expected to spend either sleeping or drinking. They discovered instead that this cook and a number of his friends had arranged things so that men from Bravo had to pull their bunker guard for them.

"They must be scraping up the streets of Evans," still another man said. "Look at this pitiful piece of shit."

"What do you want me to do?" the cook asked.

"Here, you look big enough," Bresina said, shoving an M60 machine gun into the man's hands. "Take this."

The cook struggled to keep from dropping the machine gun. "But . . . I don't know how to use it."

"Then you better learn quick," a man on Bresina's right said. "If you don't, you won't be around long."

About two hours after dark, Major Montgomery flew out to the battalion LZ to discuss with Honeycutt a plan he had worked up for a two-battalion assault on Dong Ap Bia in the morning. The plan called for the 3/187th to continue its attack as before up the two ridges, but with a slight variation. Instead of trying to overrun the mountain this time, it called for the Rakkasans to move up only far enough to exert pressure on the enemy's defenses, then hold in place while the 1/506th assaulted from the south and swept across the top of Hill 900 from 937.

"And what if the 506th doesn't make it tomorrow?" Honeycutt asked. "Do you still want me to assault the mountain?"

"No, we don't want you going in alone."

Honeycutt liked the idea of a two-battalion assault, but he did not seriously think the 1/506th had any chance of making it in the morning. A quick look at their present positions on the map told the story. Alpha and Bravo, the two maneuvering companies at the moment, were each more than one thousand meters from Hill 900 and another four hundred from 937, and he did not see how they could possibly cover that much distance in the morning. And if, as he suspected, they did not make it on time—and the NVA were allowed yet another night to reinforce the mountain up the large draw southwest of Hill 900—then the fight for Dong Ap Bia was going to become nothing but a battle of attrition, a battle which the NVA, with their inexhaustible supplies of troops just across the border, could fight indefinitely.

On this night, as on the previous one, the NVA continued maneuvering around the mountain. Most of the movement was again by small reconnaissance groups seeking to locate the American NDPs and plot their locations for mortar fire. On this night, however, the NVA decided to continue the counterattack they had started during the day. Their target was the battalion CP.

About an hour before midnight, a company of NVA regulars, led by a platoon of sappers, moved across the Trung Pham River from Laos and headed up the draw toward the battalion CP. A small American reconnaissance patrol, set up in the center of the draw, watched silently as the NVA force moved by their position, then radioed a warning to the battalion CP.

The NVA were obviously aware of the location of the battalion CP and likely even aware that Charlie Company's 2d and 3d platoons were guarding the perimeter around it. They were not aware, though, that Lieutenant Trautman's 1st Platoon had set up an ambush position along a small finger 150 meters southwest of the CP. This ambush position was right in line with the NVA line of march.

As the NVA sappers started moving up out of the draw, however, they sensed Trautman's perimeter and began probing it. Unable to pinpoint its exact location in the deep darkness under the jungle canopy, the sappers started flinging satchel charges up at the perimeter, hoping the GIs would fire wildly and give away the locations of their fighting holes.

Trautman saw the ploy instantly and began moving up and down the perimeter, whispering to his men, "Don't fire. Don't give away your position. Throw grenades or use your M79."

While he spoke, the sappers threw about ten satchel charges up at the perimeter. They landed about fifteen meters short. In their light, the GIs spotted about twenty to thirty figures moving around in the jungle. They answered with a grenade shower, and the sappers, in turn, with more satchel charges.

In the light of the explosion this time, a grenadier leveled his M79 and fired a high-explosive round right into the chest of a sapper a short distance away. The man, loaded with satchel charges, disintegrated in a deafening explosion.

The NVA were not to be denied, however, and as Trautman watched, thirty more satchel charges went off in a rippling explosion across the front of the perimeter. Most of the men ducked into their fighting holes to avoid the blast, but two or three men were knocked senseless for a few minutes.

The GIs answered with another thirty to forty grenades, one of which set off a huge secondary explosion. The sappers answered again with ten to fifteen satchel charges. By their light, a grenadier hit another sapper with a point-blank shot. Like the first, the man exploded in a blinding flash, and parts of him were scattered all over the area. For the next hour it continued, with the NVA throwing satchel charges and the GIs answering with grenades and M79 rounds. The fight became more and more surreal, a chaotic jumble of noise and shouts and blinding flashes.

At the end of that hour, one of Trautman's squad leaders suddenly climbed out of his fighting hole and started crawling to the rear. "I can't take any more of this," he said over and over. Trautman found him huddled beside a tree, shaking like a frightened child. He tried to coax him back to the perimeter, but the man would not move. Trautman had considered the sergeant one of his best NCOs, but it was only too obvious now how wrong he had been. Like the RTO who bugged out on the fourteenth, this sergeant simply could not stand the shock of combat. By then Trautman was sure of one thing: you cannot tell who the real soldiers are in a platoon until the first shots are fired.

Trautman left the sergeant and crawled back to the perimeter. He thought that the NVA would sooner or later pull back and break off the attack, but instead they only increased the rain of satchel charges, and the fight went on.

The exchange continued sporadically for the next hour. About two in the morning, a Shadow gunship appeared overhead. Armed with four miniguns and a giant searchlight, the AC-119G fixed-wing aircraft came in from the northwest and swept the draw below 1st Platoon's position with minigun fire, a 24,000-round-a-minute torrent that stripped the trees in its path almost bare of leaves and cut a swathe through the jungle thirty meters wide. For the next forty minutes, the Shadow made repeated runs up and down the draw. When its ordnance was finally expended, the plane turned on its huge searchlight, holding the edge of the beam just below 1st Platoon's perimeter.

Two Cobra gunships came in next, dived in under the light and for the next fifteen minutes fired up the draw with more minigun fire. It is unknown how many enemy soldiers died under this rain of fire, but it was not enough to stop the attack. When the gunships went off station, the sappers returned and continued mounting sporadic probes against the perimeter for yet another hour. It was not until nearly five in the morning that they finally broke off the attack and pulled back, carrying their dead and wounded with them back into Laos. They left the side of the draw covered with blood, pieces of flesh, and littered with unexploded satchel charges and grenades.

Unbelievably, not a single man in 1st Platoon was wounded during the fight, though, like Lieutenant Trautman, they were all left with ringing ears and shattered nerves.

CHAPTER 15

WAITING FOR THE CURRAHEES

The morning started, as always, with airstrikes. At 0734 the first of three sets of fighters, in an attempt to knock off some of the deep bunkers, went at the mountain with 1,000-pound bombs armed with delayed-action fuses. For the next hour, the top and west slope of Dong Ap Bia rocked and shuddered from the impact of those leviathans. There was still jungle on the ridges, but the west face of the mountain was a muddy stew of leaves, tree branches, vines, splintered trees, discarded equipment, and parts of bodies.

When the bombing stopped, the artillery took over and started slamming volley after volley of 105, 155, and 8-inch howitzer rounds into the mountain. While the artillery worked, Honeycutt prepared his companies for the big assault. Delta's disastrous three days in the deep ravine had convinced the colonel of the impossibility of launching an attack against the mountain from the north. Now that they had finally cleared their dead and wounded out of the ravine, the colonel ordered Captain Sanders to move his men back up the ridge, take over Bravo's LZ, and prepare to continue the assault up the main ridge. Leading the attack up the other ridge would again be Alpha Company. Around 0830 they left their NDP near the battalion CP and started back down through the draw toward their assault positions on the other side. To complete the morning activity, Bravo moved back to the battalion CP and took over its joint security with Charlie.

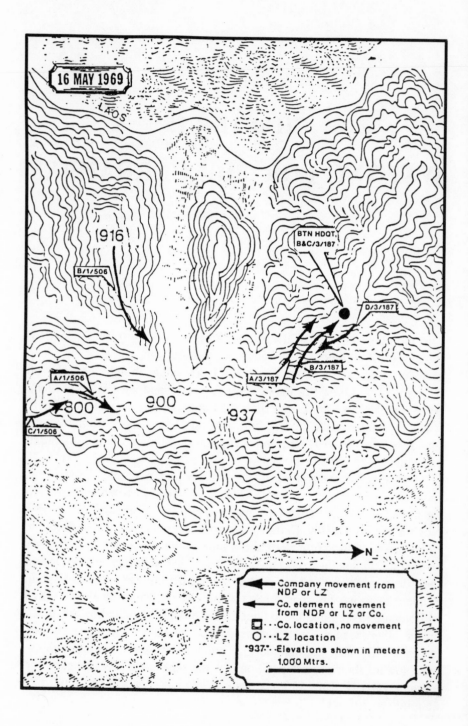

Now everything was up to the Currahees. If they could move up quickly and launch an attack against the mountain, Dong Ap Bia would likely be under the control of the 3d Brigade by evening. If not, Honeycutt realized that all his maneuvers this morning would end as little more than an exercise in futility.

Shortly after the start of the bombing, the 1/506th likewise went on the move. After breaking its NDP, Alpha Company, led by Capt. Linwood Burney, started advancing rapidly up a large ridge toward the top of Hill 800. Bravo Company, which had seized Hill 916 the day before after an easy fight, started another deliberate move northeast toward Hill 900. Charlie Company, guarding the battalion CP, followed in the trail of Alpha.

Compared to the 3/187th, the 1/506th had had an easy time of it the last three days. They had a man killed by sniper fire on the fourteenth, but each company had only one man wounded at this point, each also by sniper fire. Not a single company, however, had yet to experience any hard contact.

The situation changed quickly as they closed the distance to Dong Ap Bia. After covering about two hundred meters, the point platoon of Alpha Company was taken under intense fire by a large enemy force entrenched on Hill 800. Using RPGs, heavy machine guns, and rifles, enemy troops killed one GI, wounded eight others, and sent the rest of the platoon running for their lives back down the trail. Once they had pulled out their casualties, Alpha dug in, then hunkered down to wait out a long artillery and gunship prep of the enemy positions.

It was nearly the same scenario for Bravo Company. After moving about 150 meters down the northeast slope of Hill 916, they took heavy fire from both their front and rear. In less than a few minutes, they likewise had a man killed and eight wounded. A squad was sent down the northeast slope of 916 to ferret out the snipers, and while the company held in place, artillery fire was directed against the high ground above the saddle.

Near the top of Hill 916, Bravo quickly cut an LZ to medevac out its wounded, but the first ship in was hit by enemy fire and driven off. They tried suppressing the enemy fire with heavy doses of artillery, but the second medevac to arrive was also driven off.

After pounding the enemy positions on Hill 800, Captain Burney had Alpha again assault the enemy bunkers. The enemy, however, fled right before the attack, and Alpha swept over the four or five bunkers that had held up their advance. They did not find any bodies in the bunkers, but the surrounding area was splattered with blood. Then, strangely, while Alpha was policing up the area, nearly a platoon of NVA broke from the surrounding jungle and attacked them. Dodging from tree to tree, firing their AKs from the hip in short bursts, the enemy soldiers charged forward. Alpha was initially stunned by the suddenness of the attack, but reacted quickly and met the charging NVA with massed fire. The enemy soldiers stopped about thirty meters away and started maneuvering slowly forward, trying to hug Alpha's position. Up and down Alpha's hastily formed perimeter, recoilless-rifle gunners and grenadiers blasted the approaching enemy soldiers with HE and flechette rounds. While they fired, two Cobras arrived and began ripping into the enemy skirmishers with rockets and whirring blasts of automatic grenade fire. Facing imminent destruction from the gunships, the NVA gathered up their dead and wounded and retreated up toward the top of Hill 800. Before Alpha could go on the attack again, a wild thunderstorm broke out. Oddly, though, not one man was wounded in the enemy ground attack; two were felled by lightning and needed immediate evacuation.

On the top of Hill 916, Bravo had finally managed to medevac out their wounded, but when they tried to start a new advance down through the heavy jungle saddle between Hills 916 and 900, once again they were stopped by a blizzard of enemy fire.

Honeycutt spent most of the morning monitoring the progress of the 1/506th and by noon, after discovering that neither of the maneuvering companies had advanced much beyond their NDPs, was forced to conclude that all his preparations that morning had indeed been exercises in futility. He called brigade, nonetheless, thinking they might want him to go in again alone, but Major Montgomery instructed him to pull his troops back and postpone the attack until the next morning. To Honeycutt the news was a bitter pill to have to swallow, for he knew that with the large draw below Hill 900 still wide open, the NVA had another night to reinforce their positions on the mountain.

If the 3d Brigade's planned two-battalion attack on Dong Ap Bia had been launched that particular morning and had been subsequently successful, it is doubtful that the fight would have been remembered, let alone receive the eventual notoriety that it did. There had been a number of tough hill fights in I Corps during the preceding two years, and except for their inclusion in obscure divisional histories, they are now all but forgotten.

Around the sixteenth, however, the press got wind of the fight around Dong Ap Bia and, like besieging infantry, began slowly closing in on the story. One of the first to discover the battle was a young Associated Press correspondent, Jay Sharbutt. On the morning of the sixteenth, after visiting the battalion CP and talking with a number of soldiers in the area, Sharbutt flew to Firebase Berchtesgaden to interview General Zais.

His first questions dealt with the rationale behind the NVA's tenacious defense of Dong Ap Bia, and for them Zais had no ready answer. As mentioned earlier, both he and his assistant commander, General Smith, had already pondered this inexplicable decision on the enemy's part, but as yet could not explain it.

Eventually, however, Sharbutt posed the question that would become the epicenter for the controversy that would eventually erupt over the battle. "Why are you attacking this mountain with troops?" he asked. "Why don't you just pull back and hit it with B52 strikes?"

Sharbutt was an intelligent young reporter, but the question was hardly original. Since the second day of fighting, soldiers in all four of Honeycutt's companies had been asking the same question, and asking it over and over again. As fundamental as this question was to a discussion of the tactics being used to prosecute the battle, Zais—as he explained in a classified memorandum two months later—was stunned by it. He was not stunned because Sharbutt had uncovered some basic flaw in the tactics being used to attack Dong Ap Bia, but because he suspected quite rightly that the question represented the beginning of some controversy, which was the last thing he wanted at that moment. As the general makes clear in this same memorandum, his first reaction was to tell Sharbutt "to confine himself to writing about the battle rather than second-guessing the commander," but he instead held his tongue. To Zais, Sharbutt seemed to be a "sensitive young man" who had been in combat for the first time and was understandably "somewhat distraught," even a bit "hysterical." If his perceptions of the young correspondent proved true, Zais believed that no matter how he answered the question, Sharbutt would likely "misrepresent it."

Instead of a curt answer, though, Zais remained diplomatic, explaining that before he could bring B52s in against the mountain, he would first have to abandon the positions he already had around the mountain and move all friendly troops at least two miles back from the center of the bomb strike. He then explained further that he already had all the fire support he needed, using airstrikes that were just as powerful and far more accurate than B52s.

"Besides, you hate to give up ground you've gained," he added. "You have to fight as hard to retake it. Backing off is just not something commanders like to do."

"Look, those gooks aren't stupid," one of Zais's staff officers added at that point. "They know exactly how much damage a B52 strike will do, how deep the bombs blow. They build their bunkers to withstand that. That's what they've done out there."

It is not known from existing accounts what else Sharbutt and Zais discussed, if anything. It is known that later both Zais and Honeycutt felt that Sharbutt's subsequent newspaper accounts of the battle were both distorted and sensationalized. Whether this is true or not is a question open to debate. Regardless, his stories stunned and shocked an American public already weary of the Vietnam War and may have single-handedly set off the controversy over the battle.

The night of the sixteenth was quiet, but in the early morning hours of the seventeenth, the artillery batteries at Firebases Currahee, Bradley, Airborne, Cannon, and Berchtesgaden began an intermittent shelling of the mountain.

Rather than having Bravo and Alpha companies move into their assault positions, as on the sixteenth, Honeycutt kept them in their NDPs, ready to move should the 1/506th get close enough to launch an attack against the mountain.

At 0918 the first of a number of sets of fighter-bombers arrived with 1,000-pound bombs with delayed-action fuses. There were four or five A-frame bunkers clearly visible on the west face of the mountain, and jets were tasked with taking them out. After a number of misses, a fighter-bomber finally got a direct hit on one of the bunkers. The bomb set off a huge secondary explosion which blew the body of an enemy soldier fifty feet in the air. After two or three more direct hits, men manning observation posts on both ridges reported that the trees below the military crest of the mountain were filled with bodies, chunks of flesh, and bloody clothing.

At 0952, while the fighter-bombers were still working over the mountain, Alpha 1/506th pushed out from its NDP on top of Hill 800 and started out toward its objective, Hill 900, less than one thousand meters away. After covering less than fifty meters, the front of the column came under heavy small-arms fire from enemy positions on the northern edge of Hill 800. In a short time Alpha had a man killed and another wounded. Lieutenant Burney, Alpha's CO, sent a squad down the right side of the ridge to attempt a flanking move on the bunkers, but the NVA had positions in the draw also and drove the squad back.

Bravo 1/506th had an easier time of it. From their NDP in the saddle below Hill 916, they started up a ridge on the southwest side of Hill 900. They soon discovered some abandoned bunkers, a trench line, and some discarded NVA equipment. When they tried advancing farther up the ridge, the front of the column was ripped apart by a barrage of RPGs fired from well-concealed bunkers and spider holes. One man was killed outright, and another seven seriously wounded. Bravo's lead platoon retreated back down the ridge, dragging what they thought were all their casualties. Once they were out of the enemy's killing zone, however, they discovered that the KIA, 1st Platoon RTO, had been left behind with his radio. A squad was immediately dispatched to try to find the dead man and the radio, but they could not advance because of withering small-arms fire. Realizing the enemy had the radio, Bravo was forced to change all its frequencies.

On Hill 800, in an attempt to get Alpha moving again, Colonel Bowers ordered gunships to saturate the enemy bunkers on the northern end of the hill with CS gas rounds. Using their automatic grenade launchers, gunships pumped fifty rounds into the area, then hovered overhead to see how the NVA would react. There was little wind, and the gas settled over the bunkers like the evening fog. Seconds later, about fifteen to twenty NVA soldiers, choking and gagging, started crawling out of the bunkers. A quick burst of minigun fire brought down about ten of the men, and the rest scattered into the jungle.

In order to take advantage of the confusion caused by the gas attack, Lieutenant Burney ordered Lieutenant Dimock to lead another assault toward Hill 900. Lieutenant Dimock put his men in three columns, and they started off cautiously across the top of Hill 800. Dimock took the fourth position back in the center column, behind his RTO, Sp.4 Steve Tice. Sp.4 Paul Blackwell took point for the column, and Sp.4 Clifford Brown slack. Sgt. John Nicholas, the platoon sergeant, took point for the column on the left, and Sp.4 Larry Brook for the one on the right.

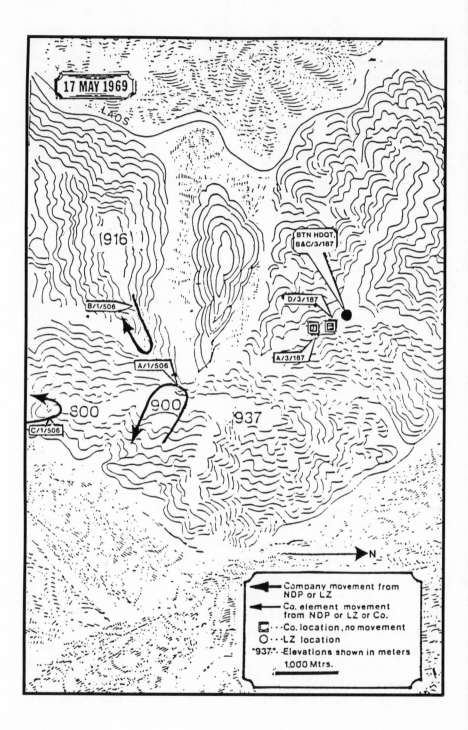

17 MAY 1969

LAOS

1916

BTN HDQT,
B&C/3/187

B/1/506

D/3/187

A/3/187

A/1/506

800   900   937

C/1/506

N

Company movement from
NDP or LZ

Co. element movement
from NDP or LZ or Co.

⬚···Co. location, no movement

○···LZ location

·937·· Elevations shown in meters

1,000 Mtrs.

After the gas attack and gunship runs, the NVA had deserted the bunkers on the northern end of Hill 800, and Dimock and his men moved quickly through the abandoned positions. At the edge of the hill, they discovered a deep saddle which led to the southern edge of Hill 900. After a short break, Dimock told the pointmen to push out again.

Aware of the danger of entering the saddle, the pointmen moved fifteen meters ahead of the rest of the platoon and slowed their pace. They moved on cat's feet toward the bottom, pushing their way silently through palm fronds, hanging vines, and stands of bamboo. When the pointmen were about halfway to the bottom of the saddle, a number of 12.7mm heavy machine guns opened up on them. The slackman in the right column, Sp.4 Joe McCants was hit in the first burst and killed. Seeing McCants fall, Dimock ordered the rest of the platoon to follow him down into the bottom of the saddle. Only seven men did. The rest either took cover where they were or scurried back up to Hill 800.

In the saddle, the seven men scrambled for cover behind rocks and trees and returned the enemy fire. The enemy bunkers were about fifty meters away on the southern slope of the saddle and so well camouflaged that the seven could do little but fire wildly. The NVA, however, had a perfect view of the GIs, and they continued pouring fire down on them. In a short time, Sp.4's William Sessions, Gilbert Page, and Sergeant Nicholas were killed.

Huddled behind a large tree, Tice, the RTO, radioed Captain Burney for help. Burney sent two Cobras, and for the next twenty minutes they rocketed and strafed the enemy bunkers through gaps in the jungle canopy. Their fire had little effect on the heavily roofed bunkers, though. Worse, some shrapnel from one of the rockets spilled over onto 2d Platoon's position, seriously wounding Brown.

When the gunships left, a number of enemy skirmishers came out of the bunkers and trenches and started maneuvering down the south side of the saddle toward the four surviving GIs. Dimock, Blackwell, Brown, and Tice repeatedly massed their fire and drove them back. Realizing that he could neither advance nor withdraw because of the heavy fire and that it was only a matter of time before they were overrun, Dimock called for napalm against the enemy bunkers. With only fifty meters separating his position from the bunkers, it was a risky call, but the lieutenant did not have much choice.

The fighter-bombers went at the bunkers with a vengeance, and for fifteen minutes the south side of the saddle was engulfed in a gigantic ball of flames. One of the bombs hit so close to their position that Tice and Brown had their eyebrows singed by the heat. Another bomb set off a series of secondary explosions which ripped through the treeline around the bunkers, scattering debris for hundreds of meters in all directions.

In the saddle the four hunkered down, waiting for the napalm fires to burn down. They assumed the napalm had finished the NVA troops manning the bunkers, but they were wrong. Without warning, a squad of enemy soldiers suddenly charged out of the shattered bunker line and down the saddle at them.

The NVA were angry, but Tice, Blackwell, Brown, and Dimock were even angrier. They had all been good friends of Sergeant Nicholas, and his death—especially coming as it did right after the young sergeant's return from an R and R trip to Hawaii with his wife and their new baby—had infuriated all of them. At the sight of the NVA, each man flipped his rifle on fully automatic and started going through magazines as fast as he could fire.

Brown, even though seriously wounded himself, seemed to find new strength at the sight of the charging enemy. "You killed Nicholas, you motherfuckers," he screamed as he fired. "You killed Nicholas, and now you're gonna die!"

Three or four enemy soldiers dropped in the first couple of volleys, and the rest scattered for cover. After the failed assault, it became strangely quiet. In the saddle the four men waited, thinking the NVA might attack again. But they did not return, and after waiting an hour, Dimock led the men back up to Hill 800 to join the rest of the platoon.

Honeycutt had again spent much of his morning monitoring the progress of the 1/506th and by noon was getting increasingly frustrated. He finally called the brigade S-3, Major Montgomery.

"What's goin' on with those guys? I can't stay here sitting on my ass. The NVA are maneuvering against me."

"They say they're movin'."

"If they are, I'd like to know where."

The 1/506th was, in fact, not moving. At one in the afternoon, with Alpha still on Hill 800 and Bravo only one hundred meters past its NDP, Montgomery called Honeycutt back with the news that the two-battalion assault had once again been postponed, again for the following morning.

Honeycutt used the rest of the afternoon to prepare his companies for the coming attack. Flak jackets were brought in and distributed to all the companies, to protect men against RPG shrapnel. Extra ammunition, including concussion grenades to be used against the bunkers, was moved up to Bravo's old LZ and stockpiled so Delta would be more quickly resupplied. At the same time, the defenses around the battalion CP were improved and RIFs sent out to the west, northwest, and northeast to try to detect any sizable enemy forces trying to reinforce the mountain. Finally a platoon each from Alpha and Delta companies moved up their respective ridges as far as they could without making contact and began searching for positions from which they could best support the attack by 1/506th.

About halfway through his preparations, Honeycutt had to stop and deal with a completely unexpected problem—newsmen! About four or five arrived at 1400, and for the next couple of hours, every chopper landing on the battalion LZ brought two or three more.

Honeycutt had a number of good friends who were newsmen—including Tom Mayer, who would eventually write the book *The Weary Falcon*—and there were many more he respected, but he generally did not like them. He felt that they almost always exaggerated their stories and portrayed the American effort in Vietnam negatively and cynically. Once, during a 101st Airborne Division operation on the plains around Hue, he discovered that a correspondent had asked a soldier in Bravo Company, "How do you feel fighting over here knowing that everybody back in the States is against the war?" It was stuff like this that infuriated the colonel and convinced him that most reporters were trying to make news rather than just report it.

When he first heard that the reporters wanted to come out, he had tried everything in his power to stop them, until General Zais himself had ordered him not only to let them land, but to treat them amiably.

"But I don't want the bastards running around here," he had told Zais; however, the general had refused to discuss the matter any further.

One of the first reporters out that afternoon was a tall, thin, long-haired, bearded man from one of the national networks. He was accompanied by a photographer carrying a 16mm camera.

"Where's the war?" the tall man asked Honeycutt as soon as he arrived at the CP. "I thought there was a fuckin' war going on out here?"

"It's everywhere," Honeycutt said, choking down his anger.

"I don't see anything."

"Come on," Honeycutt said. "I'll show you where the fuckin' war is. Follow me."

Honeycutt started off down the trail, and the reporter and cameraman fell in right behind him. The colonel intended on taking them up to Bravo's old LZ and dropping them off, but they had not covered more than seventy-five meters when an enemy soldier on Dong Ap Bia spotted them moving through an open spot on the ridge and gave them a long burst with his heavy machine gun. The bullets ripped through the trees over their heads, and all three men went flat to the ground. They were still hugging the ground when an RPG went off with a thunderous boom behind them and showered them with dirt and debris. Honeycutt looked back to see the reporter crawling around frantically on the trail gathering up his notebooks and pencils. The cameraman was in a fetal position with his arms over his face.

Honeycutt stood up and motioned them forward. "Come on. Let's get movin'." The two, however, leaped to their feet and started running back toward the battalion CP.

"Hey, don't you want to see the war?" he called after them.

The reporter looked back and yelled, "Fuck the war," then continued running.

Lieutenant Boccia likewise had little use for reporters. To him they were an arrogant, supercilious lot, more interested in promoting their own narrow ideological prejudices than in writing the truth about the war. Late in the afternoon while passing through the battalion CP, he noticed that five of them were putting up their ponchos for the night. Unable to resist playing a joke on them, Boccia sauntered over and stood watching them.

"Do you mind if I make a suggestion?" he asked after a while.

"Go ahead," one of them said.

"Do you notice how the troops don't have poncho hooches?"

"Yeah."

"Well, there's a reason for that. And that's because the moonlight reflects off the ponchos, and then the NVA just zeros in on them with their RPGs."

All five of the reporters turned to Boccia at once, their eyes as big as saucers.

"You're kidding?" one asked.

"Nope. As soon as they spot that reflection, you're a dead man."

Boccia walked away, watching out of the corner of his eye as all five men pulled down their poncho hooches. Boccia went back to his platoon and for the rest of the day prayed for rain.

About an hour after he returned to his CP, Honeycutt got a call from the intelligence shop at brigade with some information he had been expecting for the last six days. According to Captain Frederick, the S-2, the unit on Dong Ap Bia had now been positively identified as the 29th NVA Regiment. The intelligence people had not been able to tell exactly how much of the regiment was on the mountain, though they suspected as many as two battalions, each with around six hundred men.

The 29th, one of six enemy regiments operating in I Corps, was considered one of the enemy's best, an elite unit, fully equipped with heavy weapons and a full array of support groups and logistic capabilities. The 29th had fought at Hue during the 1968 Tet Offensive, where they had more than proven their mettle in a number of savage encounters with the 1st Cavalry.

For Honeycutt the information codified what he had known all along, which is that his single battalion was considerably outnumbered by the enemy force on Dong Ap Bia. It did not, unfortunately, make the job ahead any easier. A few minutes after dark, Honeycutt got another call from brigade, this time from Major Montgomery, the operations officer. Although the 1/506th's attacking companies were still five hundred meters from Hill 900 and nearly twice that distance from 937, brigade had decided that they could not afford to postpone their two-battalion assault any longer. Brigade felt—and Honeycutt agreed—that unless both battalions were moving simultaneously, the enemy could easily concentrate his forces against one or the other.

As in the original plan, brigade still wanted Honeycutt to move his two companies forward until they made contact, and then have them continue advancing until they were exerting maximum pressure on the enemy's defenses. They were not, however, to become decisively engaged until the 1/506th was ready to go for the mountain.

And to make sure the 1/506th made it this time, brigade was preparing to throw every resource at its disposal against the mountain. It had already marshaled every available fighter-bomber in the area, and for thirty minutes, starting at 0800 in the morning, they were going to hit the mountain with a deluge of high-drag bombs and napalm, to be quickly followed by sixty minutes of artillery prep. After this hour-and-a-half fire storm, brigade seemed certain that the Currahees would finally be able to initiate a breakout and get their attack on the mountain underway.

Honeycutt wished he could be as confident. "On paper this is a great fucking plan," he told Montgomery. "It's magnificent, and I hope it works. But if you want it to work, you better tell those guys to get their asses in gear and get up here where the lead's flyin' around. I don't believe this shit about how they're being held up by trail watchers. This is where the fuckin' fight is, and this is where they ought to be. But if they don't make it tomorrow and our ass is pinned to that mountain, we're gonna be in a world of hurt. You gotta let me know the minute they can't make it so we can either assault the mountain alone or get the fuck out of there."

"Don't worry, we'll let you know as soon as there's any problem."

Honeycutt wanted badly to believe that the 1/506th would be able to move up quickly enough to take part in the assault in the morning, but try as he might, he could not. Short of a miracle, it just was not possible, and he was not a man who placed much faith in miracles, especially on a battlefield. And if they did not make it on time, then he realized he had better quickly acclimatize himself to the fact that his single battalion was once again going to have to go up against the 29th NVA Regiment alone. It was not a conclusion he relished, but given the facts, it was the only one available.

Having to face the guns of the 29th NVA Regiment in the morning was not something that Captain Sanders relished either. When he discovered at the briefing a short time later that the attack was definitely "on" for the next day, he was overcome with a feeling of total hopelessness.

He hurried back to Delta's NDP and slumped down on a log in the center of his CP. Lt. Thomas Lipscomb, his 3d Platoon leader came over and knelt down beside him.

"What's the deal for tomorrow?"

"We're going up."

"No shit?"

"Yep."

"What do you think?"

"I think the whole idea sucks. You just can't attack over open ground against machine guns. That sort of shit went out with World War I at the Battle of Verdun. That's the way I feel right now—like some soldier getting ready to climb out of a trench and charge across no-man's-land."

"Do you think we got any chance at all of makin' it up there tomorrow?"

"Nope. We ain't got a chance in hell."

"I wonder what would happen if we just refused to make the attack?" Lipscomb asked. "Do you think that would stop it?"

"Nope. Not for a second. It wouldn't change things a bit. All they'd do is fire our asses and bring in two more officers. And if they refused, they'd fire their asses too."

A few minutes later, Sanders met with the rest of his platoon leaders and a few of his senior NCOs. He was again blunt. "According to the plan, we're not supposed to try and take the mountain, but they want us to move up it as far as we can without becoming decisively engaged. That's the plan. I've already reconned the place, and there's no way to do any fancy maneuvers up there. The only way we have a chance to get up that mountain is to piecemeal it. Get a platoon to the left and one to the right and then balls-to-the-wall it. Just rush the bastard. We're gonna have a lot of casualties. That's one thing you can count on. But if somebody gets hit, don't stop for 'em. Do you hear me? Let 'em crawl off on their own. When we start up the face of that mountain, we ain't stoppin' for nothin'."

When Sanders finished his briefing, he was getting ready to walk around and check his perimeter when two soldiers from 1st Platoon approached him.

"Hey, Captain!" one of the men said.

"Yeah. What's the problem?"

"You know what they're callin' this battle, Captain?"

"No. What?"

"Hamburger Hill."

"What?"

"Hamburger Hill."

"Hamburger Hill?"

"Yeah."

"Whose callin' it that?"

"Everybody, Captain. It's all over."

"Why are they callin' it that?" Sanders asked.

"Because they say this mountain turns men into hamburger," the second man said.

CHAPTER 16

ALMOST THERE

Right after first light Honeycutt got a schedule from brigade with an exact sequence of events for the attack.

0800–0830	Airstrike in support of each battalion
0830–0900	Artillery register on the hill
0900–0905	Artillery CS prep
0905–0925	Regular artillery prep
0925	Troops move out

Honeycutt agreed with everything on the schedule except the CS prep, which he thought was nothing but a gimmick and doomed to failure. When he tried to get it canceled, though, he discovered that the plan had come down from division and they were adamant about keeping it in.

Fortunately, the schedule was a flexible one, for things began to go wrong almost immediately. The fighter-bombers arrived 30 minutes late and did not finish their bomb and strafing runs until 0915. After a 20-minute artillery prep, the gas prep did not get started until 0940 and quickly turned into a fiasco. The first volley of rounds missed the registration point on Dong Ap Bia by four hundred meters and landed instead right in Alpha Company's column. A number of men barely escaped being hit in the head by the rounds, and a number of others, whose gas masks had wet filters, were sent to their knees gagging, choking, and vomiting. When the gas finally blew away, a lot of men angrily threw their masks into the draws on each side of the ridge.

The next volley of rounds managed to hit the mountain, but a strong wind blew the gas into Laos. The second artillery prep, however, went in accurately, and at 1025 Alpha and Delta companies pushed out their assault positions. For the first time in the fight, every man in the attacking companies wore a flak jacket and most of the riflemen carried about forty magazines of M16 ammo, and some as many as ten grenades.

On the point for Alpha Company was Lieutenant McGreevy and his 1st Platoon. As he moved up the southern ridge with his men, the lieutenant, like Captain Sanders, felt overwhelmed by a sense of fatalism. He had lost more than a third of his platoon attacking up this same ridge on the fifteenth and was sure it was going to be as bad today. Maybe worse. He had always wondered what a man in the first wave at Normandy during World War II must have felt before he hit the beach, and now he knew. He must have felt the same thing he himself was feeling right now, which was desperation, panic, and a sickening stomach-wrenching certainty that he and most of the men with him were going to be killed or wounded.

The platoon moved rapidly up the ridge, followed closely by the 2d and 3d platoons. For a hundred meters they received nothing but some random and inaccurate sniper fire, but as they neared the mountain, it got heavier and heavier. Most of it was high, however, ripping through the trees above the platoon. The NVA bunkers on the ridge had either been deserted or knocked out by airstrikes and artillery prep, and the platoon moved quickly past them, then down the low saddle up the other side.

At the bottom of the saddle, McGreevy put one squad on-line with two machine guns, then started up the right with another. As soon as he made his move to the right, the enemy directed their fire at the squad. Within seconds a dozen rocket grenades went off around them, and they were soon pinned down by rifle fire.

McGreevy decided to radio Captain Harkins and tell him how heavy the fire was, but could not find his RTO. He searched around frantically for the man and discovered finally that he had not advanced with him, but was still with the squad on-line, huddling behind a log. He yelled for the kid, but could not be heard over the clatter of fire and explosions. In frustration he started back down the mountain after him. About halfway down, he caught a fleeting image of Luc, the company Kit Carson Scout, standing behind a tree and laying down covering fire on the mountain. As he neared Luc, there was suddenly a loud explosion in front of the tree, and McGreevy watched in shock as Luc was blown into the air and down the ridge. It took the lieutenant a few seconds to realize that the former–North Vietnamese soldier had been hit squarely in the chest by the RPG, and a few seconds more to realize that he, too, had been hit by the blast and that he was on the ground, his stomach and chest peppered with shrapnel. Even as fatalistic as he had felt going up, McGreevy still had difficulty believing he was wounded. For some reason it infuriated him. He raised himself up on one hand and, with bullets humming over his head like angry wasps, looked up at the NVA bunkers and yelled as loud as he could, "You sonofabitches! You dirty bastards!"

They were his parting words, for a moment later two medics grabbed his shirt collar and bounced him down the mountain and into the saddle. With him gone, Alpha's first assault stalled where it was.

A few minutes after McGreevy was wounded, Delta Company started its attack. Captain Sanders sent Lieutenant Lipscomb and his 3d Platoon up to lead it, and then with 1st Platoon followed close behind. Lipscomb and his men rushed up the ridge and about thirty meters from the first bunker line spread out into a skirmish line and started advancing forward on their stomachs. They had hardly started their advance when the enemy soldiers began popping out of bunkers, trenches, and spider holes and lashing the line with small-arms fire. Three men in 3d Platoon were quickly wounded, but Lipscomb, from the left side of the line, waved his arm forward, shouting above the clatter of fire, "Let's go! Move up! Let's get these bastards!"

The men moved up in jerks and starts, firing, then rushing forward a few meters, then firing again. The enemy grenaded the line, and three more men were hit. The GIs grenaded back, and a secondary explosion ripped apart one of the enemy trenches. Enemy soldiers jumped up again from spots all over the bunker line and sprayed the advancing Americans with rifle fire. The line, however, kept advancing, slowly closing in on the bunkers. As it got closer, five enemy soldiers panicked and started running up the mountain. Lieutenant Lipscomb spotted them and, with another GI, brought down all five. A second or so later another seven or eight made a break for it, but Pfc. Paul Bellino and two other men dropped them before they had covered five meters. In the center of the bunker line, an enemy soldier was starting to bring his arm back to throw a grenade when someone shot him. The man slipped back into the trench and dropped the grenade. It went off and set off more explosives in the trench.

"Let's go," Lipscomb screamed again. "Move up, everybody!" The line jerked forward again, stopped momentarily, then swept over the enemy bunkers. On the right side of the line, two GIs rushed forward and fragged two bunkers. Others sprayed fire into spider holes and killed three NVA crouching there.

Captain Sanders had now moved up and was following closely behind the skirmish line. Behind him trailed Lieutenant Walden and his platoon. Up ahead, the line had tried to advance past the bunker line, but two claymore blasts wounded three men and sent everyone else behind cover.

"Keep moving," Sanders screamed at Lipscomb.

"They've got claymores all over up here," Lipscomb yelled down. "If we try to move, they'll blow 'em on us."

"You've got to move, claymores or not. Shoot them if you have to, but you've got to get those men up that hill. That's our only chance. If we stay here, they'll kill us all."

Lipscomb nodded and, while three men laid down covering fire, charged a trench line with two other men. He made it about halfway before a grenade exploded at his feet and blew him back down the hill. Two medics rushed to him and pulled him behind a log, but he was already dead. In almost that same instant, Bellino also made a rush forward. When an NVA soldier came out of a trench ahead, Bellino shot the man, then spun to his left and shot another. Bellino was pivoting back to the right when an NVA sniper shot him in the head and killed him.

The attack stalled, and Sanders called down for Lieutenant Walden to move his men up and join the assault. Walden and his men came at a run, pumping their feet to move up the steep slope.

Sanders was directing the men into position when he was shot in the arm. He crawled over to his battalion RTO and honked up Honeycutt. "I'm hit bad, Blackjack. I'm turning over command to Lieutenant Walden."

Walden bent down and took the handset from Sanders and yelled over the din of firing, "Blackjack, if you want me to take this hill, then get some ammo up here to us because we ain't backin' off. No matter what it takes, we're gonna take this sonofabitch."

Walden began moving his men into position. He sent one squad forward to join the skirmish line, then began feeding men into the line piecemeal. When the line started taking enfilading fire from the draw on the left, he ordered Sp.4 Howard Harris and Pfc. Jack Little to set up a machine gun and suppress the fire. When they started receiving fire from the draw on the right, he moved another machine-gun team over on the right flank to stop it. Then with the rest of his men he rushed to the right and extended the line about ten meters into the draw.

The fight was now a wild melee, a slugging match. Firing, the GIs advanced a few meters, then leaped behind logs or into shell and bomb craters. Enemy grenades sailed down on them three or four at a time, and RPGs whooshed over their heads like small, toy airplanes, but they kept moving up.

To Sp.4 Little, the assistant machine-gunner covering the right flank, the scene around him was unreal, dizzying. While Harris fired at the enemy soldiers maneuvering against their left flank out of the draw, Little fed the belts of ammo into the gun and tried to make sense out of the action around him. What is going on? he thought. Is this really happening to me? A moment later, Harris was shot in the side of the neck and slumped over the gun. Little took over the gun and kept pouring fire down into the draw while Pfc. Roy Mathew crawled over and took over as AG.

Little kept firing until Sgt. Joe Bell, his squad leader, yelled for him to move up to the line. It was a struggle going up the mountain. It was like running through an obstacle course. Fallen trees were scattered all over the ridge. He fell three different times on the way up. On the third fall, a stick-handled grenade exploded right beside him. Miraculously he was not hit by any of the shrapnel, but did lose all the hearing in his right ear. He finally reached Sergeant Bell, who told him to place fire on the ridge to their left. He set the gun up on a log and began going after enemy muzzle flashes all over the side of the ridge. He fired in seven- and eight-round bursts, moving the gun back and forth across the ridge. After about five minutes of steady firing, the gun jammed, and he and Mathew could not get it to work again.

He tossed the gun aside and started up the ridge toward his squad. Mathew followed close behind, but a moment later was shot in the throat and killed. Little came across another dead GI about halfway up and took his rifle, bandoleers, and bag of grenades. Then with a final burst he rushed forward and joined the rest of his squad and, like everyone else, began pouring fire on the enemy positions up ahead.

Nearby, Pfc. Steve Korovesis was experiencing the same feeling of unreality as Little, the feeling that he was moving in slow motion through a bad dream. Korovesis had been in Vietnam only a few weeks, and this was his first experience with combat. He had no idea what was going on around him or what he was supposed to do. All he knew was that he was carrying an M79 grenade launcher and with three or four other men was running like crazy behind his squad leader, who seemed to know what he was doing. Korovesis did not know how far they ran up the mountain, but along with everyone else he had to dive for cover to avoid a long burst of machine-gun fire. He ended up in a large bomb crater. He looked to his left to see a man from his squad in a fetal position, cowering in absolute terror, and just to his left was a man who had been shot in the throat. Bullets were hitting everywhere around the bomb crater, and there was a roar of other sounds. Overhead a Cobra was hovering and pouring minigun fire into the top of the mountain.

In the midst of all this fire, Korovesis's squad leader got up on one knee and shouted down, "Throw up the blooper. I've got a line on a bunker."

Korovesis threw up the M79 and a sack of twenty rounds, then watched enthralled as the young sergeant took careful aim and fired an HE round right into the aperture of an enemy bunker. The round exploded inside the bunker with a muffled boom, and the sergeant methodically reloaded and fired again.

Korovesis was getting ready to move up when a stick-handled grenade landed four or five feet away. His heart leaped at the sight of the grenade, but it exploded before he could move. Korovesis felt a burning sensation all along the right side of his body and discovered that he could not see out of his right eye. He did not know yet how badly he was hurt, but he knew one thing for sure, his part in the battle was over. It had lasted less than ten minutes.

The fight was over for Korovesis, but up and down the skirmish line—which twisted around the face of the mountain like a wiggling snake—it raged and roared. Every few seconds a grenade boomed. Salvos of artillery rounds crashed into the top of the mountain with hardly a pause. And dominating all the sounds was the constant crackle of rifle fire, punctuated periodically by the thunkboom of grenade launchers and the crackboom of recoilless rifles.

On the right flank of Delta's line, Lieutenant Walden moved up and down behind his men urging them on. His men responded, and the line pushed forward another five or ten meters. About 1115, however, they started taking enfilading fire from a heavy machine-gun position below the military crest of the mountain and in between the two ridges.

Braving the fire, two soldiers tried to rush forward to another position, but one was cut down after covering only a few meters. Seeing the man fall, Pfc. Willie Kirkland, 1st Platoon's medic, rushed out to help the wounded man, but was hit himself five times in the chest.

While Pfc. Rodger Murray laid covering fire on the position, Sgt. Tom McGall, a squad leader, and his RTO, Pfc. Michael Rocklen, ran up together and pulled Kirkland back down into a deep bomb crater. There another medic worked frantically to save Kirkland, only to have him die a few minutes later.

Rocklen crawled back up the mountain until he could clearly see the enemy position, then took out his compass and shot an azimuth on it. He radioed a circling FAC plane and gave him the information. A Skyraider appeared a moment later and, guided by a smoke grenade Rocklen used to mark his own position, skimmed across the face of the mountain and laid two napalm bombs right on the enemy position, obliterating it and thirty meters of enemy trenches and spider holes with a rolling ball of flames.

On the southern ridge, with their left flank now covered by Delta's advance, Alpha was also beginning to get an attack under way. After Lieutenant McGreevy was wounded, Captain Harkins rushed Lt. Daniel Bresnahan and his 3d Platoon forward, telling them to take up the attack.

They did. Bresnahan maneuvered his platoon on-line, and they started up the 30-degree slope of the mountain. It was a hard fight, but in fifteen minutes they overran the bunkers above the low saddle and killed about ten enemy soldiers, then started another move toward the enemy's second bunker line.

Around noon, Honeycutt radioed Captain Harkins for a situation report on Alpha. "How's it going up there?"

"I think we can make it," Harkins said. "One hundred meters more and we could take this SOB."

When he radioed Lieutenant Walden on Delta's situation, it was the same story. "We're pushin' hard. We've got the bastards on the run."

To Honeycutt the news seemed almost too good to be true, but it was quickly tempered by a report from brigade on the status of the 1/506th, which showed that they had moved only one hundred meters since morning. And then to compound things, he got a call from Bravo Company reporting that a Cobra gunship had shot up one of their platoons while it was en route to Alpha with ammunition. One man was dead and four wounded as a result of less than fifteen seconds of minigun fire.

Honeycutt was instantly on the fire channel with the pilot. "Get the fuck out of the area," he screamed. "Do you hear me? Get out! And I don't wanna see any of you incompetent bastards out here the rest of the fight."

Fortunately for the 3/187th, it did not stop the advance, as it had on the fifteenth. And a few minutes later, Honeycutt got a call from Walden reporting that Delta had just overrun the second bunker line and that they were now only seventy-five meters from the top. The colonel had little time to rejoice, however, for a few minutes later, Walden and his first sergeant, Thomas Stearns, were both wounded by an enemy grenade shower.

With them down, Delta now had over 50 percent casualties, and not a single officer left. They were now, as Honeycutt knew only too well, just a mob of men pinned down on the side of the mountain. And worse, they were running out of ammunition.

Honeycutt radioed the remnants of the company and told them to hold fast and not try to advance any farther and that help was on the way. He then called Captain Johnson and instructed him to move Charlie Company up the ridge, take command of the remainder of Delta, consolidate the position, and continue exerting pressure on the enemy's defenses.

Just as Delta had two hours earlier, every man in Charlie Company put on a flak jacket and loaded himself down with as much ammunition as he could carry. Many riflemen carried as many as one hundred magazines, and grenadiers the same number of grenades. And everyone, medics included, draped himself with as many belts of machine-gun ammo as he could carry.

At 1230 Charlie Company started out from the battalion CP and up the ridge at a fast walk. Behind them was a platoon from Bravo with canteens of water, boxes of grenades, recoilless-rifle rounds, and more bandoleers of M16 magazines.

On the mountain the fight went on. Both Alpha and Delta were hugging the second bunker line, and NVA and GIs were firing and grenading each other only twenty meters apart. Pfc. Michael Smith of Delta's 1st Platoon was in a situation typical of many soldiers in the skirmish line. Smith had started up the mountain with more than seventy rounds for his M79, but had gone through them in less than an hour. When he could not find any more 79 rounds, he picked up a wounded man's M16 and fired more than forty magazines through it, until it finally overheated and started jamming. There was no sense in trying to fix it because there were rifles everywhere, so he picked up another and fired another twenty to thirty magazines, until it also jammed. At the moment, Smith was on his fifth rifle, and it was so hot that he did not have to pull the trigger to fire—the rounds just cooked off by themselves.

While Charlie struggled up the ridge, Honeycutt took off with Crazy Rairdon in an LOH and began hovering over the mountain. Two or three machine guns opened up on them, but Rairdon dodged through the fire. While he zipped back and forth over the mountain, Honeycutt called in an airstrike against some bunkers on the military crest of the mountain and then adjusted mortar and artillery fire against some trenches above Delta.

In the meantime, Charlie Company and the platoon from Bravo had covered the distance from the battalion CP to the saddle below the knoll and were now pushing hard toward Delta's rear with the much-needed ammunition.

"We need that ammunition bad," a sergeant in Delta radioed Honeycutt. "Tell 'em to hurry."

"They're comin'," Honeycutt said.

And they were indeed, moving as quickly up the ridge as could be expected in the 100-degree heat. But when they were about sixty meters from Delta's rear and just coming out of the jungle, a dozen enemy positions opened up on them with a rain of machine-gun fire, and the column ground to a halt.

Honeycutt told Rairdon to drop his LOH down right over the column, then radioed Captain Johnson. "Why aren't you moving?"

"We're pinned down. We're taking heavy fire from our left and right."

"Spread those men out and get them moving. You can't just sit there. Delta's running out of ammunition, and you've got to get up there to them right now."

The captain did as he was told, broke the column into smaller groups and spread the men out in staggered lines across the ridge. When they tried to move once again, enemy fire raked the ridge and drove the men to cover.

"What's the problem now?"

"We still can't move. The fire is just too heavy."

Finally Honeycutt exploded, "Damnit, you get those men moving up that mountain! Are you listening to me? You're being paid to fight this war, not discuss it on the radio!"

A few minutes later, Charlie Company started advancing again, but Honeycutt now had a call from Captain Harkins, who said he was receiving heavy fire from the ridge on his left.

"You can't be," Honeycutt told him. "That's where the 506th is."

"I know what I see, boss."

Honeycutt and Rairdon turned the ship south. They zipped across the draw and were soon over the ridge. He thought possibly some people from the 506th were mistakenly shooting at Harkins's men, thinking they were NVA. He discovered instead that the ridge was swarming with enemy soldiers. A number of them opened up on the ship with their AKs and riddled its tail before Rairdon pulled sharply away.

Honeycutt called brigade and asked, "Where's the 506th? I thought those guys were on the ridge south of my Alpha Company?"

Brigade radioed back Bravo 1/506th's coordinates, which should have put them somewhere northeast of Hill 916, the area he and Rairdon had just taken fire from. "They can't be there," Honeycutt said. "That entire area is swarming with gooks."

Honeycutt finally honked up Bravo 1/506th himself. "Where in the hell are you guys?"

They gave their coordinates, but he still could not locate them in the area. "Mark your position with a smoke grenade," he said. When Honeycutt finally located the smoke, it was two hundred to three hundred meters from Bravo's reported position. "You fuckers ain't nowhere near where you think you are," he told them.

* * *

There was a good reason, however, for Bravo 1/506th's confusion. Only an hour earlier they had been advancing rapidly up the ridge overlooking Captain Harkins's column, but about 1130 their lead platoon stumbled into a huge enemy ambush. In a matter of minutes, the platoon had twenty casualties and fled in disarray and confusion back down the ridge about two hundred meters. There the company formed a hurried perimeter to protect the wounded, then beat off a swift enemy counterattack which came at them from four different directions.

The news was not as bad from Alpha 1/506th, though hardly encouraging. They had managed to get up the saddle to the edge of Hill 900, but were at the moment pinned down by a large enemy force in bunkers on the south side of 900. The Currahees' Charlie Company was not even moving toward Dong Ap Bia, but cleaning out some enemy bunkers on the south side of Hill 800.

To Honeycutt the conclusion was again inescapable: the 1/506th was not going to make it, short of some miracle. And here he had two of his companies eyeball to eyeball with the enemy and another moving quickly into position to join them. He knew only too well what would happen if he tried to pull all three companies back now when they were so close to the top of the mountain. As soon as the withdrawal started, the NVA would launch a big counterattack and chop them up.

He felt there was really only one logical decision to make at this point, and he made it. "We're not gonna hold anymore," he told Harkins and Johnson. "Fuck it! We're gonna continue the attack. I'm not gonna turn tail and have you all shot in the back. We're gonna push those bastards off that hill!"

Honeycutt was certain with Johnson's reinforcements moving up that he could take the hill, but he was not certain he could hold it. There was no doubt in his mind that the NVA would launch a counterattack during the night and try to retake it, a counterattack he may not be able to stop with three understrength companies.

He needed reinforcements, and he needed them immediately. "I need some people out here," he told Major Montgomery over the brigade net. "But don't send me any individual replacements, because I don't have the command structure to integrate them. I need an entire unit."

"You'll have a new company out there before the day's over," Montgomery said. "We'll have them moving in ten minutes."

* * *

When Captain Johnson finally reached what was left of Delta Company, he sent a platoon over to help with the wounded and stabilize the position, then spread the rest of his men out toward the left, extending the skirmish line another twenty to thirty meters.

Honeycutt watched the maneuver from the LOH. "Start maneuvering some men up that small finger on the left," he told Johnson at one point.

"There's too much fire up there," Johnson said.

"Do what I told you," Honeycutt said. "Do it now."

Johnson called over Lieutenant Trautman and pointed up the small finger. "Blackjack wants us to get a flanking attack up the left side. See that little finger up there? I want you to take a squad up there and secure it."

Trautman looked at his CO incredulously. "Are you crazy? That's suicide."

"Goddamnit, do what I told you. Blackjack is on my ass. Get going!"

Trautman crawled to his left behind Sgt. Tom Valentine, his best squad leader. Valentine was behind a huge fallen tree and, like everyone else on the line, was rising up every few seconds, letting loose with a burst of M16 fire, then dropping behind cover again. Enemy bullets were thudding continuously into the log and throwing up showers of bark and wood splinters. Trautman grabbed Valentine's shoulder, and as he did, two grenades went off in front of them, showering them with mud and gravel. "Val, grab about five or six men and assault the hill up that finger on the left."

"Are you kidding?"

"No. It's gotta be done."

Valentine yelled out the names of five men, and they crawled over behind the log. When he told them the mission, all five protested angrily.

"I ain't goin' up there!" one soldier said.

"Bullshit!" another yelled.

"You gotta go," Trautman said.

"The fuck I do," the first man said.

"That's right," yet another said.

Trautman looked at all five men and realized that they were not bluffing and that they were indeed not going to go—and, strangely, he did not blame them. Not one bit. But, still, the mission had to be carried out. He did not have a choice in the matter.

Finally, he said, "Look, damnit, if I go with you, will you go?"

"If you'll lead us, I'll go," the first man said.

"Yeah," another said.

"What about the rest of you?"

"I'll go, if you'll go," still another said.

Trautman turned to the last two. "And what about you guys?"

"Okay," one said, and the other nodded his head.

"Come on, follow me," Trautman said. "Val, lay down covering fire." Trautman moved to the left about ten meters, then, pumping his legs like a sprinter, started up the 30-degree slope, leaping over logs when he came to them, dodging around tree stumps and rocks, jumping over shell craters, and skirting the edge of the huge 1,000-pound bomb craters. Up ahead he could see the crest of the mountain less than one hundred meters away, but it seemed like miles. Bullets hummed in a steady stream over his head, and others stitched the ground around him. Two or three times in twenty meters he dived into bomb craters to avoid being hit, but was up in seconds and running again, thinking: Am I really doing this? Every few seconds, he looked back to see if the men were still following him and was surprised each time to see that they were. He kept running, and the meters clicked through his mind, ten, twenty, thirty. Up ahead the mountain loomed closer and closer. We're going to make it, he thought. I can't believe it, but we're going to make it. And then suddenly he heard a dull thud and looked back to see that the men behind him had stopped, that they were huddling around someone.

"Crutts is hit in the stomach," someone yelled.

Trautman was taking a step back toward the men when a machine-gun bullet hit him in the left thigh. The force of the bullet spun him around, and he tumbled into a pile of leaves and debris and passed out.

He was unconscious about fifteen minutes. When he came to, it was to a dull, throbbing pain and the sight of his left leg covered with blood. The leg was turned under his body, and when he straightened it out, an excruciating pain shot up through his hip. He gasped at the pain and stifled a scream, thinking: I'm going into shock. I've got to fight it off. I've got to have help! I've got to get out of here.

He craned his neck in all directions looking for his men, but could not see them anywhere. Where were they? He looked again, but still could not see them. My God! he thought finally, they've left me behind. The realization brought a surge of panic, and again he felt himself slipping into shock. He fumbled in his shirt pocket for a cigarette, then lit it and inhaled deeply. The smoke was slightly nauseating, but it calmed him. He turned so he was facing the mountain and straightened out his legs. With his hand he felt the wound and to his relief discovered that it had stopped bleeding. To his rear and to the left about thirty to fifty meters he could see the skirmish line.

"Help me!" he screamed at the men, waving his arms. "Over here. Somebody help me."

No one seemed to hear him, though, and so he screamed louder. This time two men seemed to look in his direction for a moment, but then turned away again. They were looking right at me, he thought. Right at me! He yelled yet again, but this time no one even turned his way.

Around him the firing continued, a wild roar of explosions and a clatter of rifle and machine-gun fire. Overhead artillery rounds were slamming without stopping into the enemy bunker line with a whooshbang! whooshbang! The artillery stopped for a moment, and a fighter-bomber dived down and hosed the top of the mountain with cannon fire.

Trautman craned his neck on the military crest of the mountain and caught a fleeting glimpse of an enemy soldier throwing a grenade, then ducking into cover again. A second later, he rose and threw another.

He looked back down the mountain and once more screamed, "Help me! Over here! Somebody help me!"

The screaming, coupled with the loss of blood, left him exhausted, and he slumped back against the slope of the mountain. He tried to fight off a creeping feeling of despair, but could not. He finally found himself thinking the unthinkable: I'm going to die. I'm going to be left up here, and I'm going to die. The attack will fail, and everyone will pull back down off the mountain, and I'll be up here all by myself. With nightfall, the NVA will come down off the mountain looking for bodies, and they'll find me, and that will be the end. It would be nice to think they might take me alive, but they wouldn't. What would they want with a badly wounded American? They'd have no place to put me, even if they wanted a prisoner, and they wouldn't. After what they've been through up here—after all the casualties they've suffered— there's no way they would have any sympathy for me. No way in hell!

With death now looming as a certainty, Trautman found that he was not afraid any longer. Still, even though he did not feel fear for himself, he did for his wife and new baby. His death would leave them without support, and that frightened him much more than the thought of three or four NVA regulars pumping bullets into his body. He closed his eyes and prayed silently: Dear God, please take care of them for me.

He looked around for his rifle and bandoleers and finally located them in some trampled elephant grass a few meters to his right. They were too far to reach, so he used a stick to pull them over to him. He laid the rifle in his lap and counted his magazines. There were twenty-four of them. He took five of them out of their cloth pockets and laid them in his lap for quick access and thought: Well, they'll probably kill me, but a lot of them will die before I do.

Overhead, Honeycutt was still hovering in the LOH with Crazy Rairdon, flying back and forth across the west side of the mountain, calling in airstrikes, adjusting artillery and mortar fire, giving instructions to Johnson and Harkins.

"Can you take the sonofabitch?" he asked Harkins a little after noon.

"Seventy-five meters and it's ours, boss," Harkins said.

Honeycutt honked up Johnson next. "How's it going?"

"I've got things stabilized. We're pushing again."

"Can you make it?"

"Yeah, we can do it."

Honeycutt instructed Rairdon to fly him back to the battalion LZ. He was certain now that his three companies were going to top the mountain, and when they did, he wanted to be there to personally control the final push. When he reached his CP, he picked up his CAR15 rifle, threw a bandoleer of magazines over his shoulder, and stuffed his fatigue shirt pockets with grenades. Then he called over Major Collier and his three RTOs and told them to get their personal weapons and follow him.

Honeycutt led them at a quick pace, almost at a run. So many men had moved up and down the trail since Lieutenant Denholm's ill-fated assault on the eleventh that it was now more than ten feet wide in spots. The jungle over the top, however, was still intact, and the air underneath thick and oppressive.

It took them about thirty minutes to cover the nearly six hundred meters to Bravo's old LZ, which was filled with wounded. Honeycutt stopped for a few moments to talk with some of the men, then pushed on up the ridge. When they were about one hundred meters past the LZ, the air started becoming misty and cool. Honeycutt stopped the column and looked around suspiciously. The colonel found himself inexplicably overcome with a premonition that something terrible was about to happen, but he could not translate the feeling into any kind of logical thought.

What was wrong?

He looked back down the trail toward the LZ and thought: What am I worried about? My rear is covered. What possibly could go wrong?

He was about to start out again when one of his RTOs shouted, "Get down!"

Honeycutt hit the dirt and looked up right at a pith helmet on the right side of the trail. Then he saw the AK pointed at his chest and heard the dull bap-bap-bap as it fired. He raised his CAR15 at the same moment and squeezed off a long burst, then watched the NVA soldier flung backwards by the blast. But a second later, he was himself rocked by two or three grenade explosions. He kept from falling, but saw Collier sprawled out on the trail, knocked senseless. The colonel looked to the right just as two NVA were coming up out of the draw. He emptied his magazine, and both went down, but before he could reload, three or four more came charging out of the draw. In a second Collier was on his feet and with the three RTOs also started firing. Their first bursts brought down three more NVA.

Honeycutt thought: We can't let them get out of the draw. He charged forward firing, and the three RTOs and Collier came on a step behind. Four or five were coming up out of the draw at the very moment. Seeing the five charging Americans, they turned around and started back down. When Honeycutt got to the edge of the draw, he stopped, took careful aim and shot three or four more of the retreating enemy in the back, then watched as the three RTOs and Collier send a fusillade of automatic M16 fire into three or four more.

Honeycutt did not feel the slightest remorse over killing the men because he knew what the intentions of the enemy soldiers had been—to shoot the few men guarding the LZ, then move through it and slaughter the wounded as they lay helpless on the ground.

After sending an RTO back to warn the men guarding the LZ to be on their toes and after making certain the NVA were not going to come out of the draw, Honeycutt started up the trail again. He had not moved more than fifty meters before a huge gust of wind ripped through the jungle canopy. It was followed by another, then another, each stronger than the first. Through holes in the canopy he could see thick clouds swirling and thickening, slowly blotting out the sun. A moment later, lightning struck, exploding across the sky like a series of 1,000-pound bombs, and a wall of water came crashing down.

On the mountain all the shooting stopped instantly. Visibility dropped to zero, and the men in the three assaulting companies pulled out their ponchos as quickly as they could and huddled under them.

"Hold in place until the rain stops," Honeycutt told Harkins, "and then continue the attack."

But the rain did not stop, or even slow. Fifteen minutes passed, and then twenty, and still it continued, falling from the sky in sheets, filling bomb and shell craters to the top, roaring down the west side of the mountain in flash floods six to twelve inches deep.

"Can you advance in this shit?" Honeycutt asked Harkins.

"No way, boss. Guys are up to their butts in mud. They can barely move. In some places the mud is three feet deep."

"Can you dig in and hold?"

"Yeah, we can do that. But we're gonna have to have some reinforcements up here before long."

The facts hit Honeycutt like a club. Reinforcements were on the way, but if the companies could not advance in the mud, how could he expect fresh troops, overloaded with ammunition and supplies, to slog their way to the top of the mountain through knee-deep mud, under fire every inch of the way. The answer was simple: he could not. It was impossible. They would never make it, or if they did, they would suffer so many casualties on the way up that he would be forced to detail entire platoons of stretcher bearers to deal with them. The only other option was to have the three companies dig in and try to hold until morning, but to Honeycutt that was even worse. With nightfall, the NVA could easily concentrate all their forces along the west side of Dong Ap Bia and charge down on his men with a vengeance. Exhausted from fighting all day in the 100-degree heat, low on water, and nearly out of ammunition, they simply could not beat off more than two or three assaults before they would be either overrun or forced into a chaotic retreat down the mountain in the middle of the night.

After coming so close to taking the mountain, just the thought of ordering a withdrawal infuriated Honeycutt. Yet it had to be done. There simply was no other alternative. After clearing it with Colonel Conmy, he ordered it started at 1432.

As Honeycutt ordered, Alpha Company held its position below the second bunker line and kept a steady stream of fire on the mountain while Charlie and Delta started pulling back. The withdrawal was orderly, but the fight was hardly over. The NVA had snipers in trees all along the ridge to the northeast of the main ridge, and they pecked away at the mud-caked, weary men with deadly accuracy.

The men of Charlie and Delta fought back angrily. Recoilless-rifle teams took up positions along the ridge, and when they spotted an enemy muzzle flash, they blasted the top of the tree with HE rounds. Grenadiers did the same, pumping round after round into the treetops, and one by one the snipers began crashing to the ground.

By 1530, with the rain just a hard drizzle and most of Delta and Charlie down, Alpha started its withdrawal. They did not have to endure any sniper fire, but as the last platoon was pulling down through the saddle, a platoon or better of NVA charged down out of the second bunker line and launched a hard counterattack. Seeing them, Harkins took personal command of the last platoon and rushed them back into positions facing the mountain and met the attacking enemy with a volley of rifle and machine-gun fire, killing a number of enemy soldiers and driving the rest back up the mountain.

Still on the mountain, Lieutenant Trautman watched the withdrawal with a sinking feeling in the pit of his stomach. For the past thirty minutes he had been furiously screaming, trying to get someone's attention before everyone pulled back off the mountain, but again he had had no luck. Now there were just a few men visible below, and he decided to give it one more try. "Over here!" he screamed. "Somebody help me! Please help me!" Exhausted, he slumped back against the mountain and closed his eyes. It's no use, he thought. They're going to leave me behind.

Trautman was wrong. Seventy-five meters southwest of where he sat, five or six men from Charlie Company had indeed spotted him and at that very moment were trying to figure out what to do about him.

"I need some volunteers to go up after the guy," a young sergeant said. "Who wants to volunteer?"

One man bristled at the suggestion. "Are you crazy, Sarge? You ain't getting me up there."

"You wouldn't get ten yards; they'd blow your shit away," another man said.

"Somebody's gotta do it," the sergeant said. "We can't just leave the dude up there."

"I can," the first man said.

The sergeant turned to Sp.4 Leonel Mata. "What about you?"

"I'm on the machine gun. I can't go."

"Okay, but somebody's gotta go."

"I'll go," Pfc. Edward Merjil said.

"Me too," another soldier said.

While Mata laid down covering fire, the three men dashed up the hill, with enemy bullets tracking them all the way. Three or four times they were driven into water-filled craters by the fire, but started forward again, drenched and muddy. They crawled for a while when the fire became too heavy, then ran, then crawled again. By the time they reached Trautman, all three were caked with mud from head to foot.

Huddling over the lieutenant, with bullets splatting in the mud around them, they wasted no time on amenities. Working quickly, they straightened Trautman's leg and splinted it with the lieutenant's M16 rifle and three cloth bandoleers. Then the sergeant and Merjil grabbed Trautman's shirt collar and took off down the mountain, dragging him behind them like a sack of potatoes. Trautman howled like a banshee at the pain, though anything was preferable to spending a night on Dong Ap Bia.

At the bottom of the saddle, Captain Harkins was supervising the last stages of the withdrawal for Alpha. When he was positive that all his dead and wounded were accounted for, he moved down through the saddle and came up the draw into Charlie and Delta's rear. There he encountered a platoon sergeant from Delta whom he knew.

"Where's Captain Sanders?" he asked the sergeant.

"They medevacked him out. He was hit in the shoulder, but he's going to be okay. Sergeant Stearns also got hit."

"Are all the wounded out?"

"Yeah."

"Where's the bodies?"

"We left them up there."

"You what?"

The sergeant started to say something, but, seeing the anger on Harkins's face, stopped.

"We stayed up on that mountain for nearly an hour so you could come down in an orderly fashion and bring everybody back, and then you go and leave your dead behind. I don't believe it!"

The sergeant had a sheepish, embarrassed look on his face.

"If you had intended to turn tail and run, I could have brought my company down an hour earlier and saved a lot of my own casualties."

Harkins stepped over to his RTO, snatched up the handset angrily, and honked up Honeycutt, "Guess what, boss?"

"What?"

"Charlie and Delta left some of their KIAs on the hill."

"What?" Honeycutt screamed. "You're shitting."

"I wish I was."

"Go back up and get them then."

"Okay. We'll try."

Harkins went back to his company and organized a number of two- and three-man teams and sent them up the mountain, but forty minutes later they came back without a single body.

"They can't find those kids in the rain," Harkins told Honeycutt. "Nobody knows where they are, and they're takin' heavy fire."

Honeycutt ignored Harkins's suggestion and called Captain Johnson. "Dean, you did a good job up there handling those two companies, and I'm proud of you. I really am. But you get your goddamn ass back up that mountain and bring back those KIAs. Do you hear me?"

"Yes, sir."

"And if you can't do it with your company, I'll send the whole fucking battalion up there. I told you once, and I'm gonna tell you again—we don't leave anybody behind. Now get movin'."

As ordered, Johnson organized more search parties, though it would take until late that night before they located the last of the KIAs and brought them back down the mountain.

Although Honeycutt had requested reinforcements from 3d Brigade and had been assured by Major Montgomery that they would be out shortly, General Zais had refused to okay the request until he had a full update on the present condition of the 3/187th. And their condition, he discovered, was not good. During the day's fighting, Alpha and Charlie companies had lost nine men each, Bravo four, and Delta thirty-nine. Though all the companies had been getting replacements during the battle, most were raw recruits just in from the States or rear-area personnel totally unfamiliar with infantry tactics. The real key to a company's strength was how many veterans they had on their rosters, and in that regard, they were all in bad shape. Since the start of the fight, Alpha and Bravo had each lost nearly 50 percent of the men on their original rosters, and Charlie and Delta nearly 80. To make matters worse, two of the original four company commanders were now casualties, as well as eight of the twelve platoon leaders, not to mention numerous NCOs.

As he states in his confidential memorandum, General Zais took a long, hard look at casualty figures sometime in the late afternoon of the eighteenth and was once again faced with the decision of whether to call off the attack on Dong Ap Bia or order yet another assault. Although he makes no mention of how he arrived at his decision, it must have been one he sweated blood over, as would any commander in his position. Regardless, sometime around three that afternoon, he decided to not only continue the attack, but also to throw in three fresh battalions. Two of the battalions—the 2d Brigade's 2/501st and the ARVN 1st Division's 2/3d—he earmarked to launch their own attacks against the mountain. The third—the 3d Brigade's 2/506th—he designated to completely replace the 3/187th and to take up full responsibilities for the attack from the west. It is not known exactly why Zais decided to replace the Rakkasans at this point, but he must have felt they were finished as a fighting unit. Regardless of his reason, the decision was unknown to Honeycutt, who thought he was merely being reinforced.

Shortly after making these decisions, General Zais flew in the rain to Phu Bai for a scheduled meeting at XXIV Corps Headquarters with Secretary of State William P. Rogers, who was on a fact-finding tour of Vietnam.

At the landing pad at Phu Bai, Zais was greeted by Lt. Gen. Richard Stilwell, the corps commander; then they both hopped in a jeep for the short ride to Stilwell's headquarters. During the ride, Zais mentioned the tough decision he had just had to make, and Stilwell said, "That's exactly the decision I would have expected from you."

Inside Stilwell's quarters, Zais discovered Gen. Creighton Abrams, the commander of all U.S. Forces in Vietnam. Abrams greeted Zais warmly and asked, "How are things going in the A Shau, Mel?"

"General Abe, we're doing well," Zais said, "but it's a hard fight, and I'm taking more casualties than I'd like. I had a tough decision to make about an hour ago, and I decided to reinforce an action where we had been pushed off the top of a hill. I believe it was the right thing to do."

"Nobody in Vietnam knows better what is right for the A Shau than you," Abrams said.

Although Zais would later claim that the decision to continue the fight for Dong Ap Bia was his and his alone, he felt that both Stilwell and Abrams, both his superiors, fully supported it.

After speaking with Abrams, the situation took a bizarre turn for Zais. About thirty minutes later, he had a casual conversation with Samuel D. Berger, the deputy ambassador to Vietnam. During the course of the conversation, he described the fight raging around Dong Ap Bia and then related Honeycutt's contention that the enemy was reinforcing the battle from Laos.

"Why don't you describe this to the secretary of state?" Berger suggested. "I am sure he would be very interested."

Zais did not want to make an issue of the situation around the mountain, but about five minutes later Berger called him into another room to meet Rogers.

"Tell him what you just told me," Berger said.

Zais repeated Honeycutt's contention and was astounded at the reaction he got from Rogers. The secretary of state was not only "shocked" and surprised to hear that the enemy was reinforcing the battlefield from Laos, but also "that they were enjoying sanctuary within a few miles of a pitched battle." The problem was discussed in more detail for another ten to fifteen minutes, after which Rogers, still incredulous, swore that when he got back to the States, he was going to do something to "rectify the situation."

If Rogers was incredulous, Zais was stunned. Try as he might, he could not fathom how the secretary of state could not know what any "well-informed citizen in America" knew, which was that the NVA used Cambodia and Laos as a sanctuary. Apparently Zais never found out, for, shortly after the conversation, he asked to be excused because the fight for Dong Ap Bia "was weighing heavily" upon him and he wanted to return to the area immediately.

About the same time that Zais was departing Phu Bai, Lt. Col. Gene Sherron, the CO of the 2/506th, was hovering in his command and control helicopter over the 3/187th's LZ, waiting for clearance to land. Sherron's Alpha Company was on its way across the A Shau at this very moment, and as soon as Sherron discussed a few things with Honeycutt, he planned on bringing them in to start the process of relieving the 3/187th.

At the moment, however, he was waiting on a bevy of medevacs, one after the other of which was roaring into the LZ, picking up loads of wounded, and then roaring out again. After hovering about thirty minutes, Sherron finally got clearance, and his pilot started the ship down. The LZ was hot. As the ship descended, enemy rifle fire cracked through the treetops. In an attempt to suppress the fire, the men guarding the perimeter around the LZ lashed the surrounding jungle with rifle and machine-gun fire. In order to get out quickly, Sherron's pilot set only one skid down, and the colonel leaped five or six feet to the ground and landed in the knee-deep mud. As the ship was pulling out, an RPG exploded in a tree ten meters away, and the perimeter guards once more cut loose in response.

The path from the LZ to the CP ran right through the center of the positions, and both sides of it were lined with body bags awaiting evacuation. In the drizzling rain, they were a depressing sight, and Sherron decided that they would have to be removed before he brought in his men, for fear of demoralizing them before they even got into the fight.

Sherron found Honeycutt all alone in the center of the CP. Without discussion, Sherron walked up to Honeycutt and told him that he had been ordered to relieve him. Honeycutt looked stunned, but claimed that he did not know anything about being relieved. But when Sherron said he wanted the bodies out before he landed his first men, Honeycutt agreed to take care of it.

Before anything would be done about the bodies, however, General Zais landed on the LZ and hurried over to the CP. Zais told Sherron to get airborne again, then walked over to Honeycutt.

"Is it true I'm being relieved, General?" Honeycutt asked.

"You already talked with Sherron?"

"Yes, sir."

"I take it you don't like it."

"I think it stinks, General."

"Why's that?"

"After all the fighting this battalion has been through, after all the casualties we've taken, if you pull us out now, it will forever be viewed as a disgrace by everyone in the division."

"Do you really think the Rakkasans are in any shape to continue this fight?"

"General, for the next attack I could use a company," Honeycutt said. "One company is all I need. You give me one company, and I can take this sonofabitch tomorrow."

"You think that would be enough?"

"Yes, just one company. That's all I need."

"I don't know . . ."

"General, you've got to remember that we've already been up that sonofabitch twice, and the enemy has yet to throw us off. It was the bombs, the ARA, and the rain that threw us off that hill—not the fucking NVA. If it wasn't for all this ARA crap, we'd have taken that sonofabitch three days ago."

"The ARA has definitely been a problem."

"General, if there is anybody that deserves to take that sonofabitch, it's the Rakkasans—and you know that as well as I do. And there just is no goddamn way in hell I wanna see Sherron and the 2/506th come in here and take that mountain after all we've been through. And if it ain't gonna be that way, then you just better fire my ass right now. Right this minute!"

Zais turned away and walked around the CP for a minute, then came back and faced Honeycutt. "Okay, you can have your company."

"Thank you, General."

Once again hovering over the LZ, Sherron got a call from General Smith, the assistant division commander. Smith told him that there had been a change of plans and that the 2/506th would not be relieving the 3/187th. Sherron was, however, to bring in his Alpha Company and put it under Honeycutt's operational control. Although Sherron was given no reason for the change, he assumed quite correctly that Honeycutt had influenced Zais's decision.

About 1600, while the 3/187th was still pulling back and medevacking out its wounded, the rain let up temporarily and the 1/506th went back on the attack. Unlike the west face of Dong Ap Bia, which the constant bombing and shelling had turned into a giant mud slough, the south face was still covered with jungle, and the infantry had little trouble advancing up it.

Led by its CO, Lieutenant Burney, Alpha 1/506th continued its push up a large ridge straight west toward Hill 900. The company moved with ease for fifty to seventy-five meters, but soon hit another enemy bunker complex. In the initial firefight, Alpha lost two men killed and seven wounded.

Not wanting to risk a costly frontal assault on the bunkers, Lieutenant

Burney ordered Lt. Roger Leisure and Lt. Robert Schmitz to lead their platoons up a draw to the south of the ridge and try to get in behind the bunkers. Once they were above the bunkers, Leisure's job was to set up a defensive perimeter facing Hill 900, while Schmitz and his men swept down on the bunkers from the rear.

The draw had steep sides, and the climb was difficult. To advance, the men in the two platoons had to hold on to small trees and vines and move sideways. Both platoons made the climb, however, in about thirty minutes, and Lieutenant Leisure and his 3d Platoon rushed forward and started setting up their perimeter facing the top of Hill 900. While 3d Platoon got into position, Lieutenant Schmitz sat down on a large rock and told his squad leaders to gather around so he could explain how he wanted to organize the sweep back down the ridge. Schmitz was just spreading his acetate-covered map out on his lap when he thought: God, this is stupid. Here I am sitting in the open, and this mountain is literally crawling with snipers.

The lieutenant got up to move behind a large bush, but had taken only a few steps when an NVA soldier came out of the back of a bunker less than twenty feet away and fired an RPG right at the spot where he had been sitting. The rocket grenade missed him by only a few feet and went off with a fiery boom against a tree behind the rock. Schmitz was knocked off his feet by the concussion, and when he tried getting up found that his left leg was a pincushion of shrapnel.

Without being told, two of Schmitz's men charged the bunker, firing their M16s on automatic. When the NVA soldier ducked back inside, one of the GIs flipped a grenade in the front aperture. The explosion shook the log-and-dirt roof of the bunker, but a second later, the NVA soldier came out the back entrance again and fired off a long burst with his AK. While one GI drove him back into the bunker with rifle fire, another rushed forward and this time threw a grenade into the rear opening. Again the bunker shook from the explosion, but seconds later the enemy soldier was up firing.

Realizing now that the bunker had a grenade sump to absorb the explosion, a GI rushed the bunker and threw in a concussion grenade. The soldier waited a few seconds after the explosion, then crawled into the bunker and pulled the dead NVA soldier out by his shirt collar.

Since he could barely walk himself, Lieutenant Schmitz turned over control of the platoon to his platoon sergeant. He formed the men into a line, and they started down the ridge. Lieutenant Burney's decision

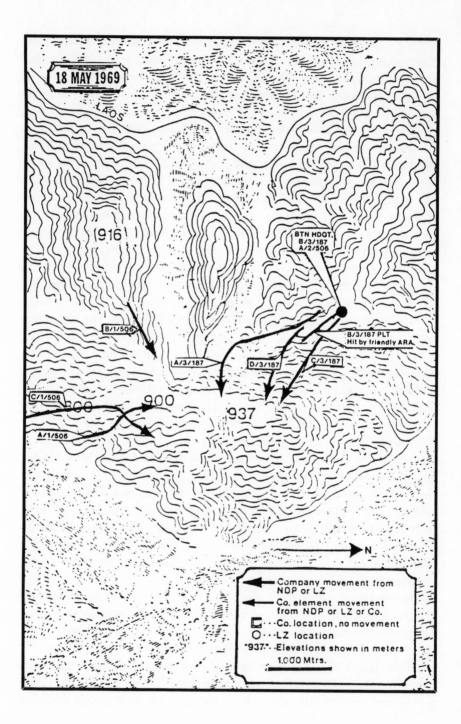

to hit the enemy from the rear proved to be a wise one. There were enemy bunkers, trenches, and spider holes all up and down the ridge, and Schmitz's men had a field day cleaning them out with grenades and rifle fire. Within thirty seconds, they destroyed ten bunkers, killed about fifteen enemy soldiers, and linked up with Lieutenant Burney and the rest of the company.

After the linkup, Lieutenant Burney led the three platoons back up the ridge. About two hundred to three hundred meters from the top of Hill 900, they joined with Lieutenant Leisure and his 3d Platoon, expanded the perimeter, and dug in for the night. As always, however, the NVA only grudgingly gave up the ground. As Lieutenant Dimock, the 2d Platoon leader, was setting out his observation posts, an NVA sniper crept up and shot the lieutenant in the throat, killing him instantly.

While Charlie 1/506th had mostly a quiet day guarding the battalion CP and maneuvering a single platoon near Hill 800, Bravo 1/506th, after losing twenty wounded and two killed in a disastrous early-morning enemy ambush, was still mired in a hard fight and making little progress.

Bravo was, in fact, quickly becoming a demoralized company. They had seized Hill 916 on the fifteenth and for the last four days had been futilely trying to fight their way to the top of Hill 900. They had been attacking through some of the most impenetrable jungle in the northern A Shau, and many men had been fighting in the 100-degree heat for ten to fifteen hours at a time without water because of the inability of chopper pilots to drop supplies through the towering thick canopy.

In the late afternoon, Bravo again tried to mount another attack on Hill 900 but was driven back yet again with five wounded. Because of the heavy fire in the area, they could not use the jungle penetrator to take out their wounded, but instead had to haul them nearly two hundred meters back up the ridge toward Hill 916, where they already had a small one-ship LZ.

For Bravo there was no escaping the bad luck which seemed to stalk them like a predator. At the LZ they evacuated out all the wounded except a young sergeant who had a bad arm wound and had been heavily sedated with morphine. When the last ship arrived for him, it went into a hover about five feet off the ground. With the help of Pfc. Jerry Hoffman, an RTO, the sergeant staggered toward the hovering ship and reached out and grabbed the ship's skid with his good hand. Hoffman was getting ready to give the sergeant a boost up into the ship when an enemy machine gun raked the LZ. Some of the rounds hit the ship's tail, and the pilot panicked and lifted off suddenly. The sergeant was so drugged that he was not even aware that he was still holding on to the skid and went right up with the ship.

A gasp went up from the ten or fifteen men standing around the LZ, and Hoffman screamed into his handset, "There's a man on your skid! There's a man on your skid!"

"What?" the pilot asked.

"I said, there's a man on your skid."

"Oh, Jesus!"

Around the LZ, the men watched in shock as the sergeant, now aware of what was happening, tried vainly to hold on, then dropped two hundred feet to his death. Watching nearby, Pfc. Robin Huard gasped for his breath and felt for a second as if he were actually going into shock. Another man on the edge of the LZ started crying like a baby.

Below the west face of Dong Ap Bia, the 3/187th was still withdrawing at 1800 and in the process of medevacking out the last of the dead and wounded. As they had after the previous assaults, all the casualties were carried down the mountain to Bravo's old LZ on the northwest side of the large saddle. From there, Crazy Rairdon once again started shuttling them in his LOH the seven hundred meters back to the battalion LZ, where they were transferred to the larger Hueys for the trips to the Army hospital at Phu Bai.

As on the fourteenth, Rairdon had to endure enemy antiaircraft fire, intermittent rain showers, gusting mountain winds, and a swirling, ghostly fog. His luck, however, did not hold out this time. After making more than twenty trips, the young pilot was shot through both ankles and forced to crash-land his ship. About thirty minutes later, the fog closed in on the clearing, and the rest of the wounded had to be carried overland to the battalion CP.

For the last hour, the men of Alpha, Charlie, and Delta companies had been coming down off the mountain and drifting back to their NDPs on the southeast side of the saddle. Almost every man was covered with mud and soaked to the skin. They walked like zombies, a stumbling, deliberate, plodding walk. Some wore rain jackets, others huddled under ponchos or pieces of plastic. Most had gotten only two or three hours of sleep a night since the start of the fight, and many men were teetering on the edge of complete physical collapse. On reaching their NDP, some men literally collapsed on the ground, covered themselves with their poncho or poncho liner, and fell into a deep sleep. Others fell asleep sitting against trees or rocks, oblivious to the rain trickling down through the jungle canopy, to the RPGs exploding periodically in the surrounding trees, to the artillery barrages that pummelled Dong Ap Bia without a stop.

But not all the men slept. Many—even those who did not have to go out on listening posts or ambush patrols—did not want to sleep. Angry, frustrated, bitter, they were too strung out to sleep, too pumped up with adrenaline and fear. Instead, they sat around the NDPs with other men and talked. As could well be expected, much of the talk, like the feelings of many men, was angry and bitter.

Numbers of reporters were now all around the mountain, and most were more than eager to hear the men's complaints. Near the battalion CP, Jay Sharbutt, who had earlier bedeviled General Zais, asked Pfc. Anthony Tolle of Bravo Company his impressions of the battle and got a bitter response.

"After all those air and artillery strikes," Tolle said, "those gooks are still in there fighting. All of us are wondering why they just can't pull back and B52 that hill. I've lost a lot of buddies up there. Not many guys can take it much longer."

Later, Sharbutt interviewed a wounded soldier awaiting evacuation at the battalion LZ.

"That damn Blackjack won't stop until he kills every one of us," the man said angrily.

Two days later both those statements would appear in newspaper and magazine articles across the country, becoming in the process the focus for the initial controversy over the battle.

General Zais would later claim to have had the interview with Tolle investigated and discovered that Dong Ap Bia was the young Pfc.'s first experience with combat, which explained why he was so "emotionally distraught." In fact, Tolle had been in Vietnam eight months at the time and had seen combat numerous times. All of this is beside the point, for Tolle was hardly the only man disgruntled and angry that evening.

At Charlie Company's NDP later that night, Pfc. Michael Jones talked with numerous men who were threatening not to make another assault. After a while the threats became so blatant that one of the company's senior NCOs started walking around the NDP with a notebook and pencil, saying over and over again, "Anybody who's going to refuse to go up again, I want you to sign right here. Come on now—just sign right here."

No one signed the paper. Like Jones, everyone assumed that you would be signing your court-martial papers.

Nearby, in Alpha Company's NDP, men were making similar threats. Around ten that night, Sgt. Tim Ard, a squad leader in the 3d Platoon, had a soldier come up to him and announce categorically, "I ain't goin' up that sonofabitch again."

"If you don't go up, you'll go to LBJ," Ard said, referring to the tough Army stockade at Long Binh, referred to by most soldiers as Long Binh Jail.

"Ain't nobody getting killed in LBJ," the soldier answered back.

Ard did not want his name associated with anyone court-martialed for mutiny, and so as soon as one of his men made a similar threat, he said matter-of-factly, "If you don't go up, you go to jail. It's as simple as that."

Sergeant Ard's CO, Captain Harkins, also got wind of the grumbling at about the same time. He was sitting down having a cup of coffee near his CP when Lt. Daniel Bresnahan, his 3d Platoon leader, approached him.

"Sir, we got a problem," Bresnahan said.

"What is it?"

"We have three kids who say they're not going back up that hill."

"Bring them over here. I want to talk with them."

"Yes, sir."

Bresnahan returned with the men a few minutes later. All three had embarrassed sheepish looks on their faces. Harkins had them all sit down, then poured each of them a cup of coffee.

"Now what's the problem?" Harkins asked.

"Sir, we don't wanna go back up that hill," one of the soldiers said.

"That's right, sir," a second said.

"Why don't we just use B52s on the hill?" the third asked.

"Yeah," the first cut in. "And where's the other battalion? How come they're not here to help us? How come we have to attack the hill all alone?"

"There's other battalions on their way to help us right now."

"When are they gonna get here?" the second said.

"They're on their way. They'll get here tomorrow."

"I'm scared, sir," the third said.

"So am I," Harkins said. "Everybody out here's scared. Only a fool wouldn't be scared of going up that mountain again. Only an idiot. But we're soldiers, and our job is to do what we're ordered to do. And if we're ordered to go back up that hill, then that's what we're going to do."

Honeycutt was very much aware of the grumblings going on around him, though he was not bothered by them. If he had been a grunt, he knew that he likewise would have been angry over being ordered to attack Dong Ap Bia. Nobody liked to be put in a situation where he might be killed or wounded, and he knew that there were many soldiers who hated him for pushing these attacks.

To Honeycutt the rifleman in combat was nothing but a ball of frustration and anger. Everything came down on him, and no matter how well you planned an attack, he was still the guy who had to pick up a rifle and go out and kill someone—or be killed himself. To think that he liked the man who ordered him to do so was absurd. But, then again, he was not out here to win a popularity contest, but to do what General Zais had ordered him to do, which was to take Dong Ap Bia.

CHAPTER 17

REINFORCEMENTS ARRIVE

Rain fell intermittently the rest of the evening, then right after nightfall, the mountain was once again rocked by a wild thunderstorm. It stopped quickly, however, and then a cold drizzling rain again set in. It stopped raining completely just before midnight, and over the battalion LZ, the drifting fog lifted momentarily.

With this break in the weather, Major Montgomery flew out to the battalion LZ to discuss with Honeycutt a plan brigade had worked up for a four-battalion assault on the twentieth. The attack had originally been planned for the next morning, but had to be moved back a day in order to insure that the two fresh battalions and the 1/506th could get close enough to the mountain to have a bearing on the battle. Except for an attack by the 2/501st from the northeast and the 2/3 ARVN from the southeast, few of the specifics of the plan brigade had put together on the fifteenth had been changed. Montgomery still wanted the 3/187th to again move as far as it could up the west face of the mountain, then fix the enemy in place while the other three battalions overran it. When Montgomery finished laying out the plan, he asked Honeycutt's opinion.

"You want my honest opinion?"

"Yes."

"Are you sure?"

"That's what I came out here for."

241

"I don't like it."

"For what reasons?"

"Because we ain't goin' through that fix-the-enemy-in-place routine again. The next time we get to the top of that mountain, we're gonna take the sonofabitch. If the 506th gets there, that's fine. And if the 2/501st gets there, it'll be great. And if the ARVN get there, I'll be fucking thrilled. But we ain't gonna sit there like today and get our asses shot off waiting for them."

Montgomery agreed to change the plan to include the 3/187th in the attack plan, then asked, "Is there anything else you need for the twentieth?"

"The only thing I need is for those other battalions to get involved in this fight."

When Montgomery left, Honeycutt went back to monitoring his companies. With most of the men completely exhausted after the day's fight, he suspected that the NVA might launch a ground attack against one or more of the NDPs. As a result, he had all his companies on a 50-percent alert during the night. While the NVA did not launch any attacks, they were on the move all night shuttling ammunition, supplies, and fresh troops up to the mountain from their base areas in Laos. Aware of this movement, brigade brought a Shadow gunship out about one in the morning, and it began hosing down suspected enemy trails with long bursts of minigun fire. About 0200, the gunship hit what was likely an ammunition-carrying party near the Trung Pham River, setting off two giant secondary explosions. After the initial explosion, a fire started and ammunition cooked off for the next thirty minutes. The NVA had numerous other trails, however. Undaunted, they continued resupplying and reinforcing the mountain the rest of the night.

In the early morning hours, the first of seven sets of fighters began softening up the east side of Dong Ap Bia, the area the ARVN and the 2/501st would be attacking on the twentieth. The fighter-bombers went at the east side with Snake and Nape, a combination of high-drag bombs and napalm. Between each airstrike, the artillery batteries at Firebases Airborne, Bradley, Currahee, Cannon, and Berchtesgaden kept a concentrated fire on the area.

While the first airstrike was ending, the 2/3 ARVN moved by Chinook from Hue to its staging area at Firebase Currahee. From there, the South Vietnamese troops moved by lift-ships into a two-ship landing zone one thousand meters southeast of Dong Ap Bia. After landing, the four hundred men moved quickly northwest up a large ridge and got into their assault positions five hundred meters from the crest of Hill 900.

Simultaneous with the ARVN move, three companies from the 2/501st were picked up by lift-ships at Firebase Airborne and CA'd into a landing zone eight hundred meters northeast of Dong Ap Bia. They soon closed the gap another four hundred meters and took up assault positions in a small river valley at the base of Hill 937.

About this same time, Honeycutt called his commanders to the battalion CP in order to give them a final briefing for the attack on the twentieth. When they arrived, he introduced them to Capt. Bill Womble, the CO of Alpha 2/506th, the company now under Honeycutt's operational control. After the introduction, he took them all up in his C and C ship for a visual reconnaissance of the mountain and their assault positions.

Once back at the CP, he had everyone sit down, then had Major Collier lay out for them the specific details of the plan. As before, the main thrust of the Rakkasan attack would be against the western face of the mountain, with Charlie Company attacking up the main ridge and Alpha up the large southern one. In order to suppress the enemy fire that had raked Charlie and Delta's left flank on the eighteenth, Collier's plan called for Captain Womble to swing to the left and attack into the trees on the northern face of Hill 937, the same area where Lieutenant Trautman had gotten stranded on the eighteenth.

"Okay, boys," Honeycutt said once Collier finished, "you know as well as I do what it's gonna be like tomorrow. I don't need to kid you—it's gonna be a sonofabitch. You know it, and I know it. But tomorrow we're gonna take that fuckin' hill—and that's final! No ifs and buts about it. Now . . . I want you to listen to what I'm sayin' here and listen good. If any of you don't think you can command your company in the kind of fighting we'll be facing tomorrow—or if any of your officers or NCOs can't command their platoons—I wanna hear about it right now. Right now! Right this minute! Because tomorrow I don't wanna hear any shit over the radio about how you're running into this or you're running into that and you can't advance. Because if I do, I'm gonna jump square in your shit, and I'm gonna move you out of that company before you can blink an eye."

Honeycutt looked Capt. Butch Chappel, Bravo's CO, in the eye. "What about you? Can you handle it tomorrow?"

"No problem, sir."

"Are you sure?"

"Yes, sir, positive."

"What about you, Harkins?"

"No problem, boss."

"And what about you, Johnson? Am I gonna have any problems with you tomorrow?"

"No, sir."

On the southern side of Dong Ap Bia, the 1/506th went back on the attack. Their Alpha Company led the way. At 1030, they moved out of their NDP on the southern edge of Hill 900 and started pushing for the peak. Lieutenant Leisure's 3d Platoon took the point and almost immediately ran into two heavily fortified bunkers flanking the ridge. Airstrikes were called in, and a direct hit from a napalm bomb knocked out one of the bunkers and incinerated the two NVA inside. When another airstrike failed to take out the second bunker, a squad from 3d Platoon maneuvered against it and knocked it out with a recoilless rifle, killing three NVA inside.

The 3d Platoon moved up and overran the two destroyed bunkers, but when they started higher up the ridge, they ran into the most intense fire they had encountered since the start of the battle. The NVA had the ground below the peak of Hill 900 covered with bunkers and interconnecting trenches, and Alpha found themselves caught in a hail of machine-gun fire and RPGs. In the first volley, Alpha suffered five wounded, but quickly countered by calling in another napalm strike. Behind the napalm, Alpha started advancing in three columns up the ridge and started the slow process of cleaning out the bunkers. Alpha's men went at the deadly work with recoilless rifles, grenades, rifles, and pistols. In all, it took three hours to clear the ridge. During that time, they destroyed twenty bunkers and killed over fifteen NVA, at the cost of nineteen wounded of their own.

When the last bunkers were cleared, Alpha moved onto the top of Hill 900. There, in a sharp firefight, they killed six more enemy soldiers and routed ten more guarding a large command bunker. The bunker—probably a battalion headquarters—was equipped with field telephones, detailed maps of the mountain and northern A Shau, and large quantities of ammunition.

Alpha consolidated their position around the command bunker, but when they tried to mount another attack toward Hill 937, they were once again pinned down by fire from a large enemy bunker complex. Exhausted after the three-hour fight to the top of Hill 900 and burdened with nineteen wounded, Alpha did not have the energy to mount yet another attack.

Charlie 1/506th, who had been following in Alpha's rear, knocking out any bunkers that had been inadvertently bypassed and collecting all the enemy weapons and ammunition, was ordered by Colonel Bowers to swing to the right and start another move up Hill 900 from the southeast.

After being injured on the tenth, Capt. William Stymiest was in command of Charlie Company again, and he double-timed his men forward in an attempt to get to Alpha's aid as quickly as possible. When Charlie was about 150 meters from Alpha's rear, Stymiest split the company, sending Lt. Ian Shumaker and 3d Platoon up a small finger to the left and Lt. Timothy LeClair and 2d Platoon up a small ridge to the right. Stymiest, with 1st Platoon and the company CP group, followed close behind.

Pfc. Joe King, a squad leader, took the point for 2d Platoon and Pfc. Danny Williams slack. It was about six in the evening when King started the platoon moving. He followed the trail upward slowly and cautiously, his rifle flipped on automatic and pointed straight up the trail, aware that he was almost certainly heading straight for some kind of trouble. Two hundred meters ahead he could hear the furious gunfire around Alpha's position on Hill 900. Through gaps in the jungle canopy, he would occasionally catch glimpses of Cobra gunships zipping by and letting loose with volleys of rockets against enemy bunkers and trenches between Hills 900 and 937. The trail King moved up was open for a while, but soon became choked with bamboo and interwoven with vines. After about fifty meters of the bamboo, the trail opened up again, finally dead-ending at the edge of a small ravine. At the bottom of the ravine was a clear, swift-flowing mountain stream and a small cleared area. About ten meters on the other side of the stream, the ground sloped gradually back up to another ridge.

King stopped about ten meters from the edge of the ravine, then crawled forward on his hands and knees. The trail went down into the streambed, then up the other side—and every inch of it, King could see, was a perfect spot for an ambush!

King sent word back through the column for Sgt. Dan Brinkle, the platoon sergeant, to come forward and have a look.

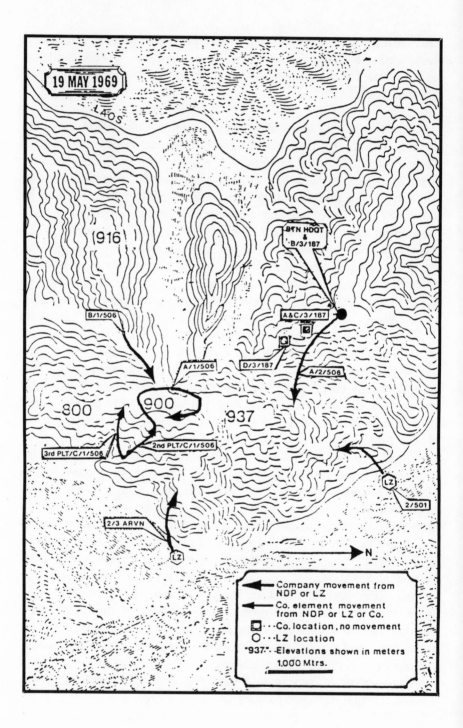

"Sure spot for an ambush," King whispered. "Don't you think?"
"Yep. Looks bad."
"I think we ought to circle the clear area," King went on, "and
see what's on the other side before we try to cross. What do you think?"
"I agree."
While they were discussing the situation, Brinkle got a call from
Lieutenant LeClair, who was near the rear of the column. "What's the
problem up there? What's the holdup?"
King took the handset from Brinkle's RTO and explained the situation,
but LeClair got very impatient and ordered him to cross. When King
objected, LeClair got angry and walked forward to the front.
"What's the problem here?" LeClair said when he arrived.
"I don't think it's safe to cross here," King said.
"Me neither, Lieutenant," Brinkle said.
"Let me see." LeClair moved up to the edge of the ravine, looked
it over carefully, then crawled back. "I don't see any problem there."
"I don't think it's safe," King said.
"If you're afraid to cross, I will," the lieutenant said. "Put your
men out for security."
It was exactly the type of reaction King had expected from LeClair.
Exactly! King considered for a second arguing with the lieutenant further
on the matter, but quickly decided against it. It would have been futile.
A waste of time. Although LeClair had been in the field only a few
weeks, he had already made it abundantly clear to everyone in the platoon
that he was running the show and that he did not welcome suggestions
from the men around him. A few days before, when one of the company
veterans had suggested something to LeClair, the lieutenant had snapped
at the man, "You speak when you're spoken to, troop. If I want any
suggestions, I'll ask for them. Got that?" After the incident, the veteran
came to King and Brinkle and said angrily, "You can't teach that man
nothin'!" His was a feeling quickly shared by everyone in the platoon.
Instead of arguing, King put one of his fire teams on the right side
of the trail, facing the clearing, and another on the left. While he was
moving his men into position, a North Vietnamese soldier suddenly
came out of the jungle and knelt down by the stream to fill his canteen.
Seeing him, LeClair opened up with his rifle, but the soldier quickly
ducked back into the jungle. LeClair told Sgt. Howard Petersen, Sp.4
Randy Mee, and Pfc.'s Edwin Murray, Johnny Young, and Tom McKay
to follow him, then started down the side of the ravine after the NVA

soldier. He ran quickly down the bank, through the stream, and up the other side. When Mee was coming out of the streambed, however, an NVA soldier came out of the back of a bunker and shot him in the head. The shot knocked him backwards to the edge of the stream, and Doc Jones, the platoon medic, rushed down through the stream in a futile attempt to save him.

At that same moment rifle fire poured down on LeClair and the other four men from half a dozen bunkers up the ridge. LeClair dived into a deep bomb crater, and Murray, Young, and McKay jumped in beside him.

At this point, with bullets hitting all around the edge of the crater, Sergeant Petersen did something so bizarre and inexplicable that the men of Charlie Company would discuss it for months afterwards. Rumor would later have it that he had gotten a letter from home that morning— possibly a Dear John letter—and that it had thrown him into a fit of depression, but no one ever found out for sure. Regardless of the cause, Petersen suddenly just stood up, turned around, and began walking slowly back down the ridge toward the streambed. Every man in the bomb crater and on the opposite bank watched in shock, knowing exactly what was about to happen. In the same instant, four or five AK47s cracked, and Petersen, riddled with bullets, was sent sprawling into the streambed.

What happened next was just as inexplicable. LeClair, who had always seemed so arrogant and self-assured, went into a blind panic.

"What should I do?" he screamed to Captain Stymiest over the radio.

"Assault their position," Stymiest said.

"I can't. We're pinned down. I can't move."

LeClair next honked up Lieutenant Shumaker, whose 3d Platoon was maneuvering on the ridge to the left, and asked the same question. The call shocked Shumaker, who had also had a lot of difficulty dealing with LeClair.

"Get everybody under cover," Shumaker said, "and I'll see if I can maneuver up the ridge and sweep down on those bunkers from the rear."

Shumaker started his platoon forward, but they were quickly pinned down by rifle fire from an enemy bunker to their front. The lieutenant put two squads on-line, then while one laid down covering fire, the other, led by Sgt. Phillip Tierney, advanced toward the bunker at a fast walk, with everyone pouring rifle fire into the bunker aperture. While his squad kept fire on the bunker, Tierney rushed forward and flipped a grenade into the back entrance of the bunker. The enemy soldier caught the grenade and threw it back out. Tierney tried to scramble away from it, but slipped and fell on his face and had his foot and leg peppered with shrapnel.

Angry, Tierney pulled another grenade and was crawling back toward the bunker when Shumaker yelled for him to stop. "Throw this in first," Shumaker said, tossing the sergeant a smoke grenade.

A grenade in each hand now, Tierney crawled back and flipped in the smoke grenade. Then when the bunker was filled with smoke, he tossed in the fragmentation grenade and killed the NVA soldier. With the bunker knocked out, Shumaker led his men forward again.

His relief effort, however, would prove to be futile, though through no fault of his own. On the other ridge, LeClair, still pinned down by withering fire, suddenly had a mood change, stood up, and ordered everyone to assault the bunkers. The lieutenant managed to take only a single step forward before an enemy soldier shot him in the head. He slipped back into the bomb crater and sprawled out on his back. At the sight of him, Private First Class Young, who was experiencing combat for the first time, started crying and screaming, "God, we're all gonna die!" Unafraid, though, he rose up over the lip of the crater and emptied a full magazine at one of the enemy bunkers, then, still crying, dropped back down, popped in a fresh magazine, and started firing again.

On the other side of the streambed, King and Brinkle had a hurried discussion and decided that if they did not start maneuvering against the enemy bunkers, the other men in the bomb craters were going to die. They agreed to have Sergeant Brinkle and about ten other men lay down covering fire while King and Pfc. Dan Williams tried to maneuver to the right against the bunker.

Before they left, King crawled with Williams to the edge of the ravine. "There's a gook behind the fifth tree up from the bottom of the ridge," King told Williams. "I counted. While they lay down covering fire, we'll both rush across to the right side of the ridge and get behind the second tree. Then you fire, and I'll rush behind the fourth tree. Then you move up with me, and we'll get that gook together."

"Okay."

Everything went according to the plan. While Brinkle and his men poured fire on the enemy bunker, King and Williams ran like madmen down through the stream and dived behind the second tree.

"Okay, open up," King yelled over the clatter of rifle fire. "Here I go."

King rushed forward to the fourth tree, then felt his heart leap in his chest like a startled frog. On the other side of the tree was an NVA soldier, squatting, his AK across his knee. On the edge of panic, King thought: My God, I counted wrong. He's behind the fourth tree, not the fifth.

Both men spun to fire at the same moment, but King was a millisecond faster. With a single terrified squeeze of the trigger, he let off half of his 20-round magazine and sent the NVA soldier, his eyes bulging in shock, flying backwards.

At almost the same moment, another NVA soldier rose up out of the rear of a bunker to King's left and let off with a long burst from his AK. King ducked behind the tree and was hit with a shower of bark. He backpedaled away from the fire, and as he did, the NVA soldier let off with another long burst. In a fleeting instant, King saw the muzzle flash of the AK and fired at it, letting rip with the rest of his magazine. He watched as the NVA soldier dropped his AK on the roof of the bunker and slid down out of sight.

King was not sure if he had killed the NVA, but Williams made sure. Angry over the death of his best friend, Randy Mee, he rushed up, stuck his M16 into the back of the bunker, and emptied an entire magazine into the head of the NVA soldier, all the time screaming, "You asshole!" Then with bullets hitting all around him, he rushed back down the ridge and joined King behind the tree.

There were still four bunkers higher up the ridge, and the NVA inside cut loose at Williams and King with a torrent of fire. Both men retreated five or ten meters to get away from the fire and took up safer positions. There they laid down covering fire while Murray, Young, and McKay dragged the bodies of Petersen, LeClair, and Mee into an abandoned NVA bunker. Then while Brinkle and the men laid down covering fire on the opposite side of the stream, all five men rushed back across the stream and joined the rest of the platoon.

There Sergeant Brinkle took command of the platoon, put everyone in a skirmish line, and started maneuvering it to the left in an attempt to flank the enemy bunkers. Seeing the flanking movement, the NVA shifted their fire and pinned down the platoon. Second Platoon returned the fire and were starting to advance again when they saw three men pop into view on the ridge above the enemy bunkers.

"Hold your fire," someone shouted. "Those are GIs."

The men were the point element for Shumaker's 3d Platoon. Leading them was Pfc. Paul Skaggs. Skaggs had a .45 automatic in his right hand and a claymore bag filled with grenades around his neck. On each side of him was a man with an M16 rifle.

When Skaggs spotted the first NVA bunker, he calmly took out a grenade and flipped it in the back entrance. A second after the explosion, he jumped down into the bunker and opened up with his pistol, then jumped back out and moved down to the next one. There he did the same, flipped in a grenade, then went in shooting. Out again, he took two or three steps down the ridge, located a third bunker, and fragged it also. Rather than jumping in this time, he lowered his head in and pumped five or six shots into the enemy soldier inside. Skaggs was moving down to the fourth bunker when the NVA soldier inside, suspecting what was happening above him, started crawling out the back entrance. The NVA was bringing his AK up to fire, but Skaggs, rather than seeking cover, jumped up on a log above the startled man and shot him in the head twice.

Finished, Skaggs and the other two men turned and jogged back up the ridge. A few minutes later, Lieutenant Shumaker brought the rest of the 3d Platoon up and linked up with Sergeant Brinkle and his men. After the linkup, both platoons dug in for the night and were resupplied with ammunition in preparation for the big assault in the morning.

By nightfall, in fact, all four battalions were in their assault positions around the mountain, forming a rough cordon nearly four thousand meters in length. There were many who believed that the NVA on Dong Ap Bia, confronted now with this massive display of force and facing certain defeat and likely even total destruction, would flee during the night and head for the safety of nearby Laos. But they were wrong. Instead, they did what they had done on each preceding night: they resupplied and reinforced the mountain, then settled into their bunkers and tunnels to catch a few hours' sleep before morning. It had been a long fight, and they were prepared to carry it to a conclusion. And to conclude it, as Honeycutt discovered, arrogantly and without the slightest show of fear.

Around midnight, while the colonel was trying to catch a catnap, one of his RTOs woke him and held out the radio's handset.

"What is it?"

"Some guy named Pham or something. Says he wants to talk with you. He's using your call sign. Keeps saying Blackjack over and over again."

Just as Honeycutt took the handset, a voice said, "Blackjack! Blackjack!"

"This is Blackjack. What can I do for you?"

"Blackjack, we are going to kill all of your men tomorrow."

"Is that so?"

"When you come up the mountain in the morning, Blackjack, we will be waiting for you. All of your men are going to die. Can you hear me, Blackjack? All will die!"

"We'll see who dies tomorrow, asshole," Honeycutt snapped.

CHAPTER 18

KING OF THE HILL

The morning began for the 3/187th with a stand-to. At 0530, while it was still dark under the jungle canopy, the men guarding the perimeters around the three NDPs raked the surrounding jungle with rifle and machine-gun fire, in the hope of catching any enemy soldiers or snipers lurking in the area.

As if in response, at 0630, a squad-size group of enemy soldiers crawled within seventy-five meters of the battalion CP and pummelled it with RPGs. A platoon from Bravo returned the fire, but the NVA quickly melted back into the large draw west of the CP.

This harassing action soon escalated. Thirty minutes later a single enemy soldier, wearing a pith helmet and green jungle fatigues, was spotted by four men from Alpha 2/506th approaching their sector of the battalion perimeter. The man had a grenade in his hand with the pin pulled and was creeping slowly through the jungle looking for the perimeter. He never found it. When he was about fifteen meters away, the four GIs riddled him with rifle fire. The man fell backwards, and the grenade exploded on top of him.

On the southeastern side of the mountain, Alpha 1/506th was not so lucky. At about this same time, an enemy soldier wearing a rucksack approached their perimeter with his hands up, yelling in English that he wanted to surrender. A sergeant gestured for the man to enter the perimeter. The man moved forward slowly, yelling "Chieu Hoi!" over and over again, but when he was about ten meters away from the perimeter suddenly lowered his head and charged forward like a bull. Before anyone could respond, the man set off a giant claymore mine he had hidden in his rucksack. The NVA soldier disintegrated, and four GIs were seriously wounded.

News of the incident traveled quickly through the 1/506th. When Pfc. Joe King and the rest of the men in Charlie Company's 3d Platoon heard about it, everyone agreed that they were not going to take any more prisoners. While everyone was standing around discussing the incident, a major from division intelligence showed up and wanted to know if anyone had found any enemy documents. When the major discovered that no one had found any, he began searching the enemy bunkers in the area himself. He soon discovered a bunker nearby that was so well camouflaged that 3d Platoon had somehow missed it during the assault the day before. The major crawled into the bunker with a flashlight and discovered a badly wounded NVA cowering in one corner. The man had spent the night inside Charlie Company's perimeter and was shivering in terror and pain. Speaking Vietnamese, the major managed to coax the man out. He was too weak to stand up, but instead huddled outside the bunker, looking around with bulging eyes like a frightened cornered animal.

At the sight of the NVA soldier, everyone in 3d Platoon gathered around to stare angrily at him. There might have been a time when each of them could have felt pity for the man, but it was long past. The savage fighting during the past five days had beaten the last bit of human kindness out of each of them and had left in its place a cold, cynical fury.

"Major, we'll take care of him for you," one man said. "Why don't you just walk up the ridge and leave him here with us."

"That's right, Major," a second man said. "We'll take care of him. Don't worry."

"That's probably the cocksucker who shot Sergeant Petersen," someone screamed angrily.

"Yeah, that's the little bastard who shot Petersen," someone else yelled.

The major seemed to ignore the talk. "I need some help carrying this man," he said.

No one moved forward to help. The major looked around at all the hard faces, then said, "Did you hear what I said? I need some help with this man."

This time everyone turned and walked away. The major looked after them with a frustrated look on his face, then finally helped the NVA soldier to his feet, put his arm around the man's waist, and started up the ridge with him.

As General Zais had ordered, the prep fire that morning was the most intense so far in the battle. Beginning at 0630 and without stopping for the next two hours, pair after pair of jet fighter-bombers and propeller-driven Skyraiders plastered four sides of the mountain with an assortment of high-drag bombs and napalm. When they went off station, the artillery took over and hit the mountain for another hour and a half.

At 1000 all four battalions—with the mountain above them dotted with burning trees and piles of debris—pushed out from their assault positions and started forward.

As planned, the 2/501st, commanded by Lt. Col. Robert L. German, moved quickly into a skirmish line and started climbing up the precipitous northeast side of Dong Ap Bia. To their left, the 2/3 ARVN Battalion began a similar climb up the equally steep southeast side. On the south side of the mountain, Lt. Col. Bowers's 1/506th continued the three-prong push toward the north, with Bravo Company attacking Hill 900 from the southwest and Alpha and Charlie Hill 937 from the south.

Honeycutt's three companies likewise started up the mountain on three different axes—with Alpha on the right, Charlie in the center, and Alpha 2/506th on the far left. When the three companies reached the base of the mountain, however, they quickly formed a long skirmish line and started up the mountain abreast.

Everyone in the three companies expected to meet the same withering fire they had during each previous assault, but instead they found the mountain as silent as a tomb. No one knew for sure what to make of the silence, but most men in the attacking companies hoped it meant that the NVA had abandoned their positions and retreated into Laos during the night.

In order to orchestrate this attack more carefully, Honeycutt, piloting the LOH himself, took off with Major Collier and flew back and forth across the skirmish line shouting out a litany of orders to his commanders: "Move up there, Alpha!" "Spread your men out, Charlie!" "Put some fire into that draw on your right, Alpha!"

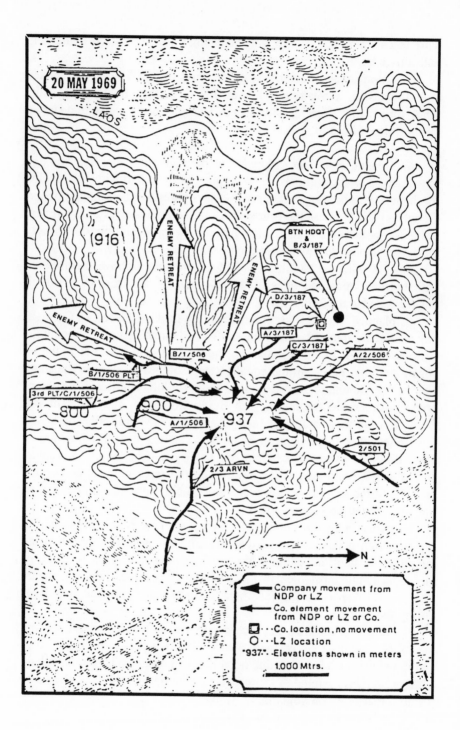

By 1010, all three companies reached the first bunker line and found it deserted. Using grenades and satchel charges, the grunts quickly destroyed or sealed each bunker before pushing on. The companies continued their methodical advance and by 1030 were only one hundred meters from the military crest of the mountain and closing in on the second bunker line. There was still no enemy fire or even a hint of enemy presence on the mountain. Up and down the skirmish line men started smiling, breathing a long sigh of relief. It was over. The bastards had bugged out during the night.

Around 1040, with the companies still abreast and closing in on the second bunker line, the NVA suddenly struck. At point-blank range, ten to fifteen NVA soldiers came out of a trench to Charlie Company's front and hit the skirmish line with a volley of RPGs. Others grenaded the line. Seven men from Charlie Company were wounded in the first exchange, and everyone else scattered for cover.

The Americans answered with a grenade shower of their own, then slashed the high ground with rifle fire, pinning the enemy in their trenches and bunkers. Rather than exposing themselves to the murderous fire, the NVA stayed in their positions and started rolling grenades down the steep face of the mountain. A dozen went off in quick succession, and four more men from Charlie Company were wounded.

Overhead, Honeycutt radioed instructions to Captain Johnson, "Keep movin'! Don't stop for the wounded. If you stay where you're at, they'll chop you up. They'll cut you to pieces. You're only seventy-five meters from the top. Keep pushin'!"

Johnson ordered his men forward, but they were soon pinned down again by a torrent of fire coming from five large A-frame bunkers.

"Use the 90mm!" Honeycutt screamed. "Knock those fucking bunkers out!"

Johnson called for the 90mm, and Sp.4 Tyrone Campbell and his assistant gunner, who had been trailing the skirmish line, rushed forward and dived behind a log.

"There, one to the right," a sergeant yelled at Campbell. "See it? Right there by that tree!"

Campbell looked over the log just long enough to locate the bunker aperture, then brought the recoilless rifle up, sighted the target, and screamed, "Look out! Back blast!" He fired, and the bunker exploded with a hollow boom.

"Over here," someone screamed down the line. Campbell and his assistant gunner ran to the left, with green tracer rounds whizzing over their heads and grenades exploding to their front like a string of fire-crackers.

"By the log," another soldier yelled.

Campbell shoved in another round and fired again. It was another perfect shot. The round exploded inside the bunker, and brown smoke belched out of the aperture. Campbell was just catching his breath when someone even farther to the left yelled for him, and he and his helper were off running again. It took three shots to knock out the third bunker, but the third caused a huge secondary explosion which blew the top off the bunker and set off a pile of phosphorous grenades inside.

Campbell was not the only man bunker hunting. On Charlie's right flank, Sp.4 Edward Merjil of 2d Platoon used his grenade launcher to silence two bunkers, then, with his squad on both sides of him laying down covering fire, rushed a third. While his men poured fire on the bunker, pinning down the enemy soldiers inside, Merjil took careful aim from ten meters away and shot a grenade right into the aperture, killing the two NVA soldiers huddling inside.

Merjil reloaded quickly, then rushed forward with the rest of his squad up the steep side of the mountain. Ten meters later, the men topped the mountain. They did not realize it at the time, but they were the first Americans to set foot on Dong Ap Bia. The time was 1145, exactly nine days and five hours after Bravo Company first made contact on the mountain.

Still, Merjil and his men had taken only a few square feet of the mountain. The NVA were still dug in all over the top of it, and before the squad could move any farther, they were pinned down by fire coming from a half-dozen enemy positions.

Below them, however, Lieutenant Sullivan was pushing the rest of 2d Platoon up the mountain with a vengeance, screaming at his men to keep advancing. When his RTO, Sp.4 Ron Swanson, tried to hand him the radio's handset to take a call from Captain Johnson, who was following fifteen meters behind the skirmish line, Sullivan pushed it away.

"It's the captain," Swanson screamed above the noise. "He wants to talk with you."

"I ain't got time to talk on the radio," Sullivan screamed. "Tell the captain to go fuck himself." Sullivan stood up and poured an entire magazine at an enemy bunker, then dashed forward five meters.

Swanson followed closely behind and once again shoved the handset at Sullivan. This time he took it.

"How's it goin' up there?" Johnson asked.

"All I know is that we're movin' up."

To the left of Sullivan, Sp.4 Leonel Mata and another squad were likewise advancing rapidly up the side of the mountain. While Mata laid down a base of fire with his M60 machine gun, six or seven other men in the squad, using smoke and fragmentation grenades taped together, were moving around the face of the mountain blowing up bunkers. The men went about the work coldly and professionally, and it seemed to Mata as if they were actually enjoying it. Within fifteen minutes, they knocked out about ten bunkers, and soon, two and three men at a time, the rest of Charlie Company started topping the mountain. Seeing the approaching men, the NVA in the bunkers on the military crest of the mountain began deserting their positions and running down the west face of the mountain, through the saddle between Hill 900 and 916, and out of the western draw toward Laos.

Honeycutt directed his 81mm mortar platoon to fire on the saddle and draw, then honked up Colonel Bowers and asked him to move some men across it to block the enemy escape route. Bowers, in turn, passed the mission on to his Bravo Company. Bravo was at the moment engaged in a fierce fight toward the southwest side of Hill 900, but they quickly dispatched two platoons back down the ridge and into the draw. There they set up a perimeter across the bottom of the draw and waited.

The retreating NVA were unaware of Bravo's new position, and as they hurried down through the deep jungle in the saddle, they ran into a wall of rifle and machine-gun fire. About ten enemy soldiers were killed in the first volley, but they quickly regrouped and pounded Bravo's blocking position with RPGs, then charged forward through the deep jungle, their AKs cracking. A group of enemy soldiers broke through the line this time, then curled around and began attacking the two platoons in the rear and flanks. In sharp, close-in fighting, Bravo lost five more wounded, but held their line and killed an estimated ten to fifteen more enemy soldiers. The fight in the draw was hardly over, however. During the next two hours, Bravo's two platoons would be in almost constant contact as group after group of enemy soldiers poured off the mountain and attempted to escape into Laos.

On the west edge of the mountain, Charlie Company had dug in, but their position was tenuous. Honeycutt, still piloting the LOH himself, flew over their position and could see that if they did not get help soon, a strong enemy counterattack could easily push them back off the mountain. And their help could come only from Alpha Company, still fifty meters from the top and in a vicious slugging match with the enemy soldiers in seven or eight bunkers and a series of trenches above them on the military crest.

Honeycutt flew over Alpha's line and honked up Captain Harkins. "Let's go, Harkins! Get those people movin'."

"We're movin', boss."

"Harkins," Honeycutt said.

"Yes, sir?"

"This is your chance for immortality, Harkins," Honeycutt continued. "This is your chance to win the fucking Medal of Honor. Take that mountain for me. Let's go!"

Harkins knew Honeycutt was joking, but he had no time to appreciate the humor. The fight in his sector was as hard as it had been on the eighteenth, and he had already lost his 2d Platoon leader, Lieutenant Bennitt, and fifteen men—and it was not getting any easier. The captain knew, however, that it was now or never and that if he did not get his men on top soon, the entire attack could come apart at the seams, disintegrate into chaos. He ran up and down behind the skirmish line screaming at his men, "Move it! Let's go! We've got to keep advancing!" He grabbed one soldier by the shoulders, who was huddling in a shell crater, stood him up, and said, "Let's go, son. Move forward." The kid responded and charged forward shooting. When one GI, frozen with terror, would not respond to two or three commands to move forward, Harkins gave the kid a hard kick in the butt and screamed, "Let's go, I said." The kid leaped forward like a horse from the starting gate and moved up the mountain.

When the line was about thirty meters from the top and pushing hard, Harkins was shot through his left ear. The bullets went in the side of his neck and lodged in his back. The captain fell down, and when he got up realized he had lost much of his hearing, could not see out of his left eye, and barely out of his right one. He staggered forward a few steps and collapsed in a shell hole. A medic rushed up and bandaged his ear and neck.

Overhead, Honeycutt watched the scene from his LOH. He radioed Harkins's RTO, and the man held the handset up to the captain's ear.

"What the fuck's goin' on down there?" Honeycutt screamed. "How come you're not movin'?"

"I've been hit bad," Harkins mumbled.

"You gotta keep moving."

"I'm hit . . ."

"I know you're hit, but you still gotta keep pushing."

"I . . ."

Honeycutt cut him off. "Harkins, if you can't fight that company, then turn it over to someone who can. Do you hear me?"

"Yes, sir."

Harkins got to his feet, told his RTO to start advancing, then grabbed the back of the man's radio and staggered forward like a blindman being led by a seeing-eye dog. Harkins lost his footing two or three times, but pulled himself to his feet and lumbered on. It was 1215.

The enemy in the last bunker line, however, held on tenaciously, and Alpha Company, after a short advance, was driven to cover by heavy fire. With the company pinned down, an enemy grenadier began rolling grenades down on the men. At the same time, a squad of enemy soldiers launched a hard attack against Charlie Company's right flank, with the obvious intention of pushing the men off the mountain.

Pinned down on the far right side of Alpha's skirmish line, Sp.4 Johnny Jackson, a machine gunner in 3d Platoon, huddled behind a log and thought: Here we go again. Another failed attack. As he cowered there, though, he suddenly remembered what he had boastfully told a friend earlier in the morning. "I'll tell you what," he had said, "if we go up that sonofabitch this time, I'm staying up. I ain't gonna be run down again and let those assholes shoot me in the back. I'm through with this retreating bullshit."

He kept thinking of his words now, and then on impulse stood up and shouted out loud so everyone in 3d Platoon could hear him, "Fuck this bullshit!" With a fluid motion, Jackson brought his M60 up to his chest and raked the enemy position above, then charged up the side of the mountain, wildly spraying bullets from side to side.

Jackson had had world-class speed in high school as a football player and track star, and he turned it on now, kicking his legs high to keep his balance as he charged through the debris covering the mountain. Dodging around shell holes, leaping logs, and all the time firing like crazy, he kept running, counting the distance in his mind. Five meters, ten, fifteen. And then suddenly the bottom seemed to fall out of the mountain, and Jackson found himself falling. He looked down in shock to see two NVA soldiers thrashing around below him. It was only then that he realized he had stepped through the bamboo mat covering a large spider hole and had landed right on top of these two men. He gasped and backpedaled away from them, watching in horror as they scrambled to bring their weapons up. He was quicker than either of them. With a long pull on the trigger of the M60, he poured a long burst into the hole and watched the two NVA soldiers crumple together.

Then at the same time, thinking: I don't have a chance in hell of surviving this, Jackson spun away and started another mad dash up the mountain. When an enemy bunker to his right opened up on him, Jackson attacked it head-on, pouring bullets into the aperture. When the enemy soldier ducked down, Jackson stuck the barrel of his machine gun into the aperture and let off with a 15- to 20-round burst.

He did not know if he killed the man, but he did not have time to worry about it. He spun again and dashed the last twenty to thirty meters to the top of the mountain. He stood there for just a second and looked around, hardly able to believe that he was actually on top of Dong Ap Bia. Out of the corner of his eye, he saw a FAC plane soaring over the draw. Then for no reason Jackson could fathom, the FAC plane turned toward the west side of the mountain and fired a phosphorous marking rocket. The round hit very close to Jackson and splattered phosphorus on his right pant leg. He dropped to the ground, scooped up a pile of loose dirt, and brushed off the phosphorus, burning his hand slightly, then looked to his left to see at least a dozen NVA soldiers pouring fire at him from trenches in the center of the mountain. Jackson dived into a shell crater and hugged the dirt, while bullets buzzed overhead and tore up the ground around him.

Down below, Sp.4 Michael Vallone had watched in disbelief as his friend Jackson charged up the hill, all the time thinking to himself: Has Jackson gone crazy? He thought for sure that at any second he would see his friend cut down. When he was not hit, Vallone suddenly felt very disgusted with himself for cowering down there while Jackson was up there fighting the NVA all alone. When the phosphorous round hit, he was sure his friend had been killed, and then he felt even worse.

Finally he screamed down the line at his squad, "Follow me!" Vallone charged forward, firing short bursts with his rifle, all the time screaming, "Come on, everybody, follow me!"

Vallone's move set off a chain reaction down Alpha's skirmish line. First his squad started forward, then all of 3d Platoon, and finally the rest of the company.

The NVA tried to stop the charge, but the line rolled over the last bunker line. Those enemy soldiers who did not escape to the top of the mountain were shot to death or fragged in their bunkers and spider holes.

Captain Harkins followed closely behind the line, still holding onto his RTO, his face covered with blood, his legs as weak as a baby's. Once he reached the top, he organized a defensive perimeter and had his company tie its line in with Charlie; then he collapsed in a bomb crater. Realizing he was too weak to be effective much longer, he turned over command of the company to Lt. Gordie Atcheson. Following that, and with the help of two men, he started the long trip back down the mountain.

On the mountain, many NVA were running toward the western draws in an attempt to escape, but others, on the eastern side of the mountain, were already mounting small counterattacks and pushing toward Alpha and Charlie's hastily formed perimeter. When a group of five or six NVA soldiers tried to mount a rush on the far left flank of Charlie's line, a grenadier hit them point-blank with a flechette round. Three of the men went down, but two kept coming. They were almost on top of the perimeter when five or six M16s cracked at once and knocked both men backwards.

In the center of the mountain, an NVA soldier popped up and fired an RPG right at Charlie's perimeter. The round narrowly missed hitting two men and sailed off toward the draw. The NVA quickly reloaded and was preparing to fire another rocket grenade when an American recoilless-rifle gunner hit him with an HE round. The force of the explosion knocked the enemy soldier backwards, and he triggered the RPG straight up into the sky like a rocket.

Still in his bomb crater, Jackson had a pile of belts for the M60 by his side and was firing like mad at the groups of NVA maneuvering all over the top of the mountain. He saw a group of five or six rush toward the south. He turned his machine gun and knocked down four of them. Then just as quickly he turned the machine gun to the north and cut down two or three more charging at him. After ten days of watching his friends get killed and wounded, Jackson was enjoying the payback.

On the southwest side of the mountain, while two platoons from Bravo 1/506th maintained their blocking near the saddle between Hill 900 and 916, the third platoon launched another attack against Hill 900.

This attack quickly became their last. When the platoon was about one hundred meters from the military crest and fifty meters from an area where four of their dead still lay from failed attacks on the eighteenth, its point squad was ripped apart by exploding claymores carefully hidden in a tree. The pointman of the column was killed instantly, and seven other men were seriously wounded. The wounded managed to crawl back down the ridge on their own, but the KIA had to be left behind.

The platoon was not expecting what happened next. Instead of hunkering down in their bunkers to wait out the usual airstrike or artillery fire, two platoons of NVA infantry came out of their bunkers and charged down on the disorganized and demoralized GIs.

Seeing them coming, the survivors in the platoon formed a hurried perimeter around their wounded, and not a second too soon. The NVA came down the jungled ridge firing RPGs and flinging satchel charges and swept right through the platoon, then turned around and charged through it again. As in the draw, the fighting was in close and savage, with many men shooting NVA soldiers from only a few feet away. When the fight finally ended fifteen minutes later, Bravo had another ten wounded and a perimeter surrounded by enemy dead.

Fearing the destruction of Bravo's platoon, Colonel Bowers ordered Captain Stymiest, the CO of Charlie 1/506th, to rush some men cross-country, relieve the platoon, then take up the attack on the southwest side of Hill 900. Stymiest, in turn, chose Lieutenant Shumaker and his 3d Platoon.

Shumaker was not happy over having his platoon chosen to make the attack. "Don't you think whoever kicked Bravo's ass will do the same to us?" he asked the captain.

"No," Stymiest said. "Because we're gonna plaster the entire area with arty and airstrikes this time. When we get done, there won't be a thing left up there alive. Not a living thing."

"I hope you're right."

Shumaker moved his platoon from its present position, south of Hill 900, down the draw to his west and up the next ridge. The men double-timed up the ridge, and it took them about thirty-five minutes to reach Bravo's beleaguered platoon. Shumaker was not prepared for what he saw next. There were dead NVA soldiers and parts of bodies all around the platoon's perimeter. Some of the GIs had taken some arms and legs and hung them in the surrounding trees with ropes as if they were Christmas-tree ornaments. An officer had even taken the bottom part of an enemy soldier's torso and buried it in the ground in front of his position, with the legs sticking up.

"What do you think?" the officers asked Shumaker, then laughed strangely. "Do you like it?"

"Yeah, that's real neat," Shumaker said and thought: My God! What in the hell have these poor bastards been through the last five days?

The lieutenant did not have time to ask. Guided by a sergeant from Bravo's platoon, he moved his men through the position and started up the ridge toward the southwest side of Hill 900. When they had moved about thirty meters, Shumaker's pointman stopped the platoon at the sight of three GIs coming toward them down the ridge.

Shumaker assumed they were some type of small reconnaissance patrol returning to the platoon position and thought little of them. A soldier about two or three men back in the column, however, suddenly started screaming, "What's going on here? How come you're letting the enemy come into our perimeter?"

Shumaker ran back and confronted the soldier. "Those are GIs. What in the hell are you talking about?"

"No, they're not," he yelled hysterically. "They're NVA. Look! They've got pith helmets on! They've got AKs!"

"What in the hell are you talking about?" Shumaker said angrily.

"I can't believe you're letting NVA come into our perimeter," the kid continued, his voice breaking. "I . . . I . . . just can't believe it!"

"Look," the lieutenant said, putting his hand on the man's shoulder, "calm down, and we'll discuss this later."

"We're not talkin' about this later!" the soldier howled.

"Look, we have to move out and help Bravo Company. We . . ."

"I'm not movin' out to help Bravo Company," he shouted. "I'm gonna be killed anyway. What difference does it make?"

At that, he fell on the ground and lay on his back, almost catatonic.

Shumaker could not be sure if the soldier was faking or actually suffering combat fatigue, but he did not have time to worry about it.

"Okay, if that's what you want," he said finally, "that's what you get." He turned to the men standing around watching, "Okay, you guys, take his rifle, take his grenades, take his rations—take everything! If he wants to stay behind and get shot, that's fine with me. We'll just leave him behind and let the NVA deal with him."

Three men moved up and started stripping the soldier of all his gear. At that same time, Skaggs, who was a close friend of the man, rushed up and started pleading with Shumaker, "I'll take care of him, sir. Don't leave him behind. He can come with me."

"I don't care," Shumaker said. "Take care of the sonofabitch if you want. But we've got to get going."

The soldier was led to the back of the column, and Shumaker started the platoon moving again. About fifteen minutes later, the guide led them to their assault position. There Shumaker put the platoon in a single column and took the third position back, behind the slackman.

The pointman moved ahead about ten meters, crawling on his hands and knees. The jungle was thick and choked with vines and bamboo. He was extremely cautious, scudding crablike a few feet, eyeing the jungle intently, then moving forward another few feet.

After covering about twenty meters, he stopped suddenly in the trail and motioned the slackman and Shumaker to come forward. He pointed up the trail at what appeared to be a GI ahead on the left side of the trail. The man was leaning forward between the fork of a tree, his rifle pointed up the ridge.

"Hey, get down," Shumaker said in a hushed voice, at the same time, thinking: Now, where in the hell did he come from?

The GI, however, did not respond.

"Hey, get down!"

Again, no response.

Shumaker and the pointman crawled up behind the GI. "I told you to get down," the lieutenant said. "Is there something wrong with you?"

The pointman went up to the GI and shook his shoulder. "Hey, Lieutenant, this guy's dead."

"He's what?"

"He's dead, Lieutenant." The pointman pulled the soldier out from the fork in the tree and laid him on the ground. "Look."

The man was indeed dead. Shumaker had no idea how he had been killed, but supposed the man had been shot during one of Bravo's failed assaults and had fallen forward into the fork of the tree.

After a short pause to check the man's identity, the guide led the column up another twenty to thirty meters, then halted them just short of a small clearing. Shumaker, the guide, and the pointman crawled up to the edge of the clearing and inspected the terrain ahead. The ridge sloped gradually upward for about sixty meters to a deep saddle, then rose sharply the rest of the way to the southwest side of Hill 900. Most of the ridge was covered by sparse jungle and low stands of bamboo and pocked by numerous bomb and shell craters. Near the top of the ridge, however, the jungle thickened. It was in this thicker jungle, Bravo's guide pointed out, that the NVA had their bunkers.

Shumaker estimated that it was around 150 meters from their present position to the bunkers. The plan he had discussed with Captain Stymiest called for a heavy shelling of the bunkers, after which his platoon was supposed to assault them on-line. Shumaker's hope was that he could get his men inside the bunker line before the NVA—still stunned by the artillery fire—had time to fully respond.

It was a hope that quickly turned sour. After a 20-minute wait for the artillery prep, he called Stymiest and discovered that it had been canceled and shifted in support of another assaulting company.

"I can't assault these positions on-line then," Shumaker told Stymiest. "Those machine guns will cut us up. If we're not going to have artillery, then I've got to have time to think up some other plan."

"You've got to make the attack," Stymiest said, "and you've got to make it right now."

When Shumaker again protested, Stymiest got angry. "The battalion commander called and said to make the attack, and that's final."

Shumaker realized that it was futile to argue, but knew that he had to come up with a plan other than a frontal assault. After more closely looking over the ridge, he decided that the only alternative was to try to work a squad up each side of it while another squad laid down covering fire. Given the terrain, it was not much better than an on-line assault, but it was all that was possible.

Shumaker put his 3d Squad on-line at the edge of the clearing with two machine guns, then split the rest of the platoon between Sgt. Raymond Baker and himself. "Just work your way up the right side of the ridge," he told his platoon sergeant. "Try and stay up with us."

Shumaker then put Pfc. Fred Rinehart on point, Sp.4 Laverino Rector on slack, followed by Pfc. Paul Skaggs, himself, and Pfc. James Ralph, the RTO.

Instead of crawling this time, they slowly edged their way along the side of the ridge, moving cautiously from tree to tree. The trail above was bare for about sixty meters, but after they passed through the saddle, they began coming across rucksacks that Bravo's troops had jettisoned during their pell-mell retreat on the eighteenth. Mixed in with the rucksacks were helmets, smoke grenades, and cloth bandoleers, and scattered everywhere were piles of spent brass and empty M16 magazines.

It was a depressing sight, but not as depressing as what they came across next. In the center of the trail was a GI who had been blown in half. His legs lay on one side of the trail and his upper body on the other. Everyone's eyes bulged at the sight, but Rinehart hurried the squad past.

Ten meters higher up, however, they came across three more bodies, and then a little farther yet another. Near the last body, Shumaker stopped the column and moved up with the pointman. About ten meters away was the enemy bunker line, but, like the entire area, it seemed deserted.

We're home free, the lieutenant thought. They've fled the area.

Shumaker moved back to his position in the column, and Rinehart started edging forward again. He stepped inside the bunker line on cat's feet, followed closely by Skaggs and Rector. Rinehart was waving the rest of the squad forward when Rector suddenly screamed. "I just saw a gook go into one of those bunkers over there. We better do something quick."

Shumaker moved up on the ridge and was just starting to run toward Rector when there was a giant explosion behind him. He did not realize it at the time, but the NVA had hidden a claymore under the body of the last dead GI. The explosion killed James Ralph, the RTO, and knocked him twenty meters down the ridge. Although hit by just the backblast of the mine, Shumaker was blown into the air, landing upside down in the top of a small tree. With twenty-two holes in his body and a dozen broken bones, Shumaker looked up to see sky between his legs. He tried frantically to move his arms and legs, but got no response from them. Instead, he wiggled his way down through the tree branches and landed on his head, a jolt that nearly knocked him unconscious.

By now there was firing everywhere. A few feet away, Rinehart, with his left arm broken by the claymore blast, charged into a bunker and, holding his M16 in his right hand like a pistol, emptied half a magazine into the NVA soldier who had set off the mine. He then threw the M16 aside, grabbed Shumaker by his shirt collar and started dragging him down the ridge. He staggered under the weight, but Rector and Skaggs rushed over and helped him, and together they dragged Shumaker down the ridge and into the saddle. From the saddle, Shumaker screamed across at Sergeant Baker, "I'm done for! Get everybody back down and call in an airstrike!"

As they had done to Bravo Company, the NVA, in groups of five and six, started coming out of the bunkers and trenches and charging down the ridge, firing their AKs from the hip. Shumaker looked up the ridge to see five enemy soldiers coming at him, their AKs barking. At that same instant, however, the two machine guns the lieutenant had put on-line at the edge of the clearing opened up at once and cut down all five. Five more followed a few seconds later, but the machine gun got them also.

This did not deter the NVA, however, and for the next fifteen minutes they kept pouring out of the bunker line and getting chopped down by machine-gun fire. Shumaker had never seen anything like it. He knew from experience how brave the NVA were, but he had never seen them so blatantly suicidal. When the fire finally died down, the ridge was covered with enemy dead.

A few moments later, Shumaker heard a roar and looked up to see the camouflaged body of a jet fighter coming over the top of him at treetop level. Rinehart and Rector lay on top of the lieutenant to protect him. All three men were bounced off the ground by the explosion of two cluster bombs which ripped through the jungle around the enemy bunkers. A second jet came in right on the tail of the first and hit the bunkers with napalm, and then the first returned for a second run with cluster bombs. When the jets finally expended their ordnance, a patch of jungle fifty meters long had been knocked flat and burned down to cinders. When another platoon of Charlie Company swept the ridge an hour later, it encountered no resistance and discovered the bodies of sixty-five enemy soldiers.

At about the same time as Lieutenant Shumaker's attack on the southwest side of Hill 900, Alpha 1/506th pushed to the edge of the same hill from the south and started fighting its way across the top of the hill toward Hill 937. After a hard, two-hour fight, during which they cleaned out numerous enemy bunkers and trenches, they reached the southern edge of Hill 937 at three o'clock in the afternoon. There they linked up with the 2/3 ARVN and dug in. Earlier in the morning the ARVN had run after two of their American advisors who were wounded, but their officers had managed to rally their men and lead them back up the mountain. During the last two hours, they had fought well, destroying dozens of enemy bunkers on the southwest face of the mountain and killing ten enemy soldiers.

The luck, however, had been with Colonel German's 2/501st. Although the battalion had come into the battle eager to avenge the beating they took at Firebase Airborne, they had not encountered a single enemy soldier in their push up the northeast side of Hill 937. At 1350, they took up positions at the northeast side of Hill 937 and awaited orders for the final push on the mountain.

It started at 1405 with a call from Colonel Conmy to Honeycutt, instructing him that while the other three battalions maintained their blocking positions around the mountain, he was to search the top of it thoroughly and destroy the last remaining enemy positions.

Although most of the troops in the 29th NVA Regiment either had been killed by now or had escaped into Laos, there were still about two platoons of enemy soldiers holding out on the top of Hill 937 in trenches, tunnels, bunkers, and spider holes. Honeycutt's men got on-line and started forward to flush them out. They moved through an apocalyptic, surreal landscape. All that remained of the triple-canopy jungle were rows of jagged tree trunks, surrounded by a muddy stew of splintered logs, bamboo, vines, and tree branches. Scattered every-where were pith helmets, pieces of clothing, bloody bandages, blankets, AK47s, stick-handled grenades, and RPG and mortar rounds. North Vietnamese dead also littered the mountaintop, their sickening sweet odor mixing with the smells of urine, excrement, tree sap, and cordite. Honeycutt's men advanced firing, fragging the bunkers and spider holes as they came to them, and pushing forward again.

It is believed that the NVA left on Dong Ap Bia had been told to fight to the end, and many did. As Honeycutt hovered in his LOH over the advancing line, he saw the strangest thing he had seen since the start of the battle. Near the center of Hill 937, eight enemy soldiers were standing stock-still around a cluster of blasted, gaunt trees. All the men seemed to be in shock and were seemingly totally oblivious to the approaching Americans. Had ten days on the mountain driven them mad? Honeycutt thought.

He would never know for sure. As the skirmish line approached the center of 937, a number of GIs spotted the NVA soldiers. Ten to fifteen rifles cracked at once, and all eight NVA fell. When one of Alpha's squads got to the cluster of trees, they discovered that all the soldiers were dead. To show their willingness to die, four of the men had chained or tied one leg to a tree. All the dead had small cloth patches sewn on the front of their shirts which read: KILL AMERICANS. On the barkless trees around them, various exhortations had been scribbled. One read: DEFEAT THE AMERICANS, HERE WE TAKE A STAND. Another: THE ENTIRE NATION IS WATCHING YOU. DON'T DISGRACE YOURSELF. And still another: STAY AND FIGHT AND NOT RUN.

Not all the NVA on Dong Ap Bia, however, were willing to die. Honeycutt saw numerous groups of NVA running in all directions off the mountain. With Bravo 1/506th still in its position blocking the large southwestern draw, most were heading into the smaller draws leading off the west side of Hill 900. In response, Honeycutt brought in two fighter-bombers who swept up and down the 1,200-meter length of the draw with cannon fire, then blasted the same ground with cluster bombs and HE. When the jets went off station, Honeycutt directed artillery and mortar fire into the same area. Although it was impossible to spot the fleeing NVA under the jungle canopy, the strafing, bombs, and artillery proved more than effective. For days after the end of the battle, troops sweeping the draw uncovered mass graves.

By 1655 the fight for Dong Ap Bia was drawing to a close. On the eastern edge of Hill 937, while the final mop-up was going on, some grunts from Charlie Company discovered two badly wounded North Vietnamese soldiers hiding in a bunker. Captain Johnson ordered the men out of the bunker, but they did not respond.

Realizing brigade might want a prisoner to interrogate, Johnson radioed Major Collier, who was circling with Honeycutt in the LOH, and asked him for advice on how to handle the situation. Collier suggested that Johnson have one of the grunts crawl to the edge of the bunker and throw in a smoke grenade.

Before Collier could finish, Honeycutt cut into the conversation. "I don't want one man hurt trying to get those little bastards out of there," he told Johnson. "If they won't come out, frag their asses."

When Johnson repeated the order a second time, the two NVA soldiers crawled out with their hands up. One of the soldiers died of his wounds shortly afterwards, but the other, 18-year-old Pham Van Hai, would later tell his interrogators a harrowing story of what life had been like on the mountain during the 10-day fight. During that time, 80 percent of Pham's 100-man company had been killed and the 29th NVA Regiment's 7th and 8th battalions, the two units defending the mountain, nearly wiped out.

That the NVA had paid dearly to hold Dong Ap Bia was substantiated a short time later by Sp.4 Johnny Jackson and his squad. While searching one of the many tunnels that honeycombed the top of the mountain, they discovered a large room containing what they estimated to be more than forty NVA dead. Stripped of all their clothing and equipment, the NVA soldiers were stacked like cord wood in one corner of the room, a horrific reminder of the ferocity of the battle.

The 101st Airborne Division intelligence shop would later claim that 633 enemy soldiers had died during the battle, as confirmed by body count. It is difficult to judge the accuracy of such figures. But if the other enemy companies on Dong Ap Bia suffered as grievously as Pham's, it is probably not far off the mark. Still, there is no telling how many other NVA soldiers were killed and wounded and carried into Laos. No telling how many were buried alive in bunkers and tunnels on the mountain or ended up in forgotten graves in the draws or along the many ridges.

As Honeycutt's troops continued searching the top of the mountain, they discovered that, like Iwo Jima's Mount Suribachi, it was honey-combed with deep tunnels, interconnected with a giant hospital, regimental CP, and numerous huge storage areas. In the storage areas they uncovered 152 individual and 25 crew-served weapons, 75,000 rounds of ammunition, thousands of mortar and RPG rounds, and over 10 tons of rice.

The final casualties for the Americans were 70 dead and 372 wounded, not counting the losses at Firebase Airborne.

Although the other three battalions would continue mopping up the surrounding area for the next seventeen days, the battle was over for the 3/187th. After a last night on the mountain, on the morning of May 21, the entire battalion was flown to Eagle Beach, a division R and R center on the South China Sea for a much-needed rest. Behind them the Rakkasans left a meat-grinder battle and a scarred, blasted mountain that they had once called Dong Ap Bia, but now referred to simply as Hamburger Hill.

CHAPTER 18

WAS IT WORTH IT?

*While few men, legislators or otherwise, have felt down the years
that they could command ships of the line or marshall air armies
without specialized training, almost any fool has felt in his heart
that he could command a regiment.*

From *This Kind of War* by T. R. Fehrenbach

A short time after the four allied battalions had secured Dong Ap
Bia and were policing up the battlefield, a GI cut out the cardboard
bottom of a C-ration box, printed the words "Hamburger Hill" on it,
then nailed it to a charred, blasted tree trunk near the western edge of
Hill 937. Another GI, passing by a short time later, added the words
"Was it worth it?" This second GI could not have realized how timely
and prophetic his question was.

Accounts about the fight for Dong Ap Bia had been appearing in
newspapers since May 14, though the general public had paid them
little attention. GI'S BATTLE ENEMY ON MOUNTAIN, the title of
a May 16 story in the *Washington Post* announced. The next day another
story appeared with the head, US JETS HIT FOE ENTRENCHED ATOP
MOUNTAIN. Both stories were nondescript accounts of the battle, not
appreciably different from the two or three reports on the fighting in
Vietnam that appeared each day in the pages of a typical American

273

newspaper. In the most antiseptic language, both described the fight for Dong Ap Bia, listed casualties, then summarized combat action for the rest of South Vietnam.

As Ward Just, a *Washington Post* staff writer, would say in an article in the *Post* on May 21, these stories, like most of the war reports during the preceding six months, appeared to have been written based on little but "the afternoon briefing at Saigon." Besides lacking what Just called "immediacy," they also failed to portray the fight for Dong Ap Bia as an event in which individual men were fighting and dying.

All this changed on the morning of May 19 with the appearance in newspapers across the country of a sharp poignant dispatch by Associated Press correspondent Jay Sharbutt. There was nothing out of the ordinary about Sharbutt's title—US ASSAULT ON MOUNTAIN CONTINUES, DESPITE HEAVY TOLL—but his gripping beginning riveted the attention of millions of readers across the country.

The paratroopers came down from the mountain, their green shirts darkened with sweat, their weapons gone, their bandages stained brown and red—with mud and blood.

Many cursed Lt. Col. Weldon Honeycutt, who sent three companies Sunday to take this 3000-foot mountain just a mile east of Laos and overlooking the shell-pocked A Shau Valley.

They failed and they suffered. "That damn Blackjack won't stop until he kills every one of us," said one of the 40 to 50 101st Airborne troopers who was wounded.

Sharbutt went on to include the discussion he had had with General Zais on the advisability of using B52 strikes on the mountain and the angry words of Sp.4 Anthony Tolle, a trooper from B/3/187th, who claimed that many men in Bravo Company were near the breaking point.

Some editions of the morning papers, like the *New York Times,* also carried the Sharbutt account of the final assault, ALLIED TROOPS CAPTURE MOUNTAIN ON ELEVENTH TRY IN TEN DAYS. Honeycutt also appeared in that account, hovering in his LOH, snorting and fuming at his men to keep the attack moving.

Although Sen. Edward M. Kennedy (D–Mass) would not respond to any of my requests for an interview, it seems more than obvious from reading his statements that, like millions of other Americans, he was very much affected by Sharbutt's accounts of the battle. In the early afternoon of May 20, in a period reserved for senators to make speeches on any topic they wished, Kennedy stood up on the Senate floor and angrily denounced the attack on Dong Ap Bia, calling it "senseless and irresponsible . . . madness . . . symptomatic of a mentality and a policy that requires immediate attention. American boys are too valuable to be sacrificed for a false sense of military pride."

President Richard Nixon had always considered Kennedy, like his brother John, a "dangerous foe." Not only was the senator possibly a future presidential contender, but also he had enormous influence over American public opinion. Kennedy's statement sent Nixon and his staff reeling.

The administration was quick to mount a counterattack, however. That same afternoon, the Senate Republican Whip, Hugh Scott (R–Penn), got up and rebutted Kennedy, telling the assembled senators that he would not attempt to "second-guess" battlefield tactics. "If our military are told to contend for a hill, it is part of the strategy which is essential to maintaining the military posture while we talk for peace."

Attack and counterattack followed like a staccato burst of machine-gun fire. The following morning in Saigon, a spokesman for Gen. Creighton Abrams defended the rationale for the battle. "We are not fighting for terrain as such," he said. "We are going after the enemy."

At a news conference at Phu Bai the following day, General Zais added his voice to that of Abrams's. "The hill was in my area of operations," he said bluntly. "That was where the enemy was, and that was where I attacked him. If I find the enemy on any other hills in the A Shau, I assure you I'll attack him there also."

When asked why the allies stormed the hill rather than hitting it with massive B52 strikes, Zais responded, "I don't know how many wars we have to go through to convince people that aerial bombardment alone cannot do the job."

When another reporter questioned the necessity for such high casualties, Zais responded passionately, his anger barely suppressed, "It's a myth somebody perpetuated that if we don't do anything, nothing will happen to us. It's not true. . . . It's just a myth that we can pull back and everything will settle down. If we pulled back and were quiet, they'd kill us in the night. They'd come on and crawl under the wire, and they'd drop satchel charges on our bunkers, and they'd mangle and maim and kill our men. The only way I can in good conscience lead my men is to insure that they're not caught in that kind of situation."

Although he did not make a public statement, General Westmoreland, the Army's new Chief of Staff, sent General Zais a telegram on May 23 congratulating him "on a gallant operation" to seize Dong Ap Bia, "which I refuse to recognize as the much-publicized Hamburger Hill."

That same day the White House entered the foray. At a news briefing Presidential Press Secretary Ronald Ziegler reiterated Zais's rationale for the battle and added that the assault had been consistent with administration "tactics and military strategy."

The feeling within the administration about the battle, however, was not unanimous. It was rumored that Henry Kissinger, Nixon's National Security Adviser, was very unhappy over the battle. The next day, journalist Hedrick Smith reported in an article in the *New York Times* that a number of high civilian officials in the administration were fearful that such costly battles "would undermine public support for the war and thus shorten the administration's time for successful negotiations in Paris."

"We are fighting a limited war," one official privately told Smith. "Now clearly the greatest limitation is the reaction of the American public. They react to the casualty lists. I don't understand why the military doesn't get the picture. The military is defeating the very thing it most wants—more time to gain a stronger hand."

Kennedy escalated his attack on the battle in a speech to the New Democratic Coalition in Washington on May 24. With rapierlike rhetoric he referred to the battle as nothing but "cruelty and savagery." Then, broadening the focus of his attack, he called the entire war "unjustified" and "immoral." A short time later, Sen. George McGovern (D–S.D.) got up and delivered another speech, during which he applauded Kennedy "for raising his voice . . . eloquently . . . in protest against a truly senseless slaughter."

This new attack brought a quick counterattack from Defense Secretary Melvin Laird. During an address to a luncheon group at the White House, Laird said that the Nixon administration's policy of keeping the "maximum military pressure on the enemy" was actually the best way to keep casualties low. Laird also reminded his audience that Nixon's policy was not appreciably different from former President Johnson's, in an attempt to remind Kennedy and his supporters that this aggressive policy had originated with the Democrats.

The following day in the Senate, Senators Margaret Chase Smith (R–Maine) and John G. Tower (R–Texas), both hawks, attacked Kennedy more directly. Tower disputed Kennedy's statement that deescalating the fighting would hasten a peace settlement, calling it "naive and dangerous. . . . Unless we are prepared to surrender to the enemy, we must negotiate from a position of strength." Chase then questioned the very notion of tactics and strategy being discussed in the Senate. "I am convinced," she said, "that trying to run the war out of Washington, as did McNamara, prolonged the war and increased the casualties. If at this point, we try and run the war from the U.S. Senate, the results may be even more disastrous."

The furor over the battle seemed to cool for the next two days. Then on May 29 Sen. Stephen M. Young (D–Ohio) started the pot boiling again. Young took the controversy a step further. Rather than criticizing the rationale for the attack, he questioned General Zais's actual tactical handling of the battle. In a lengthy speech, Young described how during the Civil War the Confederate generals Stonewall Jackson and Robert E. Lee attacked the Union forces at Chancellorsville from the rear and flanks simultaneously and routed them. "Our generals in Vietnam acted as if they had never studied Lee and Jackson's strategy," Young concluded. "Instead, they flung our paratroopers piecemeal in frontal assaults. Instead of seeking to surround the enemy and seeking to assault the hill from the sides and the front simultaneously, there was just one frontal assault after another, killing our boys who went up Hamburger Hill."

While the furor raged in Washington, the three allied battalions remaining in the northern A Shau finished securing the area around Dong Ap Bia. A short time later bulldozers were brought in; they opened a road up a large ridge from the valley floor to the top of the mountain. A number of tanks and armored personnel carriers then moved up the road and set up a defensive perimeter around the top of the mountain. Although the enemy periodically harassed the position with mortar and rocket attacks, they never did launch the ground assault the allies had been expecting.

Realizing there was nothing to be gained by having a battalion tied down in a defensive role on Dong Ap Bia, Maj. Gen. John Wright, who had recently replaced Zais as commander of the 101st, ordered the position on the mountain abandoned on June 5, unaware that his decision would reignite the controversy over the battle.

With the allies gone, the NVA once again began moving troops back onto Dong Ap Bia. The first enemy troops were part of recon units, but they were soon joined by large units of regular infantry. Finally, on June 17, when reporters began suspecting that the enemy was again on the mountain in force, allied intelligence admitted that more than one thousand NVA soldiers had reoccupied the mountain.

When questioned about the enemy presence on the mountain, General Wright said that if it should become necessary to attack again, he was "prepared to commit everything that it takes, up to the entire division, to do the job." While he admitted that he had no present plans for another ground assault, his statement infuriated Senator Young. On June 19 the senator unleashed a venomous attack on Wright in the Senate.

Mr. President, inconceivable as it may seem, if our generals in Vietnam should again be so callous over the welfare of GIs who do the fighting and dying to order an assault on Dong Ap Bia, then let us hope that General Wright will personally lead that assault and be in the forefront of those young GIs to take part in it, and encourage them with his display of leadership and bravery.
I suggest that Melvin Zais, who last month commanded the 101st Airborne Division in the attack on Hamburger Hill, be assigned to accompany him.

Young ended his speech by suggesting that Wright be reassigned and given charge of a large warehouse, which would be more in keeping with his "abilities, judgment, and discretion." Although he had little to say about the battle during the rest of 1969, Young would refer to it numerous times in Senate speeches in 1970, using it as a springboard to attack what he considered the immorality of the war and the general incompetence of the Army's high command. In another lengthy Senate speech toward the end of the year, he lambasted Zais once again following the general's promotion to lieutenant general. After briefly describing Union General Ambrose Burnside's disastrous frontal assault on the entrenched Confederate forces on Marye's Height, an attack Young considered similar to Hamburger Hill, the senator acidly concluded: "President Lincoln fired Burnside. General Zais was promoted."

To make an attack even less likely, a few days after Young's speech, the June 27 issue of *Life* magazine appeared and once again resurrected the Hamburger Hill controversy. Still recovering from the shock of the battle, the public was stunned further by *Life*'s lead article, "The Faces of the Dead in Vietnam. One Week's Toll." In a bold departure from its usual coverage of the war, *Life*'s editors printed the photos of the 241 men killed in Vietnam during the preceding week. The photos were prefaced by a one-page introduction, titled with the last line of a short letter a soldier had written to his parents during a break in the fighting for Hamburger Hill. "You may not be able to read this," he had written. "I am writing in a hurry. I see death coming up the hill."

Although only five of the photos were of men who had died during the battle, this quote confused many Americans who read the article, leading them to believe that most of those pictured had died storming Dong Ap Bia. I doubt if you could make the case that *Life* was deliberately trying to foist this ruse on the American people, but that was the result nonetheless. As military tactician and scholar Col. Harry S. Summers (Ret.) says in his book *The Vietnam War Almanac*, "American public outrage over what appeared to be a senseless loss of life" on Hamburger Hill was further "exacerbated by the publication of these photos." It became so exacerbated, in fact, that Shelby Stanton, the noted Vietnam War historian, believes the *Life* article, like the 1968 Tet Offensive, was a major turning point in the Vietnam War.

Up until that time, American commanders in Vietnam had operated under a strategy that called for them to keep "maximum pressure" on the enemy while negotiations with the North Vietnamese continued in Paris. Under the umbrella of this strategy, General Zais had felt justified in ordering the assault on Dong Ap Bia. Shortly after the appearance of the *Life* article, in what Colonel Summers says was "a reaction remarkably similar to the restrictions imposed during the closing days of the Korean War, General Abrams, the commander of all U.S. Forces in Vietnam, was ordered to avoid such large-scale battles." The new U.S. strategy for fighting the war was labeled "protective reaction." In order to hold down casualties, it called for the Americans to fight only when threatened by the enemy.

In conjunction with this new policy, President Nixon also ordered twenty-five thousand U.S. troops withdrawn by July 8 and thirty-five thousand more by early December, and the fighting gradually turned over to the South Vietnamese, officially called "Vietnamization of the war."

Ironically, the repercussions from Hamburger Hill eventually negated the very thing the battle had meant to accomplish—the destruction of enemy hegemony in the A Shau Valley. In early July 1969, General Stilwell left Vietnam and General Zais took over XXIV Corps. Although

Zais managed to complete the all-weather road into the valley, the allies' dream of installing a permanent base camp there remained just that—a dream. As Stilwell says, Nixon's troop reductions "dramatically reduced" the allies' "capability to conduct operations beyond the outer fringes of the populated areas." While the 101st did manage to launch another successful operation (Montgomery Rendezvous) in the valley, Nixon's Vietnamization policy eventually stripped them of the troops they needed to garrison a large base camp there. Before long, just as they had after the fall of the A Shau Special Forces camp in 1965, the allies once again had to concede control of the valley to the North Vietnamese.

JUDGMENTS

Critics recognized the doctrinal soundness of the operation, which was designed to clear the enemy from the A Shau Valley and Ap Bia in particular, in order to eliminate a base that could be used for further assaults on Hue and Danang. They point out, however, that its cost in lives and the disastrous public image of the American effort created in consequence make it an outstanding example of a misplaced strategy. Such an operation, they suggest, might have been accomplished, perhaps less conclusively, by firepower alone; in any case, its execution lacked stealth and tactical finesse.

> from *The War Managers*
> by Gen. Douglas Kinnard, former Chief of Staff of the Second
> Field Force in Vietnam (1967–68) and former Chief of Military
> History, U.S. Army

Here's a case where you're going up against a crack NVA unit. They had to be prepared for this battle. They had been preparing the positions on the mountains for months, maybe years. They obviously wanted to have a battle there, otherwise why would they bother to fortify and supply a position only 1000 meters from the border. Dong Ap Bia was a fortress and they could have just as easily built it right across the border in Laos and no one would have bothered them. As soon as we hit them, they hit Airborne. Why? The only reason is that they wanted to beef up the casualty figures.

> Lt. Charles Denholm
> 4th Platoon Leader, Bravo 3/187th

(Note: The men are given the rank or title they had at the time of the battle. Unless otherwise indicated, all quotes are from taped interviews with the author.)

If Hamburger Hill would have happened a year earlier, no one would have said a word about it. Look at Ia Drang and Dak To. They had similar casualties, but no one even so much as whimpered about either battle.

> Cpt. Charles Littnan
> CO, Bravo 3/187th

Knowing what we did on the 15th, we should have brought in a couple of more battalions, even an entire brigade. On the 14th, we hit that hill with a full battalion and an unbelievable amount of firepower, and the NVA brushed us off the way you would a fly. At that point Gen. Zais should have brought up a full brigade. It should have been obvious we were facing a full regiment. Military history is filled with commanders wasting their strength piecemeal, and that's exactly what Zais did. I started out with a sympathy for General Zais because of the Kennedy controversy, but the evidence is overwhelming that he failed in his primary function as an infantry commander; which is that you fulfill your mission with all available means and keep your losses at a minimum.

> Lt. Frank Boccia
> 3rd Platoon Leader, Bravo 3/187th

Lieutenant Boccia was an outstanding platoon leader who did a superb job of leading his platoon. Having been a platoon leader myself during World War II I can fully understand Lieutenant Boccia's feeling that down there on the ground eyeball to eyeball with the enemy, he was going it alone and no additional support was being provided. However, this is far from the truth.

First during the entire battle, Gen. Zais and Gen. Stilwell were above the battle area and in constant contact with the commanders on the ground. At no time was there any hesitation about committing any additional troops. From May 10–13, the 3/187th carried the battle with continuous air and artillery support. During the course of the battle, four batteries of 105s, one battery each of 155s, 175s and 8-inch artillery fired in support of the 3/187th. There was also 271 airstrikes so there was no lack of support.

Up until the 13th, Honeycutt felt he could carry it alone, and all the other battalions in the 3rd Brigade were busily engaged elsewhere in the A Shau Valley. When it became apparent the 3/187th could not carry it alone, I made the decision, supported by Gen. Zais to employ the 1/506th, commanded by Lt. Col. John Bowers, who was to attack Dong Ap Bia from the south. Honeycutt was impatient with Bowers's progress, but the 1/506th had more difficult terrain to cover than the 3/187th and were just as aggressive as the 3/187th.

> From a letter to the author
> from Col. Joseph Conmy.

Honeycutt as I'm sure you know is very bitter about the 1/506th. He felt that they didn't move up fast enough. I can't judge. We heard different things on the way up. We heard that the 1/506th had run into as much shit as we had. On the other hand the whisper went around, "Hey, those guys are just sitting back while we're taking the shit."

> Lt. Frank Boccia
> 1st Platoon Leader, Bravo 3/187th (From interview with Ray Ytzaina)

The tactics were as good as any used in the war. We had been running all over hell's half acre looking for the NVA, and we found them. It came at an unfortunate time when the 101st was spread all over I Corp from the DMZ down to the Americal Division. Because of this it took a lot of time to generate our forces. The first three days we didn't know what we were up against. All we knew is we had some people shooting at us. By the 15th we knew we had a lot of people shooting at us, and by the 18th we knew we had a whole bunch shooting at us. If we had it to do over again, we would likely do the same thing. We were there to fight soldiers. We were there to kill bad guys. We found the bad guys and decided that it was better to fight them where they were than to allow them to get down to a populated area like Hue. There was a tremendous effort on the part of Honeycutt and everyone else to use Tac Air and indirect fire. To a lot of people the big thing was the fact that we didn't use B-52s. But to do so, we would have had to pull back, and they would have gotten away. The NVA always tried to get as close as possible to us in order to negate our firepower.

If we had it to do over again, we might possibly have put a fixing attack up the center and then overloaded my route with two or three companies. When Lee Sander tried to make that end run and it failed, it had a real bad effect on the progress of the battle. It tied up a lot of resources for three days. Then when the CP and Bravo both got hit with ARA, that created even worse problems.

From my point of view Hamburger Hill was a classic attack on a bunker line.

Cpt. Gerald Harkins
CO, Alpha 3/187th

The 3/187th made contact with the 29th NVA Regiment and the 29th decided to fight. Pulling back and dropping B-52s would have alerted the enemy and they would have pulled out and hit us in the rear on another day. We found the enemy on Dong Ap Bia and that is where we fought them. We broke the back of the 29th and rendered it combat ineffective. We counted 691 enemy dead and countless weapons when the hill was taken on the 20th. General Zais was the commanding general and he helped us make the count. Also a Special Forces patrol on the Laotian side of the border led by a gentleman just retired and whom I know well advised me that they counted 1100 enemy dead and wounded carried off that hill during the course of the battle.

> From a letter to the author
> from Col. Joseph Conmy.

I didn't know what kind of tactics we were using up there. All I knew is that I was following the guy up ahead of me.

> Sp.4 Ron Swanson
> Rifleman, 2nd Platoon, Charlie 3/187th

Recognizing that the Vietnam War was a war of attrition, I don't think Hamburger Hill was a waste, unless the whole war was a waste. If the whole war was a waste, then it doesn't make any difference what battle you're talking about because it all comes out the same.

People say it was a waste because we left the hill right after we took it, but then again we left almost all territory in Vietnam after we fought for it.

I think the battle was a success for a number of reasons. For one, we won the attrition aspect of it, but more importantly it set the NVA logistics and resupply back in that area for a long time. They just didn't establish positions like Dong Ap Bia over night. This was a well fortified and strategic position and was obviously meant to control the entire valley.

> Lt. Robert Schmitz
> 1st Platoon Leader, Alpha 1/506th

It was a consensus in my platoon that there had to be a better way to get those guys off that mountain than the way we were, which was acting like a bunch of Marines making frontal assaults.

> Pfc. Michael Smith
> Grenadier, 2nd Platoon, Delta 3/187th

I didn't want to attack that mountain. I thought it was stupid. But everyone was caught in the same predicament. If I didn't go up that mountain, they would have fired me and sent up another captain. Honeycutt was actually in the same situation. There's nothing in our military tradition— and especially in the infantry—concerning retreat. They don't even teach retreat in the military schools.

The criticism that it had no importance was true. The only thing important was how many folks you killed. Obviously we killed a lot of them, but the number we killed didn't even begin to make up for the number we lost. We would have been a lot better off if we had never gone up that mountain.

But you really can't fault anybody. What was somebody going to say to Zais if he had said, "Well, we found the enemy, but decided not to attack him." These men from Zais on down were very ambitious, but when you come right down to it, would you want someone commanding an army who wasn't ambitious.

I personally never thought anything had any significance over there except defending your bases. I fault the system. I don't fault Zais or Honeycutt. I fault a system that never did figure out what the objective was over there.

Obviously the NVA were very happy we were coming up that hill. The only smart thing we did was to sit there and watch those 1000-pound bombs blow them up.

> Cpt. Luther Sanders
> CO, Delta 3/187th

Honeycutt's tactics at Hamburger Hill were aggressive, a feature of American tactics throughout the war. Aggressive tactics may produce sharp initial casualties, but they save lives in the long run, for in a protracted battle, as in a protracted war, casualties inevitably accumulate. Allowed to drag on, the Vietnam War as a whole illustrates this point.

> from *A Soldier's Report*
> by Lt. Gen. William Westmoreland

I feel Honeycutt had a job to do and he did it. I didn't like him during the battle, but I can see after reading the After Action report that there was a lot more involved in the battle than I knew about at the time.

> Pfc. Anthony Bresina
> Rifleman, 1st Platoon, Bravo 3/187th

I don't get as violently upset over this battle as Boccia does. We went in there to find the enemy and kill him. That was our job, and that was Honeycutt's job.

> Lt. Charles Denholm
> 4th Platoon Leader, Bravo 3/187th

Honeycutt was a helluva combat commander. Honeycutt used to say that a commander cannot afford to let his personal emotions get in the way of his job, or allow his personal grief to get in the way of a mission. As an infantry commander, your only reason for existence is to carry out your mission and take care of your men. If there's a conflict between the two, then your mission comes first. If your primary responsibility is to your men then you shouldn't fight a war.

> Lt. Frank Boccia
> 3rd Platoon Leader, Bravo 3/187th

We didn't need to send men up like cordwood to take Dong Ap Bia. Honeycutt would have been better in World War II making the world safe for democracy. But Vietnam was not about that. I'm not looking back as a Monday-morning quarterback because I was very bullish on the war then. But even with my bullishness, I couldn't understand how this hill was worth wasting American lives the way we did. The thing that put Honeycutt there was bigger than him. He was a product of a system.

> Lt. Joel Trautman
> 1st Platoon Leader, Charlie 3/187th

Commanders of combat units are given missions and orders and Honeycutt was doing his best to carry his out. You need to appreciate that the NVA had not stood its ground during the entire six months I'd been in the 101st. Therefore Zais, Smith and Honeycutt felt that each day the enemy would melt away as they had in dozens of previous fights. Look at the purpose of the A Shau campaign. It was to uncover supplies, interrupt the trail and overrun any NVA headquarters units. The resistance on Dong Ap Bia was so unusual that we thought we had stumbled on a command post or a large supply depot. Why else would they stay and fight?

> Lt. Col. Gene Sherron
> CO, 2/506th

I thought at first that Honeycutt was happy with the situation he found himself in, that he wanted to take that hill with just the 3/187th and was glad the 1/506th wasn't there. From reading the After Action report I can see how angry and frustrated he was that they didn't get there quicker.

> Sp4. Michael Rocklen
> RTO, 1st Platoon, Delta 3/187th

My tactics at Hamburger Hill were aggressive. That's the way you fight a war. How much ground are you gonna take being non-aggressive. How many enemy are you going to kill sitting around and waiting for him. Nobody ever won a war trying to avoid combat.

> Lt. Col. Weldon Honeycutt
> CO, 3/187th

After his statement in the Senate, Kennedy went to the top of my all-time shit list. What he said about Zais was really despicable.

> Cpt. Charles Littnan
> CO, Bravo 3/187th

What Kennedy said really pissed me off. I didn't want to think that we had gone through all that on the hill for nothing. What he said might have been true, but he was an outsider and had no right to get involved in the issue. Tactically the battle was incorrect and a waste of a lot of lives, but to use it for political gain was pretty despicable.

> Lt. Frank McGreevy
> 1st Platoon Leader, Alpha 3/187th

I remember getting the *Stars and Stripes* and reading about the reaction in the States and I have a very clear memory of Kennedy calling the battle a waste. I wish Kennedy had been there. I thought it was a very inappropriate thing for a statesman to say, especially considering the fact that the battle was still going on and that those of us involved in it had lost a lot of friends in the battle and didn't consider it a waste. If we hadn't of had that collective opinion, we wouldn't have assaulted the mountain. It was about this time, though, that we began to realize what kind of support we had back home. I mean it's one thing to have some hippie tell you you're a war criminal and quite another to have a U.S. Senator—who is obviously a very powerful force—tell you that you've wasted the lives of the men serving under you instead of giving you the moral support which during these trying times would have been great to have. At least he could have said something about the valor of the troops involved and what they accomplished. They fought under some extremely difficult conditions and conducted themselves with honor as soldiers are supposed to do. But his addressing only the political aspects of the battle . . . I don't think I can ever forgive him for that.

> Lt. Robert Schmitz
> 1st Platoon Leader, Alpha 1/506th

As I said I was very opposed to making the attack on that mountain. When I heard Kennedy's statement, however, I thought he should have been shipped to Hanoi.

> Lt. Joel Trautman
> 1st Platoon Leader, Charlie 3/187th

I always carry collective guilt for my company. You lose a life—just one life—and it means you did something wrong. No matter what you do, though, you're always going to lose people in a combat situation. But anytime one of your men dies, you question yourself about whether there might have been a better way to do something.

When I think of the boys on that hill and what they went through and then ten years later you find that all these guys who split for Canada are being offered amnesty. . . . in my mind both of us can't be right. If they were right to leave, then what we did on that hill was wrong.

> Cpt. Charles Littnan
> CO, Bravo 3/187th

An army is fielded, and if it is a good army, it fights. If it must fight against an entrenched enemy on a hill, then that is what it does. The war does not take place in a classroom or on the pages of a newspaper, and it is not fought by political scientists or journalists; it is not fought by men who read headlines.

> from an article in the *Washington Post*,
> May 21, 1969 by Ward Just, *Washington Post* staff writer and novelist

I didn't give Hamburger Hill much thought after it was over. I was just glad it was over. I heard it was the toughest fight in Vietnam. I know Charlie Company believed it because they really got their butts kicked.

> Sp.4 Johnny Jackson
> Rifleman, 3rd Platoon, Alpha 3/187th

When I think of Hamburger Hill, I always think of Luther Morgan. He played the harmonica and had a beautiful voice. He was a good friend of mine in basic training and when we went over to help Charlie Company, I helped carry his body out. He was a helluva guy, and I dreamed about him a lot after the war. I used to also dream that I was getting off this plane and going to Vietnam for my second or third tour, and all these bastards who had figured a way out of it were standing there laughing at me. And when I finally got off the plane, there was somebody there telling me that I had to go up Hamburger Hill one more time.

> Pfc. Anthony Bresina
> Rifleman, 1st Platoon, Bravo 3/187th

BIBLIOGRAPHY

Books

Blumenson, Martin. *Bloody River: The Real Tragedy of the Rapido*. Boston: Houghton Mifflin Co., 1970.

Boettcher, Thomas D. *Vietnam, the Valor and the Sorrow*. Boston & Toronto: Little, Brown & Co., 1985.

Fehrenbach, T. R. *This Kind of War*. New York: Macmillan, 1963.

Hersh, Burton. *The Education of Edward Kennedy*. New York: William Morrow & Co., 1972.

Hickey, Gerald Cannon. *Sons of the Mountains, Ethnohistory of the Vietnamese Central Highlands to 1954*. New Haven & London: Yale University Press, 1982.

Kendrick, Alexander. *The Wound Within*. Boston: Little, Brown & Co., 1974.

Kinnard, Douglas. *The War Managers*. Wayne, N.Y.: Avery Publishing Group, Inc., 1985.

Leckie, Robert. *The Wars of America*. Revised edition. New York: Harper & Row, 1981.

Lippman, Theo, Jr. *Senator Ted Kennedy*. New York: W. W. Norton & Co., 1976.

Lucas, Jim. *Dateline Vietnam*. New York: Award House, 1966.

Major Ethnic Groups of the South Vietnamese Highlands, Santa Monica: The Rand Corporation, 1964.

Millet, Stanley, ed. *South Vietnam, U.S.–Communist Confrontation in Southeast Asia*. Vol. 4. New York: Facts on File, 1974.

Mole, Charles E. *The Montagnards of South Vietnam*. Rutland, Vermont & Tokyo: Charles Tuttle, 1970.

Ross, Bill D. *Iwo Jima: Legacy of Valor*. New York: The Vanguard Press, 1985.

Russ, Martin. *Line of Departure: Tarawa*. Garden City, N.Y.: Doubleday & Co., 1975.

Stanton, Shelby. *The Rise and Fall of an American Army*. Novato, Calif.: Presidio Press, 1984.

Summers, Harry G. *On Strategy: The Vietnam War in Context*. Novato, Calif.: Presidio Press, 1982.

———. *Vietnam War Almanac*. New York: Facts on File, 1986.

The Vietnam Experience, Fighting for Time, 1969–70. Boston: Boston Publishing Co.

Westmoreland, Gen. William C. *A Soldier's Report*. Garden City, N.Y.: Doubleday & Co., 1976.

Selected Military Articles

"Apache Snow Ends; 691 Enemy Perish." *The Screaming Eagle*, June 23, 1969.
Benton, 1st Lt. Lewis E. "A Shau—Somerset Plain." *Rendevzous with Destiny*, Fall 1969.
Borders, Spec. 5 Robert. "Dong Ap Bia." *Rendezvous with Destiny*, Summer 1969.
Hair, Lt. Frank. "Massachusetts Striker." *Rendezvous with Destiny*, Summer 1969.
Horvath, Maj. Richard L. "Mystique of the A Shau." *Rendezvous with Destiny*, Summer 1969.
Johnson, Spec. 4 Kent, and Oberg, Spec. 4 Jon. "Roaming, Ranging and Prowling." *Rendezvous with Destiny*, Summer 1969.
Magary, Spec. 5 Alan, "288 Days of Nevada Eagle." *Rendezvous with Destiny*, Spring 1969.
Oyler, Lt. Harry. "Apache Snow." *Rendezvous with Destiny*, Summer 1969.

Military and Government Publications

Kelley, Col. Francis J. *U.S. Army Special Forces, 1961–1971*. Dept. of the Army, Washington, D.C., 1973.
Pearson, Lt. Gen. Williard. *The War in the Northern Provinces, 1966–68*. Dept. of the Army, Washington, D.C., 1975.
Shulimson, Jack. *U.S. Marines in Vietnam, 1966; An Expanding War*. History and Museums Divisions, Headquarters, U.S. Marine Corps, Washington, D.C., 1978.
Tolson, Lt. Gen. John. *Airmobility*. Dept. of the Army, Washington, D.C., 1973.
Westmoreland, Gen. William C., *Report on the War in Vietnam*. Govt. Printing Office, Washington, D.C., 1969.

Selected Articles

"Abrams Defends Fight for Peak." *Washington Star*, May 21, 1969.
"The Battle for Hamburger Hill." *Time*, May 30, 1969.
Esper, George. "Enemy Back in Control of Ap Bia." *New York Times*, June 17, 1969.

"The Faces of the Dead in Vietnam—One Week's Toll." *Life*, June 27, 1969.
"The Fall of a Fortress." *Time*, March 18, 1966.
"Foe Reported Back on Hamburger Hill." *Washington Post*, June 17, 1969.
Hoffman, David. "Hamburger Hill: The Army's Rationale." *Washington Post*, May 23, 1969.
Just, Ward. "The Reality of Hamburger Hill." *Washington Post*, May 21, 1969.
Peterson, Iven. "Field Commander Replies to Kennedy on Apbia." *New York Times*, May 23, 1969.
"Rebuttal on Hamburger Hill." *Time*, June 6, 1969.
Sharbutt, Jay. "Allied Troops Capture Mountain on Eleventh Try in Ten Days." *New York Times*, May 20, 1969.
———. "Mountain Battle Tough, Bloody for GIs." *New York Times*, May 18, 1969.
———. "U.S. Assault on Mountain Continues, Despite Heavy Toll." *New York Times*, May 19, 1969.
Sheehan, Neil. "Letters from Hamburger Hill." *Harper's*, November 1969.
"The Siege of A Shau." *Newsweek*, March 21, 1966.
Smith, Hedrick. "U.S. Battle Losses Stir Nixon Aides." *New York Times*, May 23, 1969.
Solheim, William G. II. "The New Looks of Southeast Asian Prehistory." *Journal of the Siam Society* 60, 1972: 1–20.
"Teddy on the Stump." *Newsweek*, June 2, 1969.
"Woe to the Victors." *Newsweek*, June 2, 1969.

Government Documents

Annex A (Intelligence) to Opord 3–69, Hdqr. 101st Airborne Division.
Appendix 5 (Terrain Analysis) to Annex A (Intelligence) to Opord 3–69, Hdqr. 101st Airborne Division.
Combat After Action Report, Operation Massachusetts Striker, 3rd Bn., 187th Infantry, 101st Airborne Division, April 25 to May 8, 1969.
Combat After Action Report, Sapper Attack on FSB Airborne, 2nd Brigade, 101st Airborne Division, July 2, 1969.
Combat After Action Report, Operation Massachusetts Striker, 2nd Brigade, 101st Airborne Division, May 25, 1969.
Combat After Action Report, Operation Apache Snow, 3rd Brigade, 101st Airborne Division, June 25, 1969.
Combat After Action Report, Operation Apache Snow, 3rd Bn., 187th Infantry, 101st Airborne Division, June 20, 1969.
Combat After Action Report, Operation Apache Snow, 1st Bn., 506th Infantry, 101st Airborne Division, June 18, 1969.

Combat After Action Report, Operation Apache Snow, XXIV Corps, August 27, 1969.

Fact Sheet: Description of Operation Vicinity of Dong Ap Bia, 101st Airborne Division, n.d.

Fact Sheet: Enemy Losses—Dong Ap Bia, 101st Airborne Division, May 24, 1969.

Fact Sheet: Hamburger Hill, A Shau Valley, Operation Apache Snow, prepared by US Army J-3, Pacific Division, n.d.

Fact Sheet: Intelligence Analysis of 29th NVA Regiment, 101st Airborne Division, n.d.

Fact Sheet: Logistical Buildup and Support Prior to and During the Action at Dong Ap Bia Mountain, 101st Airborne Division, n.d.

Fact Sheet: Ordnance Employed at Dong Ap Bia, 101st Airborne Division, May 24, 1969.

Historical Summary of the Battle at Dong Ap Bia (Hamburger Hill), 10–20 May 1969, 101st Airborne Division, n.d.

Interrogation Report of Pham Van Hai, May 21, 1969, Ref. INTSUM 140–69 (8).

Kennedy, Sen. Edward M., Senate speech, May 20, 1969.

Narrative of Operation Apache Snow, May 7 to June 7, 1969, prepared by 22nd Military History Detachment, n.d.

Operational Report, 1st Cavalry Division, for period ending April 30, 1968.

Operational Report, 101st Airborne Division, for period ending May 1968.

Operational Report, 101st Airborne Division, for period ending July 31, 1968.

Operational Report, XXIV Corps, for period ending October 31, 1968.

Operational Report, 101st Airborne Division, for period ending November 1968.

Operational Report, XXIV Corps, for period ending January 31, 1969.

Operational Report, 2nd Brigade, 101st Airborne Division, for period ending April 30, 1969.

Operational Report, 101st Airborne Division, for period ending April 30, 1969.

Operational Report, 1st Cavalry Division, for period ending April 30, 1969.

Operational Report, 101st Airborne Division, for period ending July 31, 1969.

Operation Hue, prepared by 14th Military History Detachment, 1st Cavalry Division, February 1968.

Operation Hue City, Historical Study 2–68, prepared by 31st Military History Detachment, Hdqr. Prov. Corps, Vietnam 1969.

Scott, Sen. Hugh, Senate speeches, August 1968; May 20, 1969.

Senior Officer Debriefing: Gen. Melvin Zais, June 1969.

Smith, Sen. Margaret Chase, Senate speech, May 26, 1969.

Thurmond, Sen. Strom, Senate speech, December 29, 1970.

Tower, Sen. John G., Senate speech, May 26, 1969.

US Marine Corps Oral History Program/Interviewees: Maj. Gen. Marion E. Carl and Gen. John Chaisson.
Young, Sen. Stephen M., Senate speeches, May 29, 1969; September 21, 1970; November 25, 1970.
Zais, Lt. Gen. Melvin. Memorandum for the Record: Subject: Dong Ap Bia, July 24, 1969.

Personal Accounts, Letters and Telegrams

Letter from Gen. Jim Smith (Ret.) to Ray Ytzaina, August 21, 1985.
Telegram to Gen. Melvin Zais from Gen. William Westmoreland, May 23, 1969.
The following individuals provided me with accounts of their experiences, in either original manuscripts or lengthy letters: Tim Ard, Frank Boccia, Daniel L. Cochran, Jon Fleagane, Raymond Harshberger, Robin Huard, Michael Jones, Jack Little, Rodger Murray, David Poor, Eric Rairdon, Lt. Col. Gene Sherron (Ret.), Gen. Richard Stilwell (Ret.), Steve Tice, Dick Watson, and Mark Weston.
I also utilized the following letters on file at the U.S. Marine Corps Museum in Washington, D.C.: letter to Col. F. C. Caldwell, Director of Marine Corps History, from Brig. Gen. L. E. Brown, U.S. Marine Corps, December 4, 1969; letter to F. C. Caldwell, USMC (Ret.), Director of Marine Corps History, from Maj. Gen. Marion E. Carl, U.S. Marine Corps, December 5, 1969; letter to the Marine Corps Museum from Maj. Gen. Marion E. Carl, U.S. Marine Corps (Ret.), June 1978; letter to Brig. Gen. E. H. Simmons from Col. Ray C. Gray, Jr., U.S. Marine Corps (Ret.), July 20, 1978.

Archival Sources

Bronze and Silver Star Citations from the U.S. Army Military Awards Branch, Hoffman Building II, Alexandria, Virginia.
Company Musters and Rosters for the 3/187th, 2/501st, and 1/506th from the National Records Center, St. Louis, Missouri.
Daily Staff Journals for 3/187th, 2/501st, and 1/506th from U.S. Army Adjutant General's Office, Alexandria, Virginia.

Interviews

Interview with Frank Boccia, conducted by Ray Ytzaina, n.d.
I conducted lengthy taped interviews with the following men: George Bennitt, Frank Boccia, Anthony Bresina, Greg Bucknor, John Comerford, Charles

Denholm, CSM Louis Garza (Ret.), Andrew Hannah, Lt. Col. Gerald
Harkins, Jerry Hoffman, Gen. Weldon Honeycutt (Ret.), Johnny Jackson,
Joe King, Steve Korovesis, Donald Kreiger, Lt. Col. Charles Littnan, Leonel
Mata, Frank McGreevy, Sfc. George Parker (Ret.), Richard Powell, Michael
Rocklen, Luther (Lee) Sanders, Robert Schmitz, Ian Shumaker, Mike Smith,
John Snyder, Ron Storm, Ron Swanson, Joel Trautman, and Phil Trollinger.

Miscellaneous

Ytzaina, Ray. A Study of the Casualty Figures Reported for Hamburger Hill.
n.d.

INDEX

A Loui 17, 20, 30, 40–43, 44
A Sap River 130
A Shau Camp 17 (battle for) 19–27, 29, 30, 38
Abrams, Gen. Creighton 43, 50, 229–230, 275, 279
Addison, Capt. Charles 78, 90, 92, 136–137, 140, 173
Air support 72, 99, 125–128, 138, 146, 175–176, 193, 197–198; by gunship 90–92, 164–165, 191, 216
Ambush 101–103, 106, 190–191, 245–250
Air Force 37
Ap Bia Mountain. *See* Dong Ap Bia
Ard, Sgt. Tim 139, 238
Artillery 209–210
Associated Press 197–198
Atcheson, Lt. Gordie 263

B-52 strikes 32, 275, 285
Baker, Sgt. Raymond 267–268
Barrow, Col. 50
Barski, Sgt. Roger 122–123
Bell, Sgt. Joe 213
Bellino, Pfc. Paul 211–212
Bennitt, Lt. George 7, 114, 260
Berger, Samuel D. (Ass't U.S. Ambassador) 230
Binh Dinh Province 39
Blackwell, Sp. 4 Paul 199–202
Blain, Capt. John D., IV 20, 24, 27
Bloody Ridge. *See* Dong A Tay
Boccia, Lt. Frank 8–9, 70, 75–80, 90, 99, 102–104, 109–112, 113, 125–128, 146, 131–155, 160–166, 169–170, 176, 182, 184, 186–187, 204–205, 283, 284, 288
Bork, Pfc. Alan 71

Bowers, Lt. Col. John 94–95, 130, 199, 245, 255, 264, 284
Branco, Sgt. Anthony 120
Bresina, Sp. 4 Anthony 154, 178–181, 188–189, 288, 292
Bresnahan, Lt. Daniel 85–86, 113, 215, 238
Brinkle, Sgt. Dan 245–247, 249–251
Brooks, Sp. 4 Edward 164–165
Brook, Sp. 4 Larry 199
Brown, Sp. 4 Clifford 199–202
Bucknor, Sp. 4 Greg 118
Burney, Capt. Linwood 195, 199, 201, 232–235
Burnette, Pfc. Vick 121–122

Carl, Gen. Marion E. 25–26
Camp Eagle 47, 168
Camp Evans 5, 42, 66, 115, 188
Campbell, Sp. 4 Tyrone 149–150, 257–258
Chaine Annamitique 11
Chaisson, Gen. John 29, 38
Chapman, Willie 157
Chappel, Capt. Butch 186–187, 243–244
Chuan, Gen. *See* Nguyen Van Chuan
Cochran, Sp. 4 Bill 134–135
Collier, Major 140, 223–224, 242, 271
Comerford, Sp. 4 John 9, 142, 152–153, 157–159
Con Thien 32–33
Conmy, Col Joseph 68, 124, 167–168, 225, 270, 284, 286
Counts, Sgt. Ken 122–123
Crenshaw, Lt. Russ 176
Currahees. *See* United States Army Battalion 1/506th
Cushing, Lt. Patrick 116, 122

299